# SMOKE SIGNALS
# FROM THE HEART

# SMOKE SIGNALS
## *from*
# THE HEART

## FOURTEEN YEARS
### *of the*
## FIRST NATIONS DRUM

**Editors**
**Len O'Connor**
**Natasha Netschay Davies**
**Lloyd Dolha**

## TOTEM POLE BOOKS

www.totempublications.com

**Library and Archives Canada Cataloguing in Publication**

Smoke signals from the heart / edited by Len O'Connor, Natasha Netschay Davies, Lloyd Dolha.

A selection of articles from First Nations Drum.
Includes index.
ISBN 0-9735840-0-9

1. Native peoples--Canada.  I. O'Connor, Len, 1948 June 19-
II. Davies, Natasha Netschay, 1971-  III. Dolha, Lloyd, 1960-

E78.C2S623 2004                971.004'97
C2004-904819-8

Design and layout by Low Profile Design, Victoria, British Columbia
Cover Photo by Danny Beaton

Second Edition (Revised)
Printed in Canada

5       4       3       2

# TABLE OF CONTENTS

# INTRODUCTION

## By the Editors

*Smoke Signals from the Heart* is an anthology that chronicles the first fourteen years of Canada's national Native newspaper *First Nations Drum*. The book features a selection of the newspaper's finest articles beginning in in 1990; ending in 2004. The rich and varied editorial describes the people and the stories that shaped the landscape of Native communities during this time frame, and the changes that occurred as a result.

The anthology includes an article on the unforgettable Oka crisis. *First Nations Drum* printed an article that investigated the Oka stand-off in the paper's first issue, October 1990. The article, entitled *Summer of Discontent*, illustrates how Oka changed the public's perception of Native issues. For the first time, a confrontation between the Indians and the police was given full media coverage. Natives and non-natives across the country could simply turn on their televisions or pick up a daily newspaper to follow the story as it unraveled before their eyes.

If Native issues were always given this kind of mass coverage perhaps they would be better understood by the public. Unfortunately, Oka was the exception – not the norm. Native stories that make it onto the front pages of mainstream dailies are usually full blown before the media notices them. In other words, the fuse is already lit and the (Native) situation out of hand.

The stories in *Smoke Signals from the Heart* provide the background to the events and the reasons why the issues became volatile – all

told from a Native perspective. For example, the legacy of the Residential School system is given full examination in *Wounded Leaders, Wounded Nation*. Writer John Bacher explains how the repressive educational system denied First Nations from their culture and how it was implemented by the Canadian Government.

The tragic and unjust deaths of Dudley George at Ipperwash; and Leo Lachance in Saskatchewan, are looked at in *One Dead Indian* and *White Hate*.

War hero Thomas Prince – the most highly decorated Native soldier – returns from Korea a hero but ten years later dies in poverty; his medals pawned, and his former glory replaced by bouts with alcohol. Lloyd Dolha profiles the legend of the Prince and the sad ending for one of Canada's greatest soldiers.

Other articles in *Smoke Signals from the Heart* demonstrate how Native physical characteristics affect history. For example, how the Skywalkers rushed to Ground Zero to help the survivors of 9-11. These Mohawk steel workers – famed for working on tall buildings and bridges – are profiled in *An Old Spirit Rises*.

Articles on Native artists including singers, actors, painters and sculptors provide a balance to the anthology's more solemn articles. Celebrated Native musician Robbie Robertson regarded as one of rock and roll's greatest songwriters, author of *The Night They Drove Old Dixie Down*, returns to his Native roots in his solo recordings. Robbie's impressive career, which spans more than thirty years and includes partnerships with Ronnie Hawkins, The Band, Bob Dylan and Martin Scorsese, is covered in *Robbie Robertson Puts the Weight on Native Music*.

Buffy Saint Marie became the darling of the folk movement in the sixties with her anti-war anthem *Universal Soldier*. In the seventies she went in front of the television camera for *Sesame Street* and won an Oscar in the eighties for the song *Up Where We Belong*. Buffy's multi-faceted career is covered in *Versatile Artist Covers All Bases*.

New faces of Native music include Keith Secola and his Band of Wild Indians, who appeared in Vancouver for the Music West festival**,** riding the success of their cult hit *Indian Cars*. Kashtin also appeared at Music West, and his was the first Native group to go platinum in Canada. Both groups appear as the new representatives of Native music.

Native sculptor Bill Reid, who brought international attention to Haida art, is profiled along with artist Robert Davidson who has preserved those traditional elements in his contemporary abstract work.

Environmental issues are often if not always tied to land claim issues. The picture on the cover of *Smoke Signals from the Heart* is that of Diane Reid, a Cree woman who fights a lonely struggle against the Québec government for the ecological survival of James Bay.

The Grassy Narrows First Nation, survivors of water contamination in the seventies from a pulp and paper mill, is dealing with the effects of mercury poisoning. The community is at war with forestry giant Abitibi Consolidated (the company that supplies the Knight Ridder newspaper chain, *The New York Times* and *The Washington Post* with newsprint), who has made a bid to take over The Whiskey Jack Forest. Abitibi's history of clear cutting could decimate not only the forest but all wildlife that survives within its boundaries. The forest is on Grassy Narrows First Nation land and since fifty percent of the forest is already clear cut, the band says no to the paper moguls. With all the makings of a blockbuster film, this true story is covered in *Grassy Narrows First Nations Fights for Its Future*.

Author John Goddard's *Last Stand of the Lubicon Cree*, is reviewed by Peter Cole. The book tells the story of the Lubicon, who have lived in traditional ways for centuries, but in the last twenty years 400 oil and gas wells have destroyed all their surrounding wildlife and ruined the environment. The land generated revenues of $1.2 million per day for the oil companies and for the provincial government yet the Lubicon people have never seen a penny of it.

The Nisga'a land claim and British Columbia's Premier Gordon Campbell's failed attempt at blocking its implementation is covered by Lloyd Dolha in *Nisga'a Treaty Passes into History*. The negotiations, which began at the turn of the century, were finalized in 1998 when Chief Joe Gosnell signed the agreement in Victoria.

The Mohawks of Akwesasne were not as lucky. The construction of the St. Lawrence Seaway destroyed their lifeblood, which was fishing and hunting. The smuggling and the rise and fall of the warrior society is given an in-depth look in *Tobacco Road* as the traditional Mohawks and the Great Book Of The Law (as taught by Jake Thomas) triumphs over the criminal activities of the Warriors.

The last land claim issue covered in this anthology is the struggle of the Chippewas of Nawash against land developers. The proposed six pipelines would divert Lake Huron water to distant communities when the Georgian Bay was already experiencing record low levels. The Chippewas, robbed of most of their lands in 1836, would not stand by to see history repeat itself. "It's about time the First Nations point of view is upheld. Any diversion of water into a pipeline will have an effect on the shore. What good are our boats if there's no water?" Chief Ralph Akisenzie explains in *Chippewas of Nawash Defend Lake Huron and Georgian Bay.*

In *A Funny Thing Happened on the Way to the Supreme Court of Canada* writer Lloyd Dolha explains how in the 1997 Delgamuukw decision, the Supreme Court of Canada ruled that aboriginal title exists and that governments must justify any infringement on aboriginal title. Respect is paid to the passing of Native leaders Joe Mathias, Simon Baker and Fred House, and the legacies they left behind in articles *Legacy of a Legend, Renowned Squamish Elder Passes Away*, and *A Nation Mourns the Passing of National Métis Hero.*

In *An Elders Gathering*, a stunning pictorial illustrates a gathering in Saanich. Photographer Cher Bloom captures the wizened faces of elders and the spirit that exudes from Native men and women who celebrate the autumn of their lives.

Female Native artists and role models profiled in *Smoke Signals From the Heart* include Métis model and film producer Theresa Ducharme, who has been on a mission to promote Native culture in Japan, China and Europe. Theresa and her dance group were the first Natives to perform in China, and were seen via television by 350 million Chinese viewers. Film producer Barb Cranmer and entrepreneur Dolly Watts are also featured as Native Women who have made positive changes within their communities.

In *Native Entrepreneur on the Rise*, writer Lloyd Dolha examines Clarence Louie's role in bringing his people financial independence and reshaping his Band's future. The Chief of the Osoyoos Band has demonstrated business acumen making him a role model for Native men across the country. The Band, thanks to Clarence, own several companies including the first Native-owned winery. The Band has turned a profit in all their endeavors and provides employment for their band members.

Crime-focused stories in this anthology serve as an example of the attention and help many Native communities are in need of across the nation. *BC's Murdered and Missing Native Women* is a tragic chronicle of Native women who fell into drug addiction and prostitution. Sadly, many are now missing and presumed murdered. The indifference of the police and the judicial system to their plight is examined closely in this grim article. One unforgettable and staggering fact is that the Native population of British Columbia is two percent yet Native women make up 60 percent of the province's missing women.

The trial of three Saskatchewan men who raped a twelve-year-old girl and were acquitted is documented in *Cree Family Accuses Judge of Racism*. The urban influence on Native teenagers in Manitoba and Saskatchewan results in drugs, guns and crime. This lifestyle is exposed in *Aboriginal Gangs in Prairie Provinces in Crisis Proportions*. The death of Neil Stonechild, the teenager found frozen near Saskatoon, and the role the police played in his death is sadly is recounted in *Inquiry into the Death of Neil Stonechild*.

Native athletes are featured in two stories in *Smoke Signals from the Heart*. Hockey player Jonathan Chee Choo from Moose Factory; and Jordin Too Too from Inuvik (not exactly areas considered hotbeds of hockey talent) are two rising stars in the NHL. Chee Choo plays with the San Jose Sharks and Too Too is with the Nashville Predators. The sacrifice and dedication that was required for these young men to reach their goals turned them into overnight role models for Native youth everywhere.

In *Too Too's Train Ride to the Top* First Nations Drum follows Jordin's rise from a minor hockey player to an NHL prospect; his brother's suicide and Jordin's fight to hold on to his career. Jonathan Chee Choo's one dream – to play with the San Jose Sharks – is described in *Chee Choo's Long and Successful Journey*. Another role model for Native youth profiled in the anthology is Robert Kowbel who received the Provincial Excellence Award from the Canadian Millennium Scholarship in 2004, the Salish youth was one of 50 students to receive the award.

Finally, in *Canada's Celebrated Author Shares His Inspiration*, Thomas King is interviewed by writer Natasha Netschay Davies. King, a writer, teacher, broadcaster and promoter of First Nations writing, has an impressive list of published works including *Medicine River* and *Green Grass, Running Water*, which were both made into television movies. Last year, the Ontario-based author released his first mystery novel *Dreadful Water Shows Up*, a departure from his earlier work. In this intimate interview, King shares his advice to any one considering a career in writing: "If you can live your life without writing then do so -- it will be a lot easier that way. But if you're desperate to write because it is so much a part of you, forget about having any sort of personal life."

# ACKNOWLEDGEMENTS

*Smoke Signals from the Heart* could not be possible without all the tremendous dedication, patience and commitment to the First Nations Drum newspaper. We thank all the editors, writers, photographers, the graphic design team and countless others who helped us meet our deadlines every month for the past fourteen years.

## WRITERS AND PHOTOGRAPHERS

**The late Billy Peacock, writer and co-founder**

**Lloyd Dolha, editor & political writer**

**Len O'Connor, editor-at-large**

**Bernie Bates, humorist & social critic**

**Danny Beaton, Mohawk environmentalist & activist, Native filmmaker**

**Dr. John Bacher, author, environmentalist, activist, writer**

**Lauren Carter, freelance writer, environmentalist**

**Noelle Marten, Alberta correspondent**

**Ron Barbour, journalist & radio personality**

**Peter Cole, journalist & Native issues activist**

**Janice Mann, writer & graphic designer**

**Frank Larue, journalist**

**Natasha Netschay Davies, journalist & contributing editor**

**Cher Bloom, photographer & writer**

**James Barfett, United States correspondent**

**Cam Martin, photographer & education reporter**

**Shauna Lewis, writer**

**Angie Smith, photographer**

**Robert Galbraith, photographer**

## DESIGN TEAM

**Flynn O'Connor, design director**

**Sandy Postilla, designer**

**Mike Davies, web design**

## ADMINISTRATION

**Siobhan O'Kelley, office manager**

**Lauren Brown, administration**

## THE SALES TEAM

**Mike Morningstar**

**Rick Littlechild**

**Mike Reeder**

**Mark Elyas**

# AN OLD SPIRIT RISES FROM THE ASHES

**By Raymond Barfett**          **Published October, 2001**

It was a beautiful autumn morning in New York City — a few soft white clouds were floating against the blue sky. Most people were on their way to work and everyone was enjoying the freshness provided by the cool air from the North; it had been an extremely hot summer.

*Tower 2 of the World Trade Centre*
*September 15, 2001*
Photo: Dave Thom

Several Mohawk Ironworkers were already at work, fifty floors above the bustling city streets at a job site in Lower Manhattan. They were from the Akwasasne Reserve in upstate New York and over the past one hundred and fifty years ironwork had become a part of their long-standing tradition as architects and builders. The normalcy of their day ended suddenly and abruptly. Richard Otto and his crew looked up in amazement as an airliner flew by the building, a scant fifty feet from their crane. It was headed in the direction of the World Trade Center (WTC), just ten blocks away. A moment later it crashed into one of the Towers.

Otto quickly used his cellular phone to call Michael Swamp, business manager of Ironworkers Local 440 on the Akwesasne Reserve, to inform him of the tragedy. While they were talking, another airliner passed by heading in the same direction. This could not just be an accident, something was seriously wrong here. Otto told Swamp the plane was going to hit the second Tower. Swamp heard Otto frantically telling the workers to get out of there, then there was a thunderous boom and the phone went dead.

There were about one hundred Mohawk men from the Ironworkers Union working at construction sites in NYC and New Jersey that morning, and those who could, headed directly to ground zero. Some of these men had worked on the WTC from the beginning;

they knew their way around the buildings and they hoped they could help save some lives. Grave danger and pressure are a daily way of life for these men who toil high above the ground. They showed no fear, they knew the Great Spirit and the Spirits of their Forefathers were with them. They were some of the first rescuers on the scene, helping stunned and injured people out of the buildings. After the buildings collapsed they immediately began searching for survivors.

Meanwhile Michael Swamp had called the sister locals in Utica, Albany and Syracuse and coordinated recruitment of union members to relieve the hard-pressed workers. They would spend days, weeks and months clearing up the rubble. These brave and courageous Mohawk men followed a path that was walked before them by several generations of Mohawks from New York State, Québec and Ontario. It was a path well worn, evolving out of necessity, courage, and pride.

## HISTORY OF THE MOHAWK IRONWORKERS

In the year 1886 the Grand Trunk Railway wanted to build the Victoria Bridge. It would span the mighty St. Lawrence River and connect Montreal to the Kahnawake Reserve. They contracted out the job to the Dominion Bridge Company. In exchange for being allowed to run the railroad through Mohawk Territory, Grand Trunk arranged for Dominion to hire some of the Mohawks as laborers to work on the bridge site. This decision would have a huge impact upon the lifestyle of many Mohawks, an effect that remains to this very day.

---

*T*here were about one hundred Mohawk men from the Ironworkers Union working at construction sites… They were some of the first rescuers on the scene, helping stunned and injured people out of the buildings.

---

Their first job was to supply the stone for the large piers that would support the bridge. When their shifts ended, they would hang out on the bridge watching the other workers to see what they were doing. Even young Native children became curious and soon they were climbing all over the span, right alongside the men. The workers noticed that the Mohawk's agility, grace and sense of balance made it seem as though they had a natural disposition for heights. When management became aware of this, they hired and trained a dozen tribal members as ironworkers. The original twelve, all teenagers, were so adept at working at high altitudes, they were known as the "Fearless Wonders." They would walk on narrow beams several hundred feet above the raging river and yet it appeared as though they were just on a casual walk along a forest path.

In their book *This Land was Theirs* (1999), Oswalt and Neely state that "some outsiders have suggested that an absence of fear of height was inborn, but it seem more likely that the trait was learned." Perhaps some of these men did not fear heights and those that did likely repressed their fear in order to gain employment. Constructing bridges and skyscrapers was extremely dangerous work and many of the young Mohawks were drawn to it not only for high wages, but also perhaps for an opportunity to prove their courage. They worked very hard at learning their newfound trade and soon began to train other men from their Reserve.

The Mohawk ironworkers used their Native language while they riveted steel beams, high up on bridges and skyscrapers. They spoke to each other continuously in Mohawk and this reinforced their own language competency.

*"Going Home" 1985 painting by Bill Powless*

*K*nown as the "Fearless Wonders"… They would walk on narrow beams several hundred feet above the raging river and yet it appeared as though they were just on a casual walk along a forest path.

Sometimes they even taught Mohawk to their non-Native co-workers. The Mohawks also used sign language, signals made with the hands, which was instrumental in allowing them to communicate with each other quickly and clearly, while working on narrow iron beams, hundreds of feet above the earth.

Over the next fifty years many people from various First Nations would follow in the footsteps of the Mohawks of Kahnawake. They became renowned for their ability to walk high steel beams with balance and grace, seemingly without any fear, and ironwork became a matter of identity and great pride

> *H igh up on bridges and skyscrapers the Mohawk ironworkers spoke to each other continuously in Mohawk and this reinforced their own language competency.*

within the First Nations. The legend of their innate abilities began to apply to Native men from all over the Woodland area and thus allowed them to get hired all across the US and Canada. These men helped to shape and build the "New America."

By the early 1900s the emergence of the modern-day skyscraper occurred. Iron bridges and tall buildings, those were the future. Chicago and New York City were reaching for the stars. From the beginning of that new age of construction, the Mohawks were there, "sky-walking" on the clouds, high above it all. The men made the long journey from their reserves to the big cities alone, leaving their families and then returning once or twice a month to visit. These Mohawk men, who worked in the Ironworkers Industry of America, soon became legendary and were known in later years as the "Skywalkers."

By the 1930s the Mohawks began to move in large numbers from the Kahnawake and Akwesasne Reserves in Canada and upstate NY. They were attracted by New York's great building boom, fueled by Depression-era Public Works, and later the post-war economic revival. Entire families set up their own little communities within the midst of the unknown bustling city. It was quite a contrast to their quiet lives back home.

One such community was formed in Brooklyn in the vicinity of the Cuyler Church. Reverend Cory welcomed these Mohawk families to attend his church and treated them the same as any of God's children. He spent a great deal of time learning their language, so much so that he was able to translate religious readings into the Mohawk-Oneida dialect. He also promoted the reacquisition of Mohawk traditional culture and made the resources of the church available to the Native community for that purpose. The church also served as a community center where people would often gather to hear news from home, tell stories, trade information, and hold cultural events. By the late 1950s construction in New York city diminished, thus decreasing employment and causing numerous Mohawk families to vacate the North Gowanus enclave.

## MANHATTAN ISLAND NEEDS HEALING

The Mohawks from New York State and Canada once controlled all the land in the Hudson Valley, including Manhattan Island and most of Long Island. They were the Keepers of the Eastern Door of the Iroquois Confederacy. The Mohawks were instrumental in the construction of many of the bridges and skyscrapers of New York City, such as the Woolworth Building, the Empire State

> *"I want to convey to you the sense of seriousness that First Nations peoples hold for the September 11, 2001 events. This is our homeland. Our Elders refer to the land as "Mother Earth," and when anyone harms our Mother, be it through the destruction of the environment, or by the taking of human life that was put here, it hurts us all."*
> **National Chief Matthew Coon Come**

Building, the Waldorf Astoria, the RCA Building (now the GE Bldg.), the Chase Manhatten Bank, the Columbia Center, the George Washington Bridge, the Triborough Bridge, the Henry Hudson Parkway, and any other ironwork project that required courageous men with nerves of steel.

In his statement to the Members of Canada's Parliament, National Chief Matthew Coon Come said, "I want to convey to you the sense of seriousness that First Nations peoples hold for the September 11, 2001 events. This is our homeland. Our Elders refer to the land as 'Mother Earth,' and when anyone harms our Mother, be it through the destruction of the environment, or by the taking of human life that was put here, it hurts us all."

The damage of 9/11 had to be dealt with immediately and the Great Spirit had to be invoked to aid in the healing process. The drums started beating, word spread out quickly and millions of prayers were forthcoming from Native peoples all across North America. Deeply touched, not only did they send their prayers, they started sending millions of dollars in donations.

The Elders knew that that there was an open wound on the tip of Manhatten Island; a wound that had to be healed before everyone could move forward with their lives. They were honored when an invitation was offered to attend the 17th Annual Candlelight Vigil of Remembrance and Hope to be held at the West End Collegiate Church in NYC on April 21, 2002. This year's theme was "Bringing Honor to Victims" and would pay special tribute to the families of the 9/11 disaster. The Mohawk

peoples would lead everyone in the Healing Ceremony.

Kwan Bennett, a Cherokee member of the Thunderbird Dancers, coordinated the New York City American Indian Community's participation in the Candlelight Vigil. She told Jim Kent, a reporter for the *Native Times*, that she knows many Mohawk ironworkers who've taken part in the recovery efforts at Ground Zero and at times feels overwhelmed by the impact the tragedy has had on them and the rest of the city's American Indian population. "I know that the people of the Iroquois Nations who are taking care of this land that was once part of where their people lived are really touched to the core by what

*Kwan Bennett, a Cherokee member of the Thunderbird Dancers, coordinated the New York City American Indian Community's participation in the Candlelight Vigil.*

*The Great Spirit had been invoked and the healing process of Mother Earth was well under way.*

has happened," Bennett observed. "There's been a lot of talk, particularly by the Elders, that we actually need to have a cleansing… a healing at the site. There's a lot of spiritual work that needs to be done."

The opening procession was led by the NYC Dept. of Correction Bag Pipe Band, followed by the Pipeline Pipe and Drum Band, Mohawks from the Kahnawake and Akwesasne Reserves, and members of the First Nations from all across North America. They were wearing their traditional regalia and carrying fans, rattles, turtle shells, and smudge pots.

The opening prayer by Arthur Powless, a Medicine Elder and former ironworker, was given in his Native language and was interpreted by Jerry McDonald of Akwasasne, a member of Local 440.

Don Cardinal, a traditional healer from the Cree Nations, placed the Men's Eagle Staff and Peace Pipe on the podium and Kwan Bennett placed the Women's Eagle Staff.

The Eagle Staff has represented Native peoples for thousands of years and has ceremonial and symbolic purpose. The Eagle Staff is carried to focus the intent of those it represents and signifies a strong spiritual message for those it honors. Every Eagle Staff is unique in design; made that way through the knowledge of its maker, according to the purpose and representation. The decision to make and use such a staff is always a serious undertaking.

Survivors, family members and children read original poetry and messages of hope and recovery. The Akwesasne Women's Singers, the Heyna Second Sons, pianist Eric Alderfer, the Young People's Chorus of NYC and Luis Mofsie, Director of the Thunderbird American Dancers provided musical enrichment and entertainment.

The Candlelight Vigil included spirituality and rituals. Guests received "solace stones" as a symbol of the long journey of restoration, not only physically, but also mentally and spiritually. The Grey Elders from the Pine Ridge Reserve offered the ceremonial sage. White pine needles were brought for the ceremony from Ohswegan, the Six Nations Reservation in Canada and were lit at the same time as the candles, as a symbol of unity. During the solemn candle lighting ceremony, attendees recited the names of family members and friends who were so suddenly taken away. While loved ones offered testimonials to the civilian and uniformed heroes of 9/11, meaningful and inspirational slides were shown. A Book of Remembrance and Hope recording the names of victims was ritually dedicated.

Kwan Bennett delivered the introduction for the closing prayer recited by Rayne, Gabrielle Perez, Kia Benbow and Hunter McDonald, four children ranging in age from seven to twelve. Luis Mofsie played the Men's Drum for the closing song and healer Don Cardinal smoked the peace pipe to close the ceremonies. A marvelous feast was presented and greatly enjoyed by all. The Great Spirit had been invoked and the healing process of Mother Earth was well under way.

# WOUNDED LEADERS, WOUNDED NATIONS

**By Dr. John Bacher and Danny Beaton, Mohawk Nation**     **Published January, 2004**

Canadian Natives suffer from a crisis of leadership under the graduates of the residential school system. Find out how these sinister educational institutions robbed Natives of their traditions and ties to Earth to replace them with Euro-American values of greed and ownership.

Residential schools for Natives, which were imported from the United States prison system, were introduced to the Americas by colonists. These schools were used as a device to assimilate Natives into the ideology of Western thinking. Residential schools were part of an unrelenting war to steal Indigenous lands in order for organized imperialist to profit from and control America after the guns were silenced on the American parries.

The Canadian Residential School system was a terrible nightmare created by a federal government attempting to imitate the worst aspects of the American dream – hoping that Natives would lose respect for the earth and become obsessed with getting rich through real estate speculation like ordinary North American citizens.

Residential schools were part of an unrelenting war on Native culture after the gunfire of the American prairies was stilled. Confrontation between two ways of life shifted from the battle field to the class room. Past battles over land were coupled with newer clashes over ideals, dreams and values.

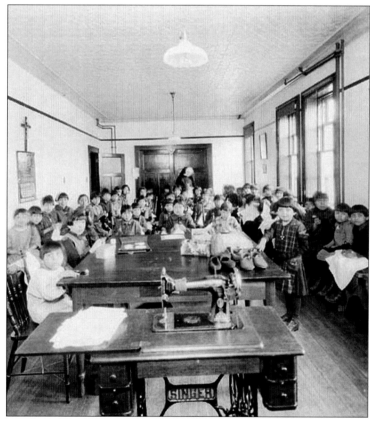

*Mi'kmaq girls in sewing class at the Roman Catholic-run Shubenacadie Indian Residential School in Shubenacadie, Nova Scotia 1929.*

*Photo: Library and Archives of Canada PA-185530*

*S*uch *extremists saw final solution in crude physical genocide reminiscent of a number of killings in the 19th century...*

After the plains wars ended, Native culture was painfully forced to adjust to life on reservations, by having cattle grazing replace the hunting of wild animals as a critical source of food. For the American government however, such a compromise was not enough. It sought to break up both the reservations and Native culture.

To conform to the American dream, Native American governments would be dissolved and the tribal lands were broken up into lots, which could be sold in the real estate market. U.S. policy hoped that individual Native Americans would break their bonds with the earth, looking at the land as a source of cash, rather than of spiritual nourishment.

The sinister school system developed at a time when moderate American political opinion supported cultural genocide. They defeated the more fanatical extremists that desired the slaughter and massacre of Native Americans. Such extremists saw a final solution in crude physical genocide reminiscent of a number of killings in the 19th century, most infamously Sand Creek.

## NARROW ESCAPE FROM NATIVE MASSACRE

The Lakota, (Sioux) spiritual leaders Sitting Bull and Crazy Horse defeated the U.S. Calvary in 1876, averting a planned massacre of Natives who were resisting seizure of the sacred Black Hills, guaranteed through a treaty with the U.S. government. A dramatic victory was won to defend traditional Native lands and the spiritual way of life based upon it. This was guarded through deep emotional bonds to the earth, reinforced by sacred ceremonies intended to promote reverence for life.

The Lakota triumph was won at a significant time. It took place on the eve of the American Centennial celebrations. These celebrated the American Revolution's victory over the Crown's efforts to defend Native territories against rich and greedy colonial land speculators such as George Washington, Thomas Jefferson and Patrick Henry.

The news of the Lakota last stand in defense of Mother Earth was received in the heavily populated eastern United States on the fourth of July. This put a great damper on the American centennial festivities, challenging widespread notions of cultural superiority. It contributed greatly to a fanatical revenge war to wipe out Native traditional ways.

At the time of the American centennial very few Euro-Americans, at least those who were significant then as a political force, had any sympathy for Native American efforts to defend their traditional culture and territories. In the 1870s, public opinion of the small number of politically active American citizens who actually concerned themselves with Native issues was divided into two basic camps.

Both disliked how Native Americans stood in the way of Euro-American efforts to exploit the earth through environmentally harmful projects such as railways, mines and agriculture on arid lands prone to erosion. The answer of one camp was to kill all Indians. The other response was to kill the cultural ways that motivated Native Americans to defend the earth from the assaults of destructive corporate agendas.

The critical architect of the residential school system was a combat veteran of the wars of the Great Plains, U.S. Army Captain Richard Henry Pratt. Considered by the American standards of the period as racially tolerant, Pratt commanded blacks and Natives who were used against their own people to seize control over the western prairies.

Pratt fought during eight years of fighting following the end of the Civil War. He played an important role in the American military victories in plains wars. This was aided greatly by the deliberate slaughter of game animals Native people needed for food and clothing. The combined policies of assaults by hunters and soldiers eventually led to the destruction of the Great Plains horse-buffalo culture.

From his Great Plains battle experience, Pratt developed a slogan that he would repeat many times: "Kill the Indian, save the man."

He wrote to the Commissioner of Indian Affairs: "If millions of black savages can become so transformed and assimilated... there is but one plain duty resting on us with regard to the Indians – that is to rescue them of their savagery."

# PRISONS PROVIDE CONCEPT

Captain Pratt developed the concept of the residential school while serving as a prison warden of Natives captured in the post-Civil War battles he fought for control of the plains. In 1875, he became the jailer of a group of Caddo, Southern Cheyenne, Comanche and Kiowa prisoners at Fort Marion in St. Augustine, Florida. They were issued military uniforms and given instruction in drill. A handful who curried his favour became guards keeping watch over their fellow Native prisoners.

Conditions for such Native prisoners of war, transported thousands of miles away from their ancestral homes on the plains, were quite traumatic. Food was scarce, disease rampant. There was terrible overcrowding. Prisoners could be jailed for 30 years in Florida cells thousands of miles from their homes. Many endured great suffering behind bars until a general amnesty in 1919, when Natives in the United States were finally given voting rights.

Pratt offered his prisoners hope for early release if they agreed to abandon their Native ways. In 1878 he had a select group of 17 prisoners released from the confines of Fort Marion. They were sent to the Hampton Institute in Virginia, then a boarding school for black children.

*"If millions of black savages can become so transformed and assimilated... there is but one plain duty resting on us with regard to the Indians – that is to rescue them of their savagery."*
**U.S. Army Captain Richard Henry Pratt**

Seeing a way of escape, the former inmates conformed to Pratt's expectations and excelled in school. From this coercive experience of forced assimilation, Pratt developed his concept of what became known as the Industrial Indian Residential Boarding School. Here he believed that distinctive Native cultural traits could be eradicated. Some of his former prisoners recruited Natives to attend these schools.

While he was a prison warden in St. Augustine, Pratt met a number of wealthy vacationers who supported his plans for the residential school; where Natives could be assimilated into American ways. Their lobbying persuaded the government to support his schemes for indoctrination, brainwashing and assimilation.

Before the 1870s, residential schools were located on or in close proximity to reservations, where parents could easily visit. They would now be deliberately located far away.

## SCHEMES TO BREAK NATIVE TIES

To obtain students for the Carlisle residential school, Pratt went to the Lakota communities which had three years earlier defeated Custer's calvary. He persuaded the chiefs to send the children to Carlisle on the deceptive grounds that gaining education would help them defend their reservation communities from white land speculators.

While Pratt spoke with the Lakota chiefs to get students for his school, one of his key supporters was Massachusetts Senator Henry Dawes. He was the author of legislation called the Dawes Act.

The infamous Dawes Act would remove 40 percent of the remaining land held by Native Americans on reservations. Much of this former reservation land, guaranteed by sacred treaties, ended up in the hands of white speculators, logging and mining interests, and ranchers.

The Dawes Act required that reservations be divided up into individual lots to teach Natives respect for American notions of private property.

Ecologists have pointed out the folly behind the Dawes scheme. Most of the land that was broken up by the Dawes Act was not suitable for intensive farming by Natives on individual plots of land. It was better suited to communal grazing for animals (such as bison) than growing crops (such as wheat) on plots that would fail during common drought periods.

Both Dawes and Pratt sought to break up what they termed the "tribal mass," and turn Indians into assimilated Americans. They had no understanding of how these Native nations had evolved over thousands of years, through cultures based on respect for the earth.

*B*efore the 1870s, residential schools were located on or in close proximity to reservations, where parents could easily visit. They would now be deliberately located far away.

# HUNGRY, HOMESICK AND PUNISHED FOR IT

The Natives Pratt lured to his school received a traumatic experience in indoctrination in American ways, which is best understood as brainwashing.

When the students arrived at Carlisle they were forced to sleep hungry on the floor on their blankets. Pratt, his wife and the Carlisle teaching staff immediately began their immersion until "thoroughly soaked." Their efforts at assimilation began by removing all outward signs of Indian appearances. Confused and homesick, the Lakota children wept as their long hair was cut and fell to the ground. A collective wail rose up, creating a wrenching sounding echo around the campus.

The Carlisle school was organized in a fashion quite similar to his management of the Fort Marion prison. Boys were dressed in military uniforms and given ranks. As in his Indian prison, Native officers were put in charge, rewarding those who sought Pratt's favor. Students practiced marching and drilling. They were given military style ranks. Marching was done to classes and to the dining hall for meals. Inspections went into considerable detail. They even tried to ensure that the regulation red flannel underwear, which many Natives found uncomfortable, was actually worn.

Cells were built to lock up students as punishment for various offenses; such as attempts to run away, a common offense.

The destruction of Native languages was one of Pratt's key objectives. Children began English lessons as soon as they arrived at Carlisle. Students were punished, sometimes severely, if caught speaking their Native languages, even in private. The few parents who were able to travel long distances to the school could only speak to their children in their Native tongues if permission was obtained from Pratt.

Eventually Carlisle became famous for its sports teams, especially in the area of football. This produced the professional superstar, Jim Thorpe. Native games such as lacrosse were never taught at any residential school in North America. Children who played Indian games were severely punished.

Climate change, separation anxiety and lack of immunity contributed to the death of many Carlisle students. More than 175 tombstones line the campus grounds today. Prayer cloths, strings of shell and beads and small bundles of sage and sweet grass embrace tree trunks in the cemetery. Those buried on the grounds represent only a small number of the Natives who perished here. Most were sent home for burial, but some had no relatives who could make the arrangements. Several hundred died on route to their families after becoming critically ill.

Although the first students at Carlisle attended voluntarily, a few years after the school was founded, compulsory methods were used. Such harsh means were applied to the children of the followers of Geronimo, many of whom attempted to hide their children. Many of these students died and were buried at Carlisle.

*Cells were built to lock up students as punishment for various offenses; such as attempts to run away, a common offense.*

## CANADA FOLLOWS CARLISLE MODEL

*Fortunately for Natives it took many decades before the Canadian government could impose the residential school model on the majority of Natives.*

Carlisle became the model for residential schools in both Canada and the United States. Most had far more serious problems of sexual abuse, torture and poor food.

While the Mohawk Institute, founded in 1829, was the first Indian residential school in Canada, it was a tiny scale operation, dependent on private British contributions, until the federal government decided to pour more money into the system.

Carlisle was founded at a critical time in Canada, 1879. This was the same time that buffalo shrank in such numbers on the plains from the deliberate extermination policies south of the border. The shrunken herds could not support Native communities on the prairies. To have education provide a means by which Natives would not have to be supported by government rations was the reason that in

1879, the Conservative Party government of Sir John A MacDonald, had an inquiry into Native education in Canada.

MacDonald's government embraced the agenda and methods of the new Carlisle academy following a report by a backbencher, Nicholas Flood Davin of Regina, to create Industrial Schools for Indians and Half-Breeds. Davin was especially impressed by the American policy of what he termed "aggressive civilization." MacDonald agreed with the approach of having the Native child "dissociated from the prejudicial influence by which he is surrounded on the reserve of his band."

Fortunately for Natives it took many decades before the Canadian government could impose the residential school model on the majority of Natives. Anticipating Native anger, schools were not formally made compulsory until 1895. Even after this step, in many parts of the country, the regulations were not enforced

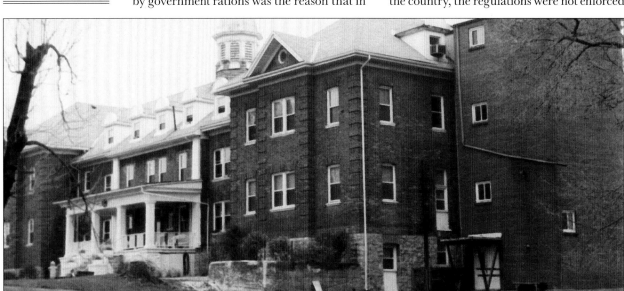

*Canada's first native residential school, The Mohawk Institute, founded in 1829 in Brantford, Ontario*

until 1933, when the Royal Canadian Mounted Police were officially empowered to act as truant officers. The system did not begin to become dismantled until Natives were finally given federal voting rights in 1962.

In the United States where Natives were granted the right to vote in 1919, the residential school system was wound down at a much faster rate, with Carlisle the model for the whole system, itself being closed down in 1918.

Even before Natives were granted the right to vote in the United States, the fanatical assumptions that gave birth to the residential school system were under public attack. This resulted in the resignation of Pratt in 1903 from the control of the school he founded.

# NEW PRESIDENT BRINGS CHANGE

The American government changed its policy of eradicating Native culture after Theodore Roosevelt became president. Roosevelt was a close friend of the American photographer Edward Curtis, who became one of the most eloquent exponents of the virtues of traditional Native culture.

More sympathy to Native American culture came about from the growth, even at the turn of the century, of the environmental movement. Many of the founders of the American environmental movement, such as the Canadian born Ernest Thompson Seton, had a profound reverence for the earth respecting cultures of Native Americans.

A Toronto born writer and artist, Seton learned to appreciate the earth from the examples of Native American leaders who defended their way of life. He was a close friend of the Lakota author Charles Eastman, who became an influential civil servant in the American Bureau of Indian Affairs. A medical doctor who treated Native victims of the Wounded Knee massacre, Eastman effectively challenged America's past manias for assimilation.

Influential opinion makers were horrified at the reality of the environmental destruction, especially the extermination of species that took place after Euro-Americans seized control of lands from Natives. Through the efforts of President Roosevelt, the Dawes Act, championed by Carlisle graduates such as Standing Bear, was eventually repealed, and much of the land returned to the control of Native communities. Natives and environmentalists worked to save the buffalo from extinction, with a herd being reintroduced to the Crow and Lakota reservations as part of the New Deal policies of Roosevelt.

Unfortunately, in Canada a strong environmental movement did not develop until after the vote was extended to Natives in 1962. This was partly caused by the fact that much of Canada, unlike the United States, remained largely wild forested environments, not subjected to industrial exploitation. At the time Natives received the vote, this was still true for most of Canada's vast and more thinly populated land mass.

*Some of the abuse of Natives in residential schools was caused by the harsh government mandates given the churches to wipe out native culture, especially languages.*

## HUMILIATION TECHNIQUES IMITATED

Some of the abuse of Natives in residential schools was caused by the harsh government mandates given the churches to wipe out Native culture, especially languages. More respectful church groups, notably the Jesuits, did teach in Native languages for a period, but this was outlawed by the Canadian government.

*A typical punishment would be to write down five hundred times that the student wouldn't "talk Indian" any more.*

Strange and cruel punishments were given to Natives for speaking in their own language. Bruises from staff punishment were signs that students were still brave enough to speak their own language. Whipping and strapping were a common penalty for speaking in Native tongues. A typical punishment would be to write five hundred times that the student wouldn't "talk Indian" any more.

The first Native residential school in Canada, the Mohawk Institute, helped to pioneer various humiliation techniques, which were used by imitators across the country. This was partly supported by the slave labour farming efforts of its students. The Principal would sell off its marketable produce, such as butter and eggs, for his personal profit. To avoid the poor fare served students, the school's higher staff and their families would eat in separate private facilities.

The only Native government which attempted to challenge the residential school system before the franchise was extended to Native peoples in 1962 was the Six Nations Iroquois Confederacy. At the behest of two parents, the Confederacy in the autumn of 1913 embarked on a campaign against mismanagement at the Mohawk Institute. This was done on the basis of hair-shearing, whipping, inadequate food, and the denial of parental visits. The Confederacy, through hauling the principal into court, did win awards against the school for whipping and the imposition of a three day water diet.

The Canadian government disapproved of the actions taken by the traditional Iroquois Confederacy. It refused to authorize the release of funds the Confederacy had authorized for legal expenses. Ten years after the Confederacy took the Mohawk Institute to court the Canadian government occupied the council house with an RCMP force, and seized its sacred wampum. This situation, which resulted in the imposition of an elected band council contrary to the traditional Great Law of Peace, still has not been corrected by the Canadian government, although a federal court ruled in 1973 that the 1923 actions were illegal.

*A group of nuns with Aboriginal students ca. 1890*

Photo: Library and Archives of Canada  PA-123707

# WOUNDED LEADERS, WOUNDED NATIONS

Canadian Natives suffer from a crisis of leadership under the graduates of the Residential school system, similar to that endured by Natives south of the border eighty years ago. Like Carlisle, which nurtured Standing Bear's advocacy of land ownership, the Canadian residential schools produced Native leaders who became advocates for disrespecting traditional bonds to the earth.

While Native leaders do not advocate policies similar to the Dawes Act, so fervently advocated by the Carlisle alumni, what they do support, in a similar disregard for Native bonds to the earth, is revenue sharing. This has been done through a denial of Native traditions of trusteeship of the earth, in favour of European models of ownership taught in residential schools.

The wisdom of elders that Natives do not "own" the land, but are its guardians for creation, is now disputed by graduates of the residential school system, such as former Assembly of First Nations Chief, Matthew Coon Come, and his colleagues, Ted Moses and Bill Namagoose. While deploring the abuse that took place in these institutions, they have only applause for the content of the curriculum, which helped shape their defense of plans for massive flooding of the waters of their Cree homeland. This formulated their innovative doctrines that caring for the land is a low status "janitor" occupation, unworthy of respect.

It is to be hoped that as in America, the leadership role played by the alumni of residential schools will be a passing phase. Coon Come was recently rejected as Assembly of First Nations Chief – as was Standing Bear by the voters at Pine Ridge who retained their love for the earth.

*Father Joseph Hugonnard, Principal, with staff and aboriginal students of the Industrial School. May 1885, Fort Qu'Appelle, Saskatchewan.*
Photo: Library and Archives of Canada  PA-118765

---

*T*he wisdom of elders that Natives do not "own" the land, but are its guardians for creation, is now disputed by graduates of the residential school system...

# "SMOKE SIGNALS" WINS AWARD

## POPULAR SMOKE SIGNALS RADIO & WEB SHOW WINS TOP AWARD FOURTH TIME

*Dan & Mary Lou Smoke*

*Photo: Dan Smoke*

**By G. Campbell McDonald, Native News Network of Canada**
**Published May, 2004**

Dan and Mary Lou Smoke's special recipe for a successful community radio show – a blending of traditional Native lore and modern news broadcasting — has won renewed recognition for the London couple's *Smoke Signals* program broadcast weekly on CHRW 94.9 FM Radio Western and webcast on the Internet at www.chrwradio. com.

In April, the show was recognized as "Outstanding Multicultural Program for 2004" at the CHRW Radio/TV Awards presentations. The occasion marked *Smoke Signals* second consecutive win and fourth year overall as title holder. The popular magazine-style program is heard on Sundays from 6:00 to 8:00 p.m. on the University of Western Ontario's FM station, which was ranked in 2003 as "#1 Campus and Community Radio Station in Canada."

The Smokes' ingredients for their award-winning recipe?

Dan: "Every week we try to give the public a look into our world in Indian Country, giving voice to our traditional perspectives and protocols. We do a half hour of First Nations music, a half hour of First Nations arts and announcements (sometimes an interview with an artist), and a half hour of First Nations public affairs and current events coverage and commentary. In the last half hour we share some of our traditional teachings and our knowings from our elders."

Mary Lou: "Evidently, people enjoy hearing what we have to say about our world and our Native culture. We get feedback in conversations when people stop us to talk on the street, and we also hear from people online. These exchanges are very gratifying learning experiences for us. The e-mails come in from across Canada and U.S. states as close as Dayton, Ohio and as far away as Del Rio, Texas; Tempe, Arizona and San Francisco, California. So we know we have a wide following and we appreciate and value that a lot."

Mario Circelli, station manager of CHRW, adds: "The Smokes take their show very seriously. They are always travelling. They go to powwows and other ceremonies all over North America and report on them." Circelli is the driving force behind CHRW's award-winning programming who launched the couple when he asked them to host *Smoke Signals* in 1991.

Elder Art Solomon, now deceased, gave the Smokes his seal of approval on their performance as Native communicators and cultural interpreters in one of his last interviews on *Smoke Signals*. He said: "It's time for us to tell our own stories. For too long, we have had the white man tell our story and now it's our turn, it's our turn to talk and it's their turn to listen."

# RENOWNED SQUAMISH ELDER PASSES AWAY

## SIMON BAKER: JUNE 15, 1910 – MAY 23, 2001 R.I.P.

**By Lloyd Dolha**                    **Published June, 2001**

With the passing of Squamish elder Chief Simon Baker at age 90, British Columbia lost one of its greatest figures of its cultural landscape.

In *Khot-La-Cha: The Autobiography of Chief Simon Baker*, author and educator Verna Kirkness described Baker as "an ambassador of his own culture and the human spirit."

Simon Baker was indeed these things and much more.

He was the last of the great "North Shore Indians," famed for their achievements in Canadian lacrosse, who he played with during his youth in the 1930s.

A dedicated husband and family man, Baker worked as a longshoreman for 41 years, eventually rising to the position of superintendent of Canadian Stevedoring.

He was a prime mover in organizing the first public powwows and sporting events for British Columbia First Nations.

A tireless volunteer, Simon Baker served as a spokesperson for countless community projects and organizations.

Chief Baker served as councilor to the Squamish Nation for more than 30 years, ten of which he served as chairman. So revered by his people, he was the only Squamish member designated Chief for Lifetime.

Baker was the recipient of numerous awards and special recognitions. He was a two-time recipient of the British Columbia Centennial

*Photo: Band Picture*

Award of Merit for 1958 and 1971. He was named to the Order of Canada in 1977, and was granted an Honourary Doctorate of Law from the University of British Columbia in 1990.

Baker was one of the most revered elders at the First Nations House of Learning and the Native Indian Teacher Education Program at UBC for many years, sharing his wisdom through stories and songs.

*Photo: Unknown*

**"*I tried to practice what they taught me, keeping up my culture from the teachings of my elders. I was glad to listen, to obey and practice our way.*"**

**Simon Baker**

Baker assisted in fundraising for the establishment of the UBC House of Learning through his extensive network of contacts.

In May 1999, Chief Baker, the only surviving member of the celebrated "North Shore Indians" of 1936, was inducted into the BC Sports Hall of Fame in recognition of his sporting achievements as Cannonball Baker, star lacrosse player of the team.

In March 2000, Simon Baker was awarded the National Aboriginal Achievement Award for Heritage and Spirituality.

As an ambassador of West Coast aboriginal culture, Baker traveled across western Europe, New Zealand and Japan throughout the 1970s and 80s, promoting aboriginal culture and heritage to the world.

In his autobiography, Baker explained the importance of home and family in the retention of cultural heritage.

"In order for me to keep the teachings of our elders, I had to keep coming home. After I left school, I had to accept the things that my grandmothers kept reminding of – my grass roots.

"I tried to practice what they taught me, keeping up my culture from the teachings of my elders. I was glad to listen, to obey and practice our way.

"I still have the knowledge, wisdom and philosophies of our elders. I had to keep learning my own culture, my language."

Khot-La-Cha, Baker's Squamish name for "Man with a Kind Heart," is survived by his wife of 71 years Emily, one sister, nine children, 38 grandchildren and one great-great grandchild.

He passed away on Wednesday, May 23, 2001.

# DOLLY WATTS: AN ENTREPRENEURIAL WARRIOR

**By Sean Devlin**                    **Published March, 1999**

*"I am a warrior. I became a fighter in order to keep afloat in the competitive world. I became fearless when faced with a real threat of losing my business. I remind myself to remain focused. I leave my home armed with years of training."*

*Per Ardua Ad Astra* is the motto for the warriors of Britain's Royal Air Force. The language is Latin, the dead tongue of the old Romans. It means "Through hardship to the stars." Such a sentiment makes an appropriate motif for the life of Dolly Watts who regards herself as a female warrior and whose son is a flight captain for United Air Lines.

Dolly's entrepreneurial savvy and determination have brought her to the point where she owns her own restaurant. Dolly has been nominated for the Canadian Women Entrepreneur of the Year Award, in the start-up division.

"I gave lots of thought to how one becomes a warrior. The myriad accounts of male warriors are etched on our totems and in the stories told at feasts. The tales that I heard when I was a child said that warriors rose while it was still dark and bathed in the river. They prayed. They used cedar branches to pummel their bodies for spiritual cleansing. They paid heed to the teachings of their parents, grandparents and ancestors. Even the spirits."

*Photo: CESO Aboriginal Services*

I met Dolly Watts amid the cedar columns and pebbled floor of the Liliget Feast House; the 52-seat restaurant designed some twenty years ago by Arthur Erickson. She is a woman of much presence. Softly spoken and looking a good 15 years less than her age of 63, she radiates centeredness and serenity.

"The family into which I was born was strong. I am Git'ksan from the house of Ghu'sen, at Gitsegukela, British Columbia, the tenth of 14 children. My mother, Chief Mel'hus, late Martha Morgan, married Chief Axtl-hix Gibu, late Wallace Morgan, from Gitwangk (also know as Kitwanga) village. His parents, who lived in Gitsegukela, were Chief Wi'get, late Stephen Morgan and Chief Ten'im'get, late Sarah Morgan.

"They lived during the time change. The government had set boundaries around their village and made laws that forbade the celebration of their culture. They and others from the village fought to keep our culture alive. They continued to hold feasts despite the threats of imprisonment. I saw the great dances, re-enactments of stories and heard chiefs speak."

The Git'ksan live on Gitwangak Reserve in northern BC along the banks of the mighty Skeena River.

> **❝***[The Gitwangak Reserve] was our food basket. The animals and birds, berries and vegetables offered us a variety of food. Tem'lax'amt or 'Sitting on something nice' was really paradise.***❞**

"It was our food basket," said Dolly. "The animals and birds, berries and vegetables offered us a variety of food. Tem'lax'amt or 'Sitting on something nice' was really paradise."

Dolly was barely walking when her mother spoke to her about the future. They were alone in a field where Mother was planting seed potatoes. It was lunchtime and she spread some food on the grass. As they ate, she said: "When you grow up like your sisters and brothers, you will go to school. You will go to school for a long time. When you finish, you have to leave home to work. There is no work in the village."

As she grew up, her mother's advice remained with Dolly.

"Every time I wanted to quit school, I remembered her words. When I became rebellious in my teens, my older brothers helped mother by forcing me to return to the boarding school. During the summer, she kept reminding me school was important and I must keep on until I graduated."

Yet circumstances conspired to block her mother's plan for Dolly. When she was seven years old, she contracted tuberculosis and landed in hospital for more than two years, where she saw many of her people die. When she was 10, she made the long trip to the Alberni Indian Residential School in Port Alberni. Upon arrival, she was stricken with rheumatic fever and spent the next year in the infirmary. It was then that Dolly displayed the innate initiative and spunk that would serve her so well in life.

"Not wanting to waste precious time, I learned to knit and crochet. I sold hats for 25 cents and diamond-patterned socks for 75 cents. The following summer I felt better. I went to a cannery close to home and worked all summer. I wanted to earn money so that I would not be a burden on my family. I was 11 years old. I was tall. At the conclusion of the summer I bought mom a beautiful coat and paid my boat fare back to school."

The next term Dolly went to school for the first time since she was seven. Classes were from 1 to 3 p.m. and the courses included English and math. The morning was spent teaching the children how to mend, sew and clean. Teaching meant that they darned piles of socks, mended clothes on the sewing and scrubbed floors.

"My attitude was that this confinement will come to an end one day," said Dolly. "Do whatever I am told and I won't get in trouble.

"There were some horror stories, however none of the incidents killed me. Some of the boys and girls were molested by supervisors; somehow I was spared. I was lonely but I could live with loneliness. I kept busy reading and knitting."

It is obvious that Dolly acquired her entrepreneurial spirit early in life. She also displayed an inherent generosity.

"I credit some of that spirit to an older brother who ordered drink crystals and tiny bottles of French perfume from the *Winnipeg Daily Free Press*. He would give me a box of the products and I sold them to the people in the village. I collected the money and gave it all to him. Mother carved small wooden items and we sold them to tourists during their walkabout. Again, I gave all the money to her. So when I knitted and crocheted at school selling was easy, only this time I kept the money. When sales dried up I ironed shirts (10 cents each) or painted posters ($10 each).

"I learned that it took constant physical and mental training right from childhood to become fearless. I learned that warriors made snap decisions took risks based, of course, on their training. I also learned that various people trained the warriors. Warriors are focused."

Dolly remained in Port Alberni for high school and married Thomas Watts from the nearby Tse-shaht village. She had three children and worked in the Woodwards store as a part-time sales clerk. She also attended night school.

When the children were grown, she decided to leave the marriage and pursue her lifelong interest in education and Native culture. She went to college and then, at the age of 49 she entered the University of British Columbia.

> **"** *There were some horror stories, however none of the incidents killed me. Some of the boys and girls were molested by supervisors; somehow I was spared. I was lonely but I could live with loneliness. I kept busy reading and knitting.* **"**

# WATTS BRINGS MEANING TO SCHOOL

Dr. Michael Kew, now retired associate professor of anthropology, recalled how Dolly, along with some other women, persuaded the department to create a special course for them.

"Here we are, First Nations people and we don't find anything of meaning to us, so why don't you do something?" Watts asked.

A course was set up for the women on how colonial oppression constructed and manipulated the image of Native peoples.

"She succeeded in passing that and doggedly went on from there," said Kew. "It was not easy for her to complete a Bachelor's degree."

But complete it Dolly did, graduating with a degree in Anthropology.

"Practically all my life has been devoted to learning. Some of it willingly and some most unwillingly. My parents were my role models for parenthood and keepers of our culture. Teachers, regardless of where I was, taught me coping skills in my new world."

After graduation in 1989 Dolly returned to Kitwanga to be band manager. She noticed a minimum of a half dozen tour buses in the village everyday during the summer and saw the potential for a small restaurant beside the gas station. She also saw the opportunity to sell Native crafts.

"I did a study for the village on tourism but my people couldn't follow up on it. They just don't have the initiative. It's been whipped out of them. They want to do something but they don't know how."

Discouraged, Dolly moved back to Vancouver, took post-grad courses and worked part-time at the Museum of Anthropology. She interrupted her studies to take a year of creative writing and is now just one year away from a Masters' degree in anthropology.

In an effort to raise money for a Native youth education program she set up a stand to sell Indian bannock bread in front of the museum. The bread smelled so good that everything just sold. People said: "It's just like Grandma's."

In 1992 Dolly formed her first company, Just Like Grandma's Bannock and began catering for profit. She never looked back and in 1995 opened the Liliget restaurant deep in Vancouver's West End, using the Git'ksan word for "place where people feast.'

"I knew it was going to be okay because the previous owners had been there for ten years each. If they could last for 10 years then surely I could be there for another 10 years," Dolly said. "I had wanted to be a writer but the bannock got in the way."

With no support from there, Dolly had obstacles to face. Once again her courage and determination took over. She turned to one of

**"*I did a study for the village on tourism but my people couldn't follow up on it. They just don't have the initiative. It's been whipped out of them.*"**

the brothers for a partnership. Her son Wallace, the flight captain, threw in start-up money.

Dolly learned to be strict and self-disciplined, paying bills in cash, re-investing in the business, contributing to savings, and rewarding herself for her own creativity.

Today she serves an array of First Nations foods, such as wild Arctic caribou, venison stew with seaweed dumplings, rabbit with rosemary compote, hazelnut rainbow trout and duck breast with cranberry chutney.

"In Git'ksan culture, parents or those who assumed that role were the first to train the child. Children learned life skills. As they grew older, extended family members (aunt or uncle) were chosen to bring the training to the next level. So if the young person showed signs of being a warrior he was assigned to someone knowledgeable in warfare. Elders empowered young people by sharing their experience."

In the beginning, many nights saw the Liliget nearly empty and Dolly worried about the years of lease payments she had committed herself to. "I had no one to fall back on. My rent depended on how well I did."

But she kept going with dogged persistence, doing her own kitchen prep work, all of the cleanup and her own catering deliveries. She worked 14 hours a day, seven days a week. With word spreading that the Native restaurant was open once again, revenues rose to $400,000 last year – bringing her to breakeven costs.

# ENTREPRENEUR WITH A HEART

With financial success achieved, Dolly has shown that the difficult transition from reserve to urban enterprises is indeed possible.

"Today we have our parents, extended families and elders. We (male or female) also have teachers in our schools, colleges and universities who have specialized in areas that can bring us closer to our goals. We have many resources, such as the Native Investment and Trade Association, where we can turn for help along the way to become warriors. The best thing is that I have been able to employ our Native people."

Her three kids and one of her grand-daughters work in the restaurant, as do six other Natives and two non-Native people.

Dolly Watts is a woman of deep compassion and liberalness.

"I'm community-minded. I have a soft spot for teens and people with AIDS."

Many folk in the West End suffer from this debilitating disease. Dolly donates dinner and coupons for dinners; she holds draws for coupons. "I try to do as much as I can, I donate here and there."

"Have aboriginal women responded in a way that warrants the name warrior? Do aboriginal women want to become warriors? Of course. Not for war, but as trail blazers

**❝*Have aboriginal women responded in a way that warrants the name warrior? Do aboriginal women want to become warriors? Of course.*❞**

for self and others. They're proving to be courageous, willing to take risks, empowered through improved self esteem in the face of competitive forces all around. Armed with knowledge and skills, standing beside our helpers (resources) and our spirit helpers. I can say that many of use have become warriors, not for militancy, but for personal challenges."

In 1996, Dolly received the Native Investment and Trade Association Entrepreneur of the Year Ward. This year she competes with three other outstanding businesswomen for the national honours, to be presented in Toronto on November 6.

Yet she is still full of dreams and ambition. Her next project is to build a longhouse beside Vancouver's Trade and Convention Centre. She has applied to the City for permission for a 300-seat structure that would include a restaurant, performance stage and art gallery.

"I want to host a conference there but the city is trying to discourage me. It seems they only want to give permission for 150 seats."

Dolly invited Arthur Erickson back to the restaurant he designed to tell him of the concept. "He seems interested. And he ate everything on his plate."

Ever the visionary, Dolly looks beyond her hoped-for conference centre to a restaurant at Ottawa's Canadian Museum of Civilization.

She continues the tradition of her strong and independent family. When "government officials" tried to pressure her family into calling her the more conventional name of Dorothy, her parents stood their ground and named their daughter Dolly because she had been born so small she fit in a little doll box.

"I am a warrior. I became a fighter in order to keep afloat in the competitive world. I became fearless when faced with a real threat of losing my business. I remind myself to remain focused. I get up early to bathe and pummel my body with Dove on my sponge. I leave my home armed with years of training."

# THE OKA CRISIS: A SUMMER OF DISCONTENT

**By Bill Peacock and Len O'Connor**
**Published October, 1991**
Photos by Robert Galbraith

It began with Jean Ouellette, the then-mayor of Oka, announcing the expansion of the Oka Golf Club, at a city council meeting in March, 1989. The golf course borders the Pine Hill Cemetery, a sacred burial place for the Mohawks of the neighboring reserve of Kanesatake. The cemetery and the bordering forest, know as The Pines, has been Mohawk territory for 270 years, however they have no title or legal documents to prove their ownership, which is the problem.

For years the Mohawks of Kanesatake have protested the presence of the golf club and any attempts at expansion. The white man's legal titles are meaningless; it is Mohawk land and always has been; pure and simple.

"We warned the president of the expansion committee: you're not going to cut down any trees. We told him that if he did, he'd be responsible for the consequences," Kanesatake negotiator Allen Gabriel told the *Globe and Mail*. He could have never known just how serious the consequences would be.

The negotiations between the mayor's office and the Mohawks didn't resolve anything. Ouellette had already sealed the deal without talking to anyone from Kanesatake. The contractors had been hired and the project already approved by both mayor and council. When asked why there was contact with the Mohawks, Ouellette replied: "You know you can't talk to the Indians."

In March, 1990 after several peaceful demonstrations, the Mohawks set up camp in The Pines and up went the barricades to ensure that the construction workers would not be allowed entrance into the native sacred territory. The occupation was meant as a bargaining ploy. But instead it infuriated the mayor and the council of Oka; who sought a federal injunction to remove the barricades. They counted on the police to enforce the law and arrest the Mohawk protesters.

Québec Native Affairs Minister John Ciacca, who had a history of dealing with First Nations on a federal and provincial level, was called to mediate a settlement. He immediately saw the danger in police intervention and tried to convince the Oka mayor that the Mohawks would not back down.

"These people have seen their land disappear without having been consulted or compensated, and that, in my opinion, is unfair and unjust, especially over a golf course. The Mohawk tradition, even that of the so-called warriors, leads me to believe that discussions conducted in a calm and serene climate can succeed. The risk that any such police intervention would degenerate into a violent confrontation is great, if not inevitable. The consequences of a confrontation would be dramatic."

The negotiations dragged on. Weeks turned into months and both sides grow impatient. The Mohawks sent out a call for help to the neighboring reserves of Akwesasne and Kahnawake. The plan was simple: there is strength in numbers and it would show a sense of collective solidarity. The real issue was the lands claim, and most bands already felt cheated. Supporters from both reserves joined the protesters including members of the warrior society from Awkesasne.

The presence of warriors led by Francis Boots made people nervous. It meant that the protesters would resort to violence to defend their land. This did not wash well with the mayor of Oka who saw police intervention as inevitable.

> **"** *These people have seen their land's disappear without having been consulted or compensated, and that, in my opinion, is unfair and unjust, especially over a golf course.* **"**
> **Québec Native Affairs Minister, John Ciacca**

> **"** *Luc Carbonneau, lawyer for the Town of Oka… later informed the media that Oka council had already chosen Wednesday morning as the deadline for the removal of the blockades. Heavy equipment would be sent in to do the job if the Indians refused to do it, accompanied by police.* **"**

Ciacca met the Oka mayor and council and convinced him to postpone construction until he went to Ottawa to discuss the problem with Prime Minister Brian Mulroney. One of his first proposals was to have the federal government buy the land and give it to the Mohawks. The mayor reluctantly agreed.

The protesters refused to speak to Ciacca. They wanted a settlement that could only be ratified by Canadian Parliament. Ciacca, who was part of the Québec caucus, represented a history of broken promises from the Québec government, which made the protesters suspicious of the proposal.

For Minnie Garrow, who stood behind the barricades for three months, there could be no compromise: "In Canada, the mayor of Oka, the provincial and the federal authorities all tell Mohawks to pull down the barricade and accept a compromise in which the federal government or Québec buys the land and puts it aside. They don't understand: the land is not for sale. The Creator gave us this land. The Creator gave us our law and our rights. We negotiate on political differences, not rights." The month of June marked the fourth month of protest. The stalemate in negotiations had created tension on both sides. The police presence in Oka was strengthened and they kept a close watch on the barricades. In the Mohawk camp, the barricades were fortified with logs and barb wire. Warriors in battle fatigues patrolled The Pines in jeeps, communicating by walkie-talkie.

There was an impending sense of doom that the police would mount an attack on the barricades. Fear became a reality when on June 30, Luc Carbonneau, the lawyer for the Town of Oka, won an injunction in civil, which meant the barricades must come down or the Natives would face criminal charges.

He informed both provincial and federal negotiators that the only discussions he would have with Mohawks would be how soon they could vacate the area. Carbonneau later told the media that city council decided on Wednesday morning as the deadline for the blockades to be removed. Heavy equipment would be sent to do the job, and the police would make sure there was no interference from the Mohawks.

## A BLACK DAY IN JULY

John Ciacca realized the urgency of the situation and promptly called the mayor of Oka with an appeal to halt the golf course and avoid all confrontation with the protesters. In return he would see that the barricades came down.

"That sign of goodwill would re-establish a climate in which to negotiate a solution that is acceptable and fair to all."

The mayor was not convinced. He told the minister that nothing would ever be resolved at the negotiating table and the town of Oka was acting within the law. In a letter to the police, he demanded action.

"We are counting on you to settle this problem without any further delays or requests on our part."

Jacques Lacaille, the lawyer for the Mohawks, knew that the police could not mount a raid without permission from the minister of security, who was on holiday. He also had Ciacca's promise that no such authority would be forthcoming.

**❝** *We heard the bang. I mean real loud, right behind our ears. Tear gas – BANG! It came again. We couldn't believe this. I ran down to barricade, yelling, 'STOP! We have women and children here.* **❞**

**Ellen Gabriel**

Lacaille was scheduled to be in court the next day, July 11, to appeal the injunction. He was convinced he would win the appeal.

Behind the barricades most of the protesters believed there was still time for a solution. Unfortunately, in the early morning of July 11, a convoy of police cars arrived at Oka and proceeded towards The Pines. Ellen Gabriel and several Mohawk women were organizing the tobacco burning ceremony when they noticed the police advancing on them.

"There were riot police dressed in gray, SWAT teams in black, and regular officers in green. It was a huge squad – maybe 100 to 120 in all. They started walking up the pavement to the path. We wanted to continue our ceremonies, but couldn't. An officer motioned for one of us to come down. When we got to the barricade, they asked us for a spokesman or leader. I told them they could talk to me or Denise and we asked them to put away their guns. We told them that women and children were present. There was no need for guns or violence."

Police weren't interested in talking to the women; they wanted to speak to the chief of the warrior society. They were here to enforce the injunction: the barricades must come down. Ellen repeated there was no need for violence and without warning the police fired a volley of tear gas canisters.

"We heard the bang. I mean real loud, right behind our ears. Tear gas – BANG! It came again. We couldn't believe this. I ran down to barricade, yelling, 'STOP! We have women and children here.'"

A yellow front end loader intent on tearing down the barricades moved forward. On both sides were the police with automatic rifles and bullet proof vests. Tear gas was now accompanied by concussion grenades covering the advance of the armed riot squad.

Francis Boots and the warriors were taken by surprise. They arrived on the scene and took their positions in fox holes and behind trees.

"Our men saw them come up the path, and the cops fanned out – a few officers trying to get in the trees, others sweeping wide to the east, trying to cut off our sides."

The advancing police opened fire and the warriors hidden in The Pines fired back. The exchange lasted less than a minute; no casualties on the Mohawk side but Corporal Marcel Lemay from the SWAT team was fatally wounded. The police retreated, leaving their cruisers and the front end loader behind. The warriors were elated they had survived but worried that the police would return.

"We were scared that they would come back right away and attack," Boots told *Village Voice* writer Rick Hornung. "We would have lost. We only had enough ammunition for a minute."

The police remained in Oka, in shock that one of their officers was fighting for his life. While they planned their next move, warriors from Kahnawake captured the Mercier Bridge – the only direct link for 60,000 commuters who drove to work daily to Montreal. The warriors stopped all traffic and threatened to blow up the bridge if the police made a second attack on The Pines.

"We did it on our own. We figured on taking the bridge to protest the SQ attacks and tell them that they had to deal with us as well as the Mohawks of Kanesatake," Cookie McCumber told the *Montreal Gazette*. He had organized the attack without consulting the leader of warriors from Kahnawake, who were taken back by the move.

> **"** *We did it on our own. We figured on taking the bridge to protest the SQ attacks and tell them that they had to deal with us as well as the Mohawks of Kanesatake.* **"** **Cookie McCumber**

The protesters at the barricades breathed a sigh of relief. "The police now had to fight us on two fronts. They could not isolate us as a group of militants in the woods. They had to see us as a major political problem, not a bunch of thugs or criminals," Francis Boots told The Village Voice from inside the barricade. He knew the police would not attack again, at least not on that day.

Sam Elkas, the Québec minister of public safety with the authority to sanction the police raid on The Pines, was not aware of the action until the next day when the police raid was on the front page of every newspaper in the world. "The whole operation broke almost every rule in the book," Elkas told the media. "What a mess! More than a hundred policemen were told to attack, and no one knew who gave the order, when they gave the order, or what the attack plan was."

The police acted on their own direction and as a result Corporal Lemay was dead. To make matters worse, the forensic pathologists at the hospital in St. Eustache who had examined Lemay, were convinced the bullet that killed the officer had come from behind or from beside him, which meant the police – and not the Mohawks – had fired the fatal bullet. It had been a costly day for the police and Elkas was left to clean up the mess; and to find a solution immediately.

John Ciacca returned to The Pines and within four days he and the Mohawk protestors had an agreement that if the police began to withdraw, the warriors would vacate the bridge and begin to dismantle the barricades. There would also be an amnesty for the warriors. Ciacca agreed on all terms.

> **"***It was a double-cross, an absolute violation of any agreement that we made. Our point was to get the police out of our land. It didn't matter whether the cops were federal or provincial. They had to leave for the barricades to come down.***"**           **Ellen Gabriel**

"We have the agreement; it's just a question of working out the details for putting it into effect."

The main condition of the agreement was in the hands of the police, unfortunately they were reluctant to leave.

"We substantially reduced the number of officers as a demonstration of goodwill and willingness to support the negotiating efforts," Ghislaine Blanchette, spokesman for the police, told reporters with a straight face. The exact number of police officers called back was not given but fewer than a hundred, and that was from a force of more than 1,000 policemen surrounding The Pines. To make things worse, Blanchette admitted that the RCMP would replace the officers they had called back.

The protesters felt betrayed. Ellen Gabriel, speaking for the people behind The Pines said: "It was a double-cross, an absolute violation of any agreement that we made. Our point was to get the police out of our land. It didn't matter whether the cops were federal or provincial. They had to leave for the barricades to come down."

As the agreement sank like a sunset, the protesters realized there would be another round of negotiations. They put together a committee to represent the different factions of their people. This was done with great difficulty because now that Kahnawake was caught in the struggle, they had concerns separate from the expansion of the golf course.

# MORE NEGOTIATIONS

Grand Chief Joseph Norton had been negotiating since January with Native Affairs and was close to reaching a deal that would give Kahnawake self-government.

"We had been making progress. Ciaccia was eager to reach an agreement that would give us our own judicial system. We took that to mean a big step toward legalizing the cigarette trade on our land, and bingo if we wanted it here. We believed that if the Mohawks could get a self-government plan at Kahnawake, then they could get one at Kanesatake and Akwesasne. Sure, I was against the expansion of the golf course and the use of the police, but I did not want our plans to be tied to the golf course."

Joseph Norton would insure that his concerns were part of any agreement that was drafted. This was the lesser of complications that would make the agreement difficult for government to accept. The warriors from Kahnawake felt that their interests were well represented by Norton. There was a working relationship that served both sides. The warriors who captured Mercier Bridge felt that since they took the risk they should be part of the negotiations. This was not well received by Norton or Allain Delaronde, the head of the warrior society in Kahnawake.

Francis Boots, Loran Thompson and the warriors from Akwesasne, had their own clauses to be drafted on any agreement. The first was that the Mohawks are a sovereign nation: the

Mohawk Nation. The implementation of this clause would require participation from the U.S. and Canadian governments along with Ontario and Québec; but the chances of that happening were zero. The second clause was amnesty for the warriors and protesters who were directly involved with the conflict; and the police would not interfere with Mohawks leaving Kanesatake and Kahnawake for 48 hours.

All of these concerns had merit, but the main concern was the expansion of the golf course. After all, this was the reason why the conflict occurred; but now it was the least important clause in the proposal that was given to the Québec government. Bourassa rejected the proposal, describing their demands

as ludicrous. He wanted the Prime Minister to step in. Indian Affairs Minister Tom Siddon had avoided any involvement so far.

"We are prepared to address the social and economic development needs of Kanesatake," Siddon told the *Globe and Mail.* "But we won't talk while there are barricades and we won't talk in circumstances where firearms are used to provoke negotiations."

Siddon would abandon this stance when 4000 protesters from Chateaugay stormed the police barricades at Mercier Bridge screaming "sauvages" at the warriors and burned a Mohawk stuffed doll in effigy. Now the police had a different group of protesters to deal with and their actions forced Prime Minister Mulroney to deal with the situation. An offer was made to the town of Oka for the land that was to be used for the golf expansion but the municipal council refused to sell.

The negotiations were not helped by federal intervention. Finally Premier Robert Bourassa, on August 5, gave an ultimatum: the barricades and the occupation would end in 48 hours or suffer the consequences. The protesters dug in, there were 1500 police officers waiting for the signal that never came. Instead, Bourassa requested the help of the military, and Prime Minister Brian Mulroney sent 4000 soldiers to replace the police.

"The object of the troops is to replace the Suréte du Québec officers who, after a month or so, are presumably fatigued. The mediation process must work. It can work. We must make every effort to settle our differences without violence," Mulroney told the *Ottawa Citizen.* He hinted that the city council of Oka were reconsidering the government offer for the disputed land and were close to making a deal.

# HERE COME THE TANKS

Military intervention was the worst news for the warriors who realized there would be no way of defending themselves against an overwhelming number of soldiers who, unlike the police, could summon a whole arsenal of weapons that could neutralize the protesters in one attack.

The police finally left but their replacements arrived in tanks and helicopters. The army set up camp and instructed the Mohawks that if negotiations failed they would take matters in their own hands.

For the people of Kanesatake, the siege had turned normal life into a nightmare. Food supplies had to be smuggled into the reserve usually by boat and at great risk. Medical supplies were scarce and the elders who suffered from arthritis and hepatitis were the first casualties. The women and children already traumatized by the siege conditions, including the daily helicopters flying at low levels; the constant threat of police attack, now with the army ready to attack; pressed the tribal council to come to an agreement that would end the siege.

*The police finally left but their replacements arrived in tanks and helicopters. The army set up camp and instructed the Mohawks that if negotiations failed they would take matters in their own hands.*

*The women and children already traumatized by the siege conditions, including the daily helicopters flying at low levels; the constant threat of police attack, now with the army ready to attack; pressed the tribal council to come to an agreement that would end the siege.*

"The federal and provincial governments recognize the band council as the only legitimate representatives of the people on our territory and we are not even on the negotiating committee," a frustrated Chief George Martin told reporters. He was growing more impatient as conditions worsened on the small reserve.

Kahnawake Grand Chief Joseph Norton was feeling the same pressure from his people who also feared the army could attack at any moment. They wanted the chief to make a separate deal. Norton, along with traditional Chief Billy Two Rivers renewed negotiations. The warriors made an amendment to their amnesty demand, which Norton hoped would make the difference. The new clause read if the army allowed small planes to airlift men and women out of the territory, the warriors would abandon the Mercier Bridge.

Government negotiators were quick to agree that this was the first time a solution without violence seemed attainable. If the barricades were removed from the Mercier Bridge traffic would return to normal and the white protesters would be appeased. They would have to renegotiate with the warriors in The Pines before the whole matter was settled, but everyone agreed that removing the barricades from the bridge was a huge step in the right direction.

On August 29 three small Cesna airplanes came and went from the reserve and several warriors went with them. The remaining warriors on the bridge waited for the soldiers to remove the barricades from the bridge.

"As far as I'm concerned we've reached a very historical period, and we can look forward to a peaceful, calm settling of this situation from here on in," Joseph Norton told the *Montreal Gazette.* Unfortunately the warriors in The Pines didn't feel the same way and would not give up under any circumstance. The result was aggravated tension on both sides: the army sensing victory at hand, were ready to move in and the warriors with no options left, were ready to make a last stand.

# A VIOLENT STANDSTILL

On September 6, the Mercier Bridge was open to traffic. Tempers in Chateauguay had cooled but most residents were still angry at the warriors who occupied the bridge. When a convoy of women and children left Kahnawake in their vehicles, they were met by an angry mob of more than 500 yelling anti-Mohawk slogans. The mob threw rocks and bricks at the cars that shattered windshields and injured nine people, including an eight-month-old baby.

The violence spread to Tekakwitha Island, which served as a marina for the Kahnawake Reserve, located south of the Mercier Bridge. On September 16, a confrontation between soldiers, police and several hundred band members became ugly. The police fired tear gas at the Mohawks, who charged the ranks of the soldiers. Seventy-five Mohawks would end up in the hospital while 19 soldiers received medical attention.

Behind the barricades at The Pines, nothing had changed. Warriors and soldiers were eyeball to eyeball, and the negotiations came to a standstill. "At the same time, inside the treatment center it was getting very, very

tense. All of the pressure, all of the deprivation, all of our differences were coming out," lawyer Stanley Cohen told the CBC. "The men had their position, the women had theirs."

On the same day as the riot on Tekakwitha Island, the Army took over negotiations; or brought them to an end, depending on one's interpretation. The warriors realized that any agreement hinged on their surrender. Their only recourse was to find a way to escape and since they were surrounded on all sides, this was not seen as an option.

Chief Joseph Norton chaired a special meeting for all factions. He told everyone that government negotiators had offered extensive proposals, land taxation, rights to natural resources, and no golf expansion at Oka. The land purchased by the federal government would be turned over to the band council of Kanesatake; the agreement hinged on the warriors surrender. On September 26, the warriors accepted the ultimatum, and proceeded to burn their weapons, tapes and anything that could be used as evidence against them. Waving the warriors flag and a banner of the Iroquois Confederacy they joined the remaining protesters in a sweet grass and tobacco burning ceremony.

When it was over they filed out of the treatment centre. The army was waiting with buses to transport them to the Farnham military base. Rather than walking towards the buses the women ran towards the forest and the men ran in the opposite direction. Both were rounded up by soldiers, who forced them into the buses with gun butts and billy clubs,

*Ronald (Lasagna) Cross*

"A few slipped through, but it was a disaster," long-time protester Minnie Garrow told the *Village Voice's* Rick Hornung. "The army was shining those blinding lights, and I can still hear the screams when the soldiers swung their rifles or knocked people to the ground. It was terrible."

Loran Thompson – the most wanted – was one of the few warriors who escaped. Ronald (Lasagna) Cross, Robert (Mad Jap) Skidders, Gordon Lazore, a.k.a. Noriega; Mark- (Blackjack) Montour and several others, were taken to army headquarters and then turned over to police to face charges. It was a humbling defeat after a heroic stand that had the world watching.

"We had shown Canada and the world the justice of our cause, and now it was time to go out. We've established our honor," Lorraine Montour said to the few journalists left at the treatment centre.

## THE LEGACY OF OKA

The first time the Canadian government sent an army to suppress Native people was to the Northwest Uprising, with Louis Riel as the designated martyr. More than a hundred years later 4,000 soldiers surfaced in Oka and Khanawake to subdue a protest. Both times the Army came out the winner. MacDonald hoped that Riel and his dream were over when the hangman put a rope around Riel's neck. He was wrong; Riel became a symbol of Native rights more powerful after he died and was recently given the official title of Manitoba's Founding Father.

Oka will have a similar effect that will resonate throughout Native communities for a long time. The protesters at The Pines can hold their heads high: they brought a sense of pride to First Nations across Canada and a collective sense of unity that will be remembered for generations to come. For a brief period, the confrontation at the Mercier Bridge and at The Pines was watched by Natives on television from Newfoundland to Vancouver Island; a sense of solidarity for the Mohawks was felt by

> ❝ *We had shown Canada and the world the justice of our cause, and now it was time to go out. We've established our honor.* ❞ **Lorraine Montour**

everyone. For once the media gave an honest picture of Natives in crisis and how tilted the odds were against them.

"The Oka crisis was, I think, in many ways a moral victory for aboriginal people," Keith Spicer, chairman of the Citizens' Forum on Canada's future told a gathering of First Nations. "For the first time anybody can remember, your causes, interests and values were on the television screens for weeks at a time."

The police (Suréte de Québec) were exposed for their irresponsible and brutal behavior. Their unsanctioned attack that caused the crisis is an example of their attitude towards First Nations. The Suréte couldn't wait to use force to suppress the protesters when force was not required. Unfortunately, when dealing with Natives, the "might is right" attitude is shared by most police forces, right across Canada.

Prime Minister Brian Mulroney's failure in dealing with the tribal council at Kanesatake which could have prevented the confrontation is another example of Ottawa's laissez-faire attitude towards Native problems. Tom Siddon, the federal minister for Indian Affairs demonstrated time after time the indifferent mentality Ottawa has maintained for years, when it comes to settling land claims.

Québec Premier Robert Bourassa fared even worse than his federal counterparts. His gauche handling of the crisis will have grave repercussions when it comes to closing the massive hydro deal with Cree Grand Chief Mathew Coon Come. It may cost him his career.

The people of Kanesetake can claim victory, since the golf expansion will not happen – ever. Unfortunately, the scars from the occupation will remain in the community and that is a heavy price to pay for defending your own land. Relations with their white neighbors in Chateaugay and Oka are damaged beyond repair. The hostility shown by the citizens of Chateaugay when they stoned the convoy of cars leaving Khanawake is one of the ugliest images of racism ever seen in Canada and unfortunately it demonstrated only too well the hatred most Québecois feel for the Mohawks.

It didn't start with Oka. The Mohawks and French have hated each other for more than three hundred years. It is a feud that will not end tomorrow or next year, and the history of the Oka crisis will only add fuel to the flames.

Oka will be remembered as the turning point in Native Land Claims. Finally a Native band said, "We are not going to take it" and stood up to the federal and provincial governments.

> **❝** *The Oka crisis was, I think, in many ways a moral victory for aboriginal people. For the first time anybody can remember, your causes, interests and values were on the television screens for weeks at a time.* **❞**
> **Keith Spicer, chairman of the Citizens' Forum on Canada's future**

# THOMAS PRINCE: CANADA'S FORGOTTEN ABORIGINAL WAR HERO

**By Lloyd Dolha**                    **Published May, 2001**

The ten war medals of Canada's most decorated aboriginal war hero Sergeant Thomas George Prince, a veteran of WWII and the Korean War, were returned to the Prince family after being lost for over 30 years.

*Photo: Unknown*

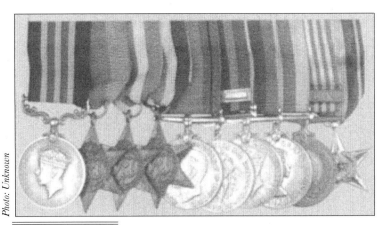

Photo: Unknown

*H*e was a crack shot with a rifle and crafty as a wolf in the field.

"I was out in Halifax for the AFN meeting when I got the call that the medals were coming up for auction. We re-organized our committee and began to write letters for a fundraising media campaign and I did some radio talk shows," said Jim Bear, nephew to the late Thomas Prince.

Money and pledges poured in from across the country. Bear, a prominent member of the Winnipeg aboriginal community has been after the medals since 1995, when the medals first re-surfaced eighteen years after the death of Tommy Prince in November 1977. The medals were auctioned off by a Winnipeg coin dealer for $17,500 in 1997.

The ten medals were bought by the Prince family at a London, Ontario auction for $75,000 on the third bid.

The medals from WWII includes the King George Military Medal and the US Silver Star, which was presented to Prince at Buckingham Palace by King George VI, for his five years of outstanding service as a member of the First Special Service Force, a combined Canadian-U.S. elite airborne unit that came to be known as the famed "Devil's Brigade.'

The wartime experience of Sergeant Tommy Prince is the stuff of legend. He was a quiet ordinary man who had greatness thrust upon him by the force of one of the greatest conflicts in the history of Western civilization. It's as if he was born and bred for one great task and then cast aside by the very society he fought for. He was a true son of his people and a great warrior.

His life story is told in the publication *Manitobans in Profile: Thomas George Prince*, 1981, Penguin Publishers Ltd., Winnipeg, Manitoba. It's a fascinating piece of Canadiana.

Thomas George Prince was the great-great-grandson of the famous Chief Peguis, the Salteaux chief who led his people to the southwestern shore of Lake Winnipeg in the late 1790s from Sault Ste. Marie, Ontario. One of eleven children, Tommy Prince was born in a canvas tent on a cold October day in 1915. When he was five, the family moved to the Brokenhead Reserve just outside of Scanterbury, some 80 kilometers north of Winnipeg, where he learned his father's skills as a hunter and trapper. As a teenager, Prince joined the Army cadets and perfected his skill with a rifle until he could put five bullets through a target the size of a playing card at 100 metres.

When war broke out in Europe in 1939 Prince volunteered at 24, and was accepted as a sapper in the Royal Canadian Engineers, which he served with for two years. In June 1940 he volunteered for paratrooper service. The training was hard and very few successfully completed. Prince was one of nine out of a hundred to win his wings from the parachute school at Ringway, near Manchester, England.

*It wasn't his ability to "jump" that made him a good paratrooper. Prince had a natural instinct for "ground". He would land, creep forward on his belly with the speed and agility of a snake and take advantage of small depressions in an otherwise flat field to conceal himself from view. He was a crack shot with a rifle and crafty as a wolf in the field.*

Manitobans in Profile, p. 19

Prince was promoted to Lance Corporal as a result of his impressive skills and in September, 1942, flew back to Canada to train with the first Canadian Parachute Battalion and was soon promoted to sergeant. It merged with the United States Special Force, the airborne unit known as the "Green Berets." The First Special Service Force was an experiment in unity comprising 1600 of the "toughest men to be found in Canada and the United States."

All the men were qualified paratroopers and received training in unarmed combat, demolition, mountain fighting and as ski troops. They were described as "the best small force of fighting men ever assembled on the North American continent" and the "best god-damned fighters in the world and a terror to their enemies."

This combined elite force was first called into action in January 1943, when the Japanese occupied Kiska, an island in the Aleutian chain of islands near Alaska in the Pacific but the Japanese had already withdrawn. They went to the Mediterranean, followed by the Sicily landing. By a daring maneuver it captured strategic Monte la Difensa, an extremely difficult piece of ground. Fighting side by side with the US Fifth Army it maintained an aggressive offensive throughout the Italian campaign. The liberation of Rome was the culmination of its daring exploits.

A natural hunter, Prince's fieldcraft was unequalled and in recognition of unique abilities he was made reconnaissance sergeant. At night, Prince would crawl toward the enemy lines, mostly alone, to listen to the Germans, estimate their numbers and report back to his battalion commander.

Before every attack, he was sent out to reconnoiter enemy positions and landscape formations that could provide cover for an attacking platoon.

Prince's most daring exploit was on the Anzio beach-head where the Special Service Force had fought for ninety days without relief on the frontlines.

On February 8, 1944, Sergeant Prince went out alone on a voluntary assignment to run a radio wire 1500 metres into enemy territory to an abandoned farmhouse where he established an observation post. From his post, Prince could observe enemy troop movements unseen by the Allied artillery and radio back their exact locations. Armed with this knowledge, the Allied artillery could lay down an accurate barrage and successfully destroyed four enemy positions.

*A natural hunter, Prince's fieldcraft was unequalled and in recognition of unique abilities, he was made reconnaissance sergeant.*

When the communications were abruptly cut off, Prince knew what had happened. Shellfire from the opposing armies had cut the line. Without concern for his own safety, Prince stripped off his uniform and dressed in farmer's clothes left behind. At that time, many Italian farmers persisted in remaining on their farms despite the war that raged around them.

Acting as an angry farmer, Prince went out into the field shaking his fists and shouting at the German-Italian line and then to the Allied line. Taking a hoe out into the field, he pretended to work the field in plain view of the enemy line while he secretly followed the radio line to where the break had occurred. Pretending to tie his shoe, he secretly spliced the line together and continued to work the field before retiring back to the farmhouse where he continued to relay enemy positions. With the positions of the enemy revealed to the Allied artillery, the enemy soon withdrew.

Only then did Prince return to his CO, Lieutenant-Colonel Gilday who recommended Prince for the Military Medal for "exceptional bravery in the field."

It was at Anzio that the Force earned the name "Devil's Brigade." In the diary of a dead German soldier there was a passage that read, "The black devils are all around us every time we come into the line."

The passage was a reference to the Force's tactic of smearing their faces with black and sneaking past Axis lines under the cover of darkness and slitting the throats of enemy soldiers.

Following the capture of Italy, the Devil's Brigade took part in the seizure of coastal islands during the invasion of southern France. The Force gained the mainland and proceeded up the Riviara until they reached mountainous defenses held by German forces.

To break the impasse, the Force would have to launch a surprise attack, destroy the enemy defensive line and quickly capture the reserve battalions before they could be brought up as reinforcements. To accomplish this daring move, the Force needed to know the exact location of enemy reserves and details of roads and bridges.

With only a private to accompany him, Prince breached the enemy line and located the reserve encampment. On the way back to report, Prince and the private came upon a battle between some Germans and a squad of French partisans. From a rear position, the pair began to pick off the Germans until they withdrew as a result of high casualties.

When Prince made contact with the French leader, the Frenchman asked "Where is the rest of your company?" Pointing to the private, Prince said "Here."

"Mon Dieu. I thought there were at least fifty of you!" said the astonished Frenchman.

The French commander recommended Prince for the Croix de Guerre, but the courier was killed en route and the message never reached the French Commander-in-Chief, Charles de Gaulle.

*One of his proudest moments and most cherished memories was when King George VI pinned on the Military Medal and the Silver Star, on behalf of President Roosevelt, and chatted with Prince about his wartime experiences.*

Returning to his own line, Prince was again sent out to the action on the frontline, despite his fatigue. Then, the enemy line was breached and an attack was launched on the German encampment reported by Prince. When the battle had ended, Prince had been without food or sleep for 72 hours, fought two battles and covered over 70 km on foot. For his role, the Americans awarded Prince the Silver Star.

One of his proudest moments and most cherished memories was when King George VI pinned on the Military Medal and the Silver Star, on behalf of President Roosevelt, and chatted with Prince about his wartime experiences.

Sergeant Thomas Prince was one of 59 Canadians awarded the U.S. Silver Star and one of three who were awarded the King George Military Medal.

In December 1944, the Devil's Brigade was disbanded. The war in Europe ended while Prince was in England. He returned to Canada and was honourably discharged on June 15, 1945.

Prince returned to civilian life on the Brokenhead Reserve and found that few things had changed. He worked in pulpwood camps and was a heavy drinker on weekends. In 1946 at a dance, a woman attacked him with a broken beer bottle and badly cut his right cheek requiring 64 stitches.

It was a major turning point for Prince. He resolved to leave the reserve and get a job in Winnipeg.

With the assistance from the Department of Veteran's Affairs, he established his own cleaning service with a half-ton panel truck and cleaning supplies and, for a time, prospered.

At the time, the Manitoba Indian Association had been seeking an influential spokesperson and on December 1, 1946 elected him as chairman. The federal government had recently announced the formation of a Special Parlimentary Committee to revise the Indian Act.

The Manitoba Indian Association were concerned about the slow encroachment on their hunting and trapping rights. They wanted better housing, roads and educational opportunities for their children and financial assistance to start up businesses.

Prince arranged for friends to run his small, but profitable business. As chairman, he consulted extensively with aboriginal communities across Manitoba. He developed clear, well-documented arguments that clearly laid out the Manitoba Association's concerns in a brief presented to the committee on June 5, 1947.

Prince was overcome and frustrated by the legalese statements government officials threw out to counter his arguments. The committee hearings dragged on for two months and Prince became increasingly frustrated. He tried to persuade other aboriginal representatives to travel to London and appeal to King George VI whom he had met.

*Prince returned to civilian life on the Brokenhead Reserve and found that few things had changed.*

*While some changes were made to the Indian Act, life for Canada's Indians remained unchanged. Prince came to realize from the committee hearings that Indian people lacked prestige in the eyes of post-war Canadian society, who generally looked down on Indian people.*

While some changes were made to the Indian Act, life for Canada's Indians remained unchanged. Prince came to realize from the committee hearings that Indian people lacked prestige in the eyes of post-war Canadian society, who generally looked down on Indian people. To change this widely-held view became a bit of an obsession with him.

He returned to Winnipeg with the intention of building up his business but instead found that his "friends" had wrecked his truck in an accident and it had been sold for scrap metal. With no recourse, Prince returned to the lumber camps and worked at a local concrete factory in the summers.

Then at the age of 34, one week after the Canadian government announced its involvement in Korea, Tommy Prince again volunteered.

As part of its UN commitments, the Canadian government formed and trained the 2nd Battalion of the Princess Patricia's Canadian Light Infantry (2PPCLI), which Prince joined as a seasoned veteran. He and other veterans were re-instated at their former ranks, in charge of training fresh recruits.

Tom Prince held an exalted position in the military tradition of the 2PPCLI, where he was the hard-boiled sergeant whose legendary exploits were held in awe by the fresh recruits.

*H*is skills as a hunter, which had made him one of the best soldiers, had no value in the urban centre of Winnipeg in the early 1950s.

Following basic training at Wainwright, Alberta, the 2PPCLI sailed across the Pacific on December 7, 1950. It was the first Canadian unit to land and to become part of 27th Commonwealth Brigade in Korea.

Prince's service on the Korean frontline was intense but brief. Second in command of a rifle platoon, the 2PPCLI were part of a commonwealth effort to push back the North Korean forces from hill and mountain strongholds.

In February, 1951, Prince led a "snatch patrol" of eight men into enemy territory and captured two guarded machine gun posts as part of a demoralization effort. The tactic was repeated successfully many times with Prince in charge. But his commanding officers felt that Prince took too many chances with the men's lives and eventually assigned him fewer patrols.

Prince was with the 2PPCLI when they, together with the 3rd Royal Australian Regiment, were awarded the United States' Presidential Unit Citation for distinguished service in the Kapyong valley on April 24 and 25, during one of the toughest actions of the war. The Patricias were to hold a defensive position on Hill 677 so that a South Korean division could withdraw during an attack by Chinese and North Korean forces. Although the battalion was surrounded and re-supply of ammunition and emergency rations could only be accomplished by air, the Patricias held their ground. The enemy withdrew. Ten 2PPCLI men were killed and twenty-three were wounded during the battle.

His knees were subject to painful swelling as a result of the constant climbing of the steep Korean country side. Following a medical examination in May 1951, he was hospitalized and then assigned administrative duties. In August, he returned to Canada.

Prince remained in active service as an administrative sergeant at Camp Borden in Ontario.

His knees responded to the added rest and in March 1952, Prince volunteered for a second tour of duty and sailed for Korea in October with the 3rd Battalion PPCLI.

In November, the training of the 3PPCLI was interrupted by fighting on "the Hook," a key position of the Sami-chon River that overlooked much of the rear areas of the UN forces.

When a Chinese battalion gained a foothold on the forward positions of another UN unit on November 18, the 3rd PPCLI was ordered in to help defend the sector. By dawn of the following day, with the assistance of the 3rd Patricias, the UN unit recaptured the post. Five Patricias were killed and nine wounded, one of whom was Sergeant Prince.

He recovered from his injury but began to have continual difficulties with his arthritic knees. He spent several weeks in the hospital between January and April. In July, 1953, the Korea Armistice was signed and Prince returned to Canada. He remained in the army until September 1954 when he was discharged with a small pension because of his bad knees.

Unskilled and unable to fit into the post-war boom, Prince retained only menial jobs and was the subject of scorn from white workers ignorant of his wartime gallantry. His skills as a hunter which had made him one of the best soldiers had no value in the urban centre of Winnipeg in the early 1950s.

In many ways, Tom's problems were typical of a certain type of returning soldier. These men had been unskilled workers prior to joining the army. From being in low socio-economic positions, they suddenly became respected and honoured men who wore a uniform and commanded attention. Men like Prince were promoted to the rank of non-commissioned officers and had authority over others. When they were demobilized from the army, all the power and respect which their uniforms generated suddenly disappeared.

*The PPCLI honoured Sgt Tommy Prince, third from left, in a ceremony held August 2, 1975.*　　　*Photo: Princess Patricia's Canadian Light Infantry*

*At his funeral, a delegation of Princess Patricias served as pallbearers and draped a Canadian flag over his coffin for the memorial service attended by active soldiers, veterans and representatives from France, Italy and United States, friends and family.*

Nevertheless, Prince met and married Verna Sinclair shortly after and had five children together. By the early 1960s, nothing had really changed for Indian people. Prince still suffered from discrimination at the jobs he could get. Often he simply quit. His arthritic knees got worse so he drank more. All of this led to money problems and he and Verna separated in 1964. His five children had to be placed in foster homes by the Children's Aid Society. Prince tried to keep in touch with his children but they were often moved to other foster homes. He could keep in touch only with his daughter Beryl, who remained in one foster home for seven years. He visited monthly and never gave up trying to keep in touch with his other children. In the years before his death, Prince was "a truly forgotten man." It was during these years that he pawned his prized medals.

Tommy Prince died at Winnipeg's Deer Hospital on November 1977, at the age of 62. At his funeral, a delegation of Princess Patricias served as pallbearers and draped a Canadian flag over his coffin. The memorial service was attended by active soldiers, veterans and representatives from France, Italy and the United States, friends and family.

*As the coffin was lowered into the ground, Beryl and Beverly Prince, Tommy's daughters, shed tears. When the officer in charge presented Beverly with the Canadian flag which had been draped over the coffin the flow of tears increased. Who were all these strangers, both military and civilian, honouring her father with apparent sadness and great respect? Where had they been these past years when her father, crippled from machine- gun wounds, was forced to do menial jobs to keep alive? Were the honour and respect given only after his death? Did these people really care or was this just a colourful pageant performed by white people for entertainment?*

Manitobans in Profile, p.6

The ten medals of Sergeant Thomas Prince have been verified as the originals by the War Museum in Ottawa and will be held in trust for the Prince family at the Museum of Man and Nature in Winnipeg.

# GRASSY NARROWS FIRST NATIONS FIGHTS FOR ITS FUTURE

**by Lauren Carter**                    **Published March, 2003**

*Protester bars entrance to company logging truck*

*Photo: Lauren Carter*

The people of Asubpeeschoseewagong (Grassy Narrows First Nation), located 80 kilometres north of Kenora, in Northern Ontario, have seen more than their share of suffering.

In the early 1960s, they were uprooted by Indian Affairs. In the '70s, the government informed them that several tonnes of inorganic mercury from a pulp and paper mill upstream in Dryden had contaminated their water and fish. While the band eventually received compensation from the Reed Paper Company and the Federal Government, the mercury remains, seriously affecting the health of the land, and a percentage of the 14-square-mile reserve's residents still suffer the effects of mercury poisoning. Add to this the ongoing flooding of their sacred sites, traditional lands and wild rice fields by Ontario Hydro, threats to dump nuclear waste on their Customary Lands, the nightmare of residential schools, sky-high unemployment, and resulting cultural and social problems and you've got a fair mix of misery.

## IT ISN'T OVER YET

In the latest threat to their well-being, Montreal-based forestry giant Abitibi-Consolidated, which pulled in over four billion dollars in 2002 and supplies Knight Ridder newspaper chain, the *New York Times*, and the *Washington Post* (among others) with newsprint, is pushing for approval of a 20-year-plan to "manage" the Whiskey Jack Forest including the last remaining stand of old-growth boreal forest on Asubpeeschoseewagong traditional lands. The Grassy First Nations might as well be on the moon for the amount of trees and plants and animals they'll have

> **"** *Over 50 percent of our traditional land has been clear-cut. There's reforestation but it's all monoculture tree farming. They plant trees they're going to harvest again. The land is turning into a tree farm.* **"**
>
> **Joe Fobister, Grassy Narrows first Nations Environmental Commitee**

*One of the massive clear cutting sites on the Reserve*

*Photo: EnviroWatch, Inc.*

around them if this plan goes through. While regeneration is seen to be the great hope, it will not assist inevitable soil erosion and the 40 percent of plant and animal species dependent on the sensitive ecosystem of the boreal forest. Irrevocable damage has already been done.

"Over 50 percent of our traditional land has been clear-cut. There's reforestation but it's all monoculture tree farming. They plant trees they're going to harvest again. The land is turning into a tree farm," says Joe Fobister, spokesperson for the Grassy Narrows First Nation Environmental Committee.

Abitibi's new plan, dubbed the "Whiskey Jack Management Plan" would secure the corporation's right to harvest the forest in five year increments from April 2004 until 2024 despite Aboriginal treaty rights set out in the Royal Proclamation of 1763, further secured by Treaty #3 and, further still, by the Canadian constitution.

The community has been battling Abitibi, the Ministry of Natural Resources (MNR), and the Ontario government for years in an effort to develop selective logging practices that would sustain the ecosystem that the local First Nation's depend on. In 2000, Joe Fobister, Willie Keewatin and Andy Keewatin Jr. initiated a case against the Ontario government (with defense from the Sierra Legal Defence Fund) arguing that Abitibi's operations infringed on their constitutional rights to hunt and trap in their traditional lands. That same year, protesters lobbied when the corporation clear-cut a large area in Wahgoshig First Nations traditional territory, cutting trees that marked graves on ancestral burial sites. This cut came irregardless of on-going talks between Abitibi, the MNR, and Wahgoshig leaders.

Despite all efforts – including raising issues in Abitibi's public consultation sessions, a process that has proved irrelevant for many – clear cutting has continued, eliminating the forest, destroying the ecosystem, bit by bit.

"We're seeing animals that are diseased. The Government of Ontario claims that it's caused by parasites but we never saw these diseases up until ten years ago. It's becoming a common thing to see animals with tumours on their lungs, white spots on their livers," Fobister says.

## AND NO ONE, IT SEEMS, WILL LISTEN

Part of the problem is that the Government of Ontario is insisting that the band's Customary Lands – 2500 square miles surrounding the 14 square miles of their reserve – is actually Crown Land. For the Government, the MNR, and the corporation, this belief, as false as it is according to Treaty 3 and the Canadian Constitution, means that there is nothing wrong with exiling 700 members of a land-based culture onto a tiny island in the middle of a weak and unhealthy forest, largely stripped bare by clear cuts.

"[The Province of Ontario] won't recognize our existence," Fobister says in

> "*We're seeing animals that are diseased. The Government of Ontario claims that it's caused by parasites but we never saw these diseases up until ten years ago. It's becoming a common thing to see animals with tumours on their lungs, white spots on their livers.*"
>
> **Joe Fobister**

frustration. "The MNR is serving the corporation. I'd say they're in bed together."

Indian Affairs Minister Robert Nault has refused to become involved in the issue, saying it is a matter for the MNR, and angering many.

In response to being ignored while the system-at-large gradually whittles away their land and their way of life – a process that suggests to many a continued cultural genocide – members of the Grassy Narrows First Nation decided to take the process into their own hands. Last December, they issued an invitation for public consultation with Abitibi and the MNR – to take place in the middle of a clear-cutting access road, five kilometres from the Grassy Narrows community. Since then, protesters have been blocking company access into the last remaining old growth of the Whiskey Jack Forest. Solidarity – from First Nation's communities and both Native and non-Native activist groups – has been strong.

And still, Joe Fobister says that in Abitibi's annual work schedule, exhibited to the public in early April, it appears they plan to continue logging on the land that the protesters are occupying. It'll be business as usual once the roads dry, and the logging trucks resume their duties.

While the corporation waits, the blockade maintains a presence with a handful of people. Two portables – out of the four used to house people and school the youth over the winter – have been taken away. But Judy DaSilva, also from the Environmental Committee says not to worry. Plans continue for further actions including a youth gathering at the blockade in June. And once the trucks have started moving again, near the end of May, the warriors will return to their positions en masse. For if they don't protect the land for themselves and for their children and their children's children, who, exactly, will?

> **"** *[The Province of Ontario] won't recognize our existence. The MNR is serving the corporation. I'd say they're in bed together.* **"**
> **Joe Fobister**

# ROBBIE ROBERTSON PUTS THE WEIGHT ON NATIVE MUSIC

**By Len O'Connor**                    **Published June, 1995**

Robbie Robertson was the keynote speaker at Music West held in Vancouver in May. The event – part conference and part musical festival – had a list of Canadian recording hot shots lecturing on all aspects of the music industry. It was also a showcase for performers who played the local clubs.

But this year's festival was different – there was the presence of Native talent, which is why Robbie Robertson made a rare appearance as a speaker, not as a musician. Native bands included Kashtin, who played to a packed house at the Commodore, and, driving his Indian Car all the way from Arizona, Keith Secola and his Wild Band of Indians. Blues guitarist Clyde Roulette and country singer and Juno winner Vern Cheechoo performed at the Friendship Centre.

*"I salute the organizers for booking as many Native bands as they did. That is the reason I'm here."*

Robbie was visibly moved and proud that Native musicians were "invited to the party." A Mohawk from the Six Nations, Robbie, along with Buffy St. Marie and the Vegas brothers who started the band Redbone, were the only Native musicians who left an impression in the sixties.

"A lot of white musicians dressed like Indians, but there was only a few of us out there at the time," said Robbie from the podium. "I've had a lot of luck over the years and my advice to Native musicians is to believe in yourself. Set goals. Remember one thing, if you can't dream it happening, it won't. But if you are willing to live the dream and work to be as good as you possibly can, the brass ring is yours."

Robbie knows the sacrifice it takes to make

*Ronnie Hawkins and the Hawks at the Brass Rail in Hamilton, Ontario, C. 1963*
*Photo: Turkey Scratch Arechives*

the dream come true. He left home when he was fifteen to play with Ronnie Hawkins and the Hawks, Canada's premier rock band in 1958. "This band," Robbie said, "played the fastest, most violent rock 'n roll that I'd ever heard. It was exciting and very explosive. I loved the dynamics, the style."

Rockabilly in overdrive with an intuitive rhythm and blues feel, with outrageous stage antics were the Hawks – the last holdouts of the fifties Memphis sound. Ronnie Hawkins was part of the second wave of southern rockers that emerged in the fifties, just before Elvis entered the army and the curtain came down. Gene Vincent, Eddy Cochrane and Ronnie would leave behind one or two classic singles, before all three would disappear in self-exile.

Ronnie had two hits released in the late fifties, *Mary Lou* and *Forty Days*, which made it onto the Billboard's top ten list. Unfortunately, he was unable to sustain a successful recording career and was forced to maintain his following mainly on the reputation of his band.

The Hawks played Alan Freed's rock shows and worked a circuit that went from New York to Dallas and all stops in-between. Yet it was in Toronto where they worked as the house band at Le Coq D'Or, that Ronnie and his crew set new standards of excellence that would influence a generation of Canadian musicians.

The Hawks would be Robbie's apprenticeship. He evolved into one of the finest guitarists of his generation and the musicians he played with were head and shoulders above most of their peers. David Clayton Thomas, who sang in Toronto bars before joining Blood Sweat and Tears, remembers the Hawks in their heyday:

"For young musicians, there were no other options. Yonge Street was the place you went and Ronnie's was the band you heard. It was that basic, if you wanted to be a musician.

The band, they were Gods to us, particularly Robbie Robertson. He was our idol. We'd go down to Le Coq D'Or with our Telecasters but because some of us were too young to get in, we'd stand beside the back door. The guys in the band would always make sure the back door was left open a crack; so on any given night you'd always see a dozen fifteen-year-olds, and maybe a twenty-two-year old like myself, peeking inside watching Robbie Robertson."

The personnel in the Hawks had changed over the years, but the final casting that started with Robbie and eventually included Rick Danko, Garth Hudson and Richard Manuel with Levon Helm (the sole American) would remain intact for the next sixteen years.

Five talented musicians in the prime of youth were ready to write their own history. They matured together as Ronnie's back up band and then moved on. For a while they played on their own but eventually were hired by Bob Dylan for his 1965 world tour.

It would be the beginning of the second phase in Robbie's career. From Ronnie Hawkins he had mastered his craft as a guitarist; now he was entering the ring with America's poet songwriter, the voice of a generation.

What Time magazine would later describe as "the most decisive moment in rock history," did not have a perfect beginning. The Hawks, rooted in rockabilly, rhythm and blues and gospel, were not inclined towards folk music. Robbie wasn't sure if this was their big break or the big bust.

"There was a lot of strumming in this music and we didn't play with strummers. Anybody who strummed, it just seemed to take the funkiness out of it. Unless of course it was rockabilly and this wasn't rockabilly. So in the beginning, there was a lot of skepticism about whether this was meant to be."

This was soon resolved when they started rehearsing and got acquainted, an instant camaraderie developed even though they were worlds apart musically. The chemistry between Dylan and the band would not be the problem – Dylan going electric was the problem; a big problem that would turn into a nightmare.

## A NEW VISION

The Prince of Folk had only performed once with a band, and that was at the Newport Folk festival where he scandalized the audience of folk purists who felt they had been betrayed by their acoustic messiah. The Dylan tour of

> **"**For young musicians, there were no other options. Yonge Street was the place you went and Ronnie's was the band you heard. It was that basic, if you wanted to be a musician.**"**
>
> **Robbie Robertson**

'65, received the same response; a chorus of boos would fill the concert hall the moment the band plugged in their instruments. *New York Times* editor Robert Palmer wrote that only two cities (Memphis and Dallas) had received Dylan and the band with applause.

"I was trying for a quality of music, an emotional experience with dynamics," Robbie explained. "This wasn't just thrashing around. And we finally discovered something while performing live although they booed us all over the world. They were really rough. And most of the time, if you were put in this position, you would say, 'Wait a minute, I must be doing something wrong. All these people must be

*Bob Dylan with Robbie, Chicago, November 1965.*
*Photo: Dean Meador*

*O*n the road, Dylan shared his new material with Robbie, making him part of the creative process. Now Robbie wanted to develop his writing that would set the stage for the band to develop its own destiny.

right.' But when we would listen to the tapes after the shows, we'd say, 'That's not that bad.' It took a lot of blindness or courage – I don't know which – to think that we were gonna persist out there. And eventually people came around. We just stuck to our guns. I had a lot of respect for Bob not giving in."

The British concerts were the turning point for the band. The Albert Hall performance was attended by the Beatles and the Rolling Stones. After the show, Robbie found himself talking with John Lennon and Keith Richards. The British Press was more receptive to Dylan's electric persona, they had high praise for *Blonde on Blonde*, the album that showcased his new material, and kind words for his back-up group.

Everyone was happy to return to New York. The band had come to terms with Dylan's material, and a new vision was sowing in Robbie's mind. On the road, Dylan shared his new material with Robbie, making him part of the creative process. Now Robbie wanted to develop his writing that would set the stage for the band to develop its own destiny. The opportunity would come under the worst of circumstances; while waiting for the tour to resume stateside, Dylan was in a motorcycle accident.

The band moved to Woodstock so they could work on Bob's new material while he was recuperating. They rented a suburban-looking pink house and set up a make-shift studio. For the next six months they worked on songs that Bob had started on the road; and for the first time Robbie contributed new songs, as did the other members, and co-wrote with Dylan.

The sessions lasted from spring until December 1967. For Robbie, they would be the mold for the band's first album.

Drummer Levon Helm noted in his biography that the recording of *Ain't No More Cane* was a breakthrough for the band. "One of the things we'd always loved about soul music was the way groups like the Staple Singers and the Impressions would stack those individual voices on top of one another, each voice coming in at a different time until you got this blend that was just magic. So when we cut a song called *Ain't No More Cane* we tried to do it like that. With those multiple voices and jumbled instruments we discovered our sound."

A record deal was signed with Capitol Records. John Simon who had produced Leonard Cohen's debut album was brought in as producer and in the fall of 1968, *Music From Big Pink* was released. The cover was a picture of their pink house and the back was a picture of all band members with their families, cousins and close friends.

The message was that The Band was not a group of rock stars living a fairy tale existence. They were working musicians who played music inspired by the artists who had spent their lives pioneering their music. In his book Mystery Train, Greil Marcus wrote a very accurate description.

"The picture inside *Big Pink of the Band* – their friends and relatives and their ugly but much loved pink house – caught some of what they had to say. Against a cult of youth, they felt for continuity of generations, against the instant America of the sixties, they looked for the traditions that made new things not only possible, but valuable; against the pop scene, all flux and novelty, they set themselves; a band with years behind it and meant to last."

The album received rave reviews and Robbie's songwriting talents didn't go unnoticed. The song that established him as the group's main tunesmith was *The Weight*. It was a white soul ballad anchored in a gospel groove, with Levon trading verses with Danko and Manuel; and all three joining in for the chorus. This was The Band, hillbilly harmonies contrasting with five cultivated musical personalities and a communal sense of feel that had no equal in rock.

The next album simply titled *The Band* would be their masterpiece. It was one of those

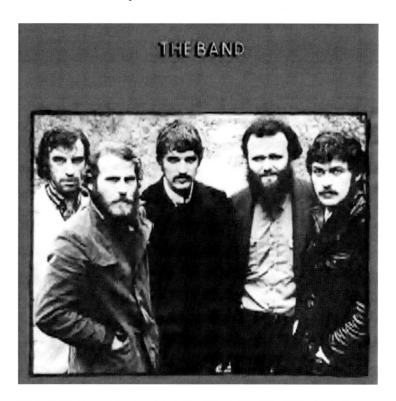

*The next album simply titled The Band would be their masterpiece. It was one of those rare albums on which all the songs were great, a seamless cycle of music with equal parts of brilliance from the first bar to the last note.*

rare albums on which all the songs were great, a seamless cycle of music with equal parts of brilliance from the first bar to the last note. Robbie wrote the best songs of his career including *Cripple Creek, Rag Mamma Rag, King Harvest, When You Awake* and perhaps none more timeless than *The Night They Drove Old Dixie Down.*

"It was information that I had gathered over the years that I didn't even know was gonna end up in a song. I remembered the first time I went to Arkansas I would hear people say that the South's gonna rise again. It was touching and it stayed with me."

*January 12th, 1970 cover of Time magazine*

## SUCCESS COMES WITH A PRICE

The album went gold with two hit singles and for the first time since pre-Dylan, the Band now had star billing. The concerts confirmed the collective talent of the group and established them as one of the premier units in rock and roll. They were also on the cover of Time magazine; the first for a Canadian band.

But success didn't come without a price. Although the Band kept most of their personal problems in check, drugs were threatening to undue the fine balance that made the unit work. Heroin found its way into Woodstock, and pianist and main singer Richard Manuel would be one of its first victims. Years later he would end his life by hanging himself.

"One of the scariest things that ever happened to us was to become successful," remembered Robbie. "We'd been together for a while – six years before we joined up with Bob Dylan and we'd spent a few years with Ronnie Hawkins and then some time on our own. We'd been around the block. We weren't guys who got some instruments for Christmas and were trying to learn how to play these things. We felt we had paid some dues.

"But all the bullshit that comes with success, some of it you're ready for, some of it you're never ready for. And it was kind of a crazy period, the late sixties. It was hard for everyone to keep their heads on straight 'cause the idea was not to… So success came as a confusing element. All of a sudden we were on the cover of Time magazine and there was a seriousness being given to this that we weren't completely clear about."

The Band would record four more albums in the seventies. *Stage Fright*, which was recorded live in Woodstock, had inspired moments but didn't measure up to the first two albums; nor did *Cahoots* or *Moondog Matinee*. Robbie wrote some good songs such as *The Shape I'm In* and *When the Moon Struck One*. But the new songs fell short of the standard he had set in the early recordings. In 1975, The Band reunited with Bob Dylan for the *Planet Waves* tour. The casting was the same, only this time The Band shared the Marquee and performed a set of their own songs.

The tour gave the band new life. They recorded *Acadian Driftwood* and *Southern Cross*, which had all the elements of a vintage Band album. But much like *Stage Fright*, it had isolated moments of brilliance and merely met, rather than surpassed, *Big Pink*. The innocence was gone. There were no surprises. Besides, public taste began to shift in the mid-seventies. Punk was getting ready to raise its shaved head and lay waste to what they described as rock dinosaurs.

Robbie must have realized it was only a matter of time. If he was to keep growing as a writer, he would have to do it with different musicians. The Band was locked into a sound and an attitude that had given them a piece of rock history, but in 1977 they had to make a radical change or fold the deck. The Band opted for the latter, there would be a farewell performance, and the curtain would come down, for the last time.

In 1977 they played their last concert at the Winterland Palace in San Francisco, where they had showcased for the first time as The Band. The concert featured the entire songbook and the invited guests provided insights into different time periods of their career. Van Morrison, Muddy Waters, Joni Mitchell, Neil Young, Dr. John, Ronnie Hawkins and Bob Dylan were all on the guest list. The concert was filmed and released as *The Last Waltz*. The movie was hailed as one of the premier rock documentaries ever made, and to this day retains that accolade.

## ROOTS REVISITED

Most of the Band members worked on solo careers after *The Last Waltz* but not Robbie. He left performing behind to concentrate on producing and writing soundtracks. Neil

*Dylan and Robbie at The Last Waltz*
*Photo: LFI*

*In 1977 they played their last concert at the Winterland Palace in San Francisco, where they had showcased for the first time as The Band.*

Diamond's *Beautiful Noise* was his first project. Robbie's friendship with Martin Scorcese gave him the opportunity to write the soundtracks for the movies *Color of Money*, *The King of Comedy* and *Raging Bull*.

In 1987, a decade after *The Last Waltz*, he returned to studio. With the help of Peter Gabriel and Bono he completed his first solo album. Self-titled, the record not only put Robertson back on the charts, but for the first time his own Native background was the inspiration for two of the songs.

"Well, I grew up a city kid, but in the summer my mom and I would go to the Six Nations Indian Reservation, where she was born and grew up. These people had spirituality, a relationship to nature that you just don't see in the city at all. My mother's people were Mohawks, but there were different tribes there, and all these people were tremendously into music. Everybody seemed to play guitar or fiddle or mandolin; everybody sang. This was the first time I could sit right in the room and see people pick up a guitar, watch what they were doing and hear fingers scrape along the strings," said Robbie.

*Broken Arrow* and *Showdown at Big Sky* was the first time Robbie used his Native background in music. His most recent project will allow him to revisit his roots.

"Ted Turner, who owns CNN, recently approached me to compose and coordinate the music for a six hour mini-series based on the history of Native Americans."

This will be the first time that First Nations history has been given such epic treatment and Robbie intends to work with several Native musicians. "Kashtin and Keith Secola – I definitely want to work with them on the project."

Robbie's reputation as a songwriter rests largely on how well he translates history into music, case in point, *The Night They Drove Old Dixie Down*. The Roger's mini-series will give him ample opportunity to put his talents to work and may prove to be a showcase for upcoming Native artists.

*Photo: Cher bloom*

**"** *I've had a lot of luck over the years and my advice to Native musicians is to believe in yourself. Set goals. Remember one thing, if you can't dream it happening, it won't. But if you are willing to live the dream and work to be as good as you possibly can, the brass ring is yours.* **"**

**Robbie Robertson**

# KASHTIN:
# RIDING THE TORNADO

**By Rick Littlechild**                    **Published June, 1995**

The most exciting Native band to play Music West was Kashtin. Riding the success of two platinum albums, the musical fraternity of Florent Vollant, Claude McKenzie and their band showed a packed house at the Commodore Ballroom (Vancouver) why they are leading the charge for Native music.

Kashtin's music, a hybrid of traditional Innu and rock with Innu lyrics, performed by two seasoned and charismatic performers, had the Commodore rockin' – quite a feat since no one had a clue what they were singing.

"The name 'Kashtin' is Innu for 'tornado' – a beautiful tornado, a good weather tornado," says Florent Vollant, singer and songwriter for the group. Both he and his partner, Claude McKenzie, are from Maliotenam, a Montagnais Reserve in northern Québec. The Montagnais are a branch of the Innu nation not to be confused with the Inuit. Only 12,000 people speak the Innu language, yet Kashtin performs its songs entirely in this language.

"We have been doing it for close to 10 years. There were some other people singing in Innu when we started, but we were the best. We would tour around all the reservations in eastern Québec and everybody knew our name. We never had the chance to work in studio. We were always worried how it would sound on record. So when this fellow from Montreal wanted us to go up there and record our music, we were plenty scared."

Guy Trepannier was the interested producer. President of Groupe Concept Musique, he had seen Kashtin on television and was so impressed with their performance

*Florent Vollant and Claude McKenzie, Kashtin at Music West, May, 1995*
*Photo: Cher Bloom*

that he offered to produce their first album. Trepannier was convinced that the power of Kashtin's songs would overcome the language barrier; in fact, he was hoping that with the

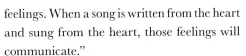

*The covers of Kashtin's first three CDs*

growing popularity of World Music, the Montagnais lyrics would add an exotic flavour to the mix.

The duo was apprehensive. They had synthesized the rhythms and language of the Montagnais into rock structures to better reach the Innu youth, but they had never considered an audience beyond their own people. "We were scared," Vollant remembers, "but also, we felt the time might be right. Our friends were telling us it was time to take our music to the outside."

The self-titled album released in 1989 was an instant success, reaching double platinum sales and establishing Kashtin as one of the best Native bands in the world. Finally convinced that their time had come, Kashtin began to play venues across Canada, the United States and Europe. *Kashtin*, the album, made it to France's top ten, and the band's concerts sold out in every city in which they performed.

"When we played last time in Toronto, I looked into the audience and I could see people crying. Almost certainly, they didn't understand the words but they understood the spirit," Vollant said.

The pressure to record in English and French was always there but Vollant and Mckenzie remained on their chosen path. "Both Claude and myself could sing in those languages but that is not the kind of communication we are after. What Kashtin has to bring to everyone are feelings. When a song is written from the heart and sung from the heart, those feelings will communicate."

The second release, *Innu*, released in 1991, followed the path of its predecessor, reaching platinum sales and proving that Kashtin were right in sticking to their vision of singing in their own tongue. "We want to show Native people who have the courage to pursue their aims non-violently but not passively. So in our music you have modern rock'n'roll and ancient traditions to show us working with, rather than against the main culture."

Kashtin have just signed a lucrative record deal with Columbia Records and the third album will be released shortly. Robbie Robertson has promised to use some of their songs in a television documentary on First Nations history that he is producing. The band returns to Europe in May for an extended tour that ends in August and comes home for the release of the new album – only to go back on the road, this time in the United States. The future is so bright they have to wear shades.

With the exception of Redbone, Kashtin has accomplished something no other Native band has done: they have achieved mainstream success without compromising their culture or heritage. More surprising is that their music has been a vehicle to promote the Innu culture.

In the liner notes of their first album, Vollant states the band's mission:

*"Our culture is often perceived as a single entity, without distinction as to nations, languages and customs. Through our music we seek to tear down the walls of indifference by captivating the listeners with the difference."*

# KEITH SECOLA: SACRED CLOWN RIDES INDIAN CAR

**By Rick Littlechild**                    **Published June, 1995**

Keith Secola's music talks about the day to day lives of Native people in a language everyone understands. He uses humour to underline what he calls the "richness of poorness." Two of his songs, *Indian Cars* and *Fryebread* are played on all Native radio stations across Canada and the United States. Keith and his *Band of Wild Indians* have toured Europe and most of the United States. Jerry Garcia from the Grateful Dead, Bono from U2, and John Densmore from The Doors are friends of his who he says believe in his music.

"Now they are starting to pay more attention to Native American music because basically the recording industry has exploited all kinds of genres. If you look at reggae, look at the blues, look at South American music; all of these things have been exploited in a repressive kind of way, and in an overexposed sense. Indian music is one that's in line for this year and the rest of the time now."

Secola, an Anishinabe from the woodlands of Minnesota now residing in Tempe, Arizona, is riding the edge of cult status, due largely to *Indian Cars*, a song he wrote years ago and is starting to get national exposure. "It's a cult type of thing. It's even alternative to alternative; definitely on the bottom feeders on the great radio chain. It's been supported by myself and no record company, but I've sold 10,000 copies."

An *Indian Car* is, according to Secola, "a gas powered vehicle moving on wheels that shouldn't be going anywhere. Hardly the flashiest model, typically old, battered, rusty and barely running, held together through Indian power and whatever available improvised means. [It's] a commentary on the general strained economic situation of Native life."

*From the cover of the album* Circle – *Keith Secola (centre) with his Band of Wild Indians*
*Photo: Jay Miles*

This satirical approach Keith credits to the traditional role of the sacred clown: "I like the sacred clown approach to seriousness. They make fun of serious things. The clowns are a way to make things balance. In Indian

*Keith Secola appearing at Music West, Vancouver, 1995*

Photo: Cher Bloom

rocker, *Zogipoon*, sung in Secola's native tongue, and the Powwow chorus of *Indian Cars* are both part of Secola's musical gumbo. He's not afraid to turn tables musically, realizing that Native musicians bring their own sensibility – the only true definition of any musical movement. Keith Secola's vision of fusion: a fine balancing act with shades of country and folk, meshing with traditional native music.

His main influences: "All the Bob's: Bob Dylan, Bob Marley, Bob Johnson, Bob Lennon, Bob Bowie and of course Bob Young," Keith replies. And what is his music? "A blend of folk, blues, reggae, country, indigenous and World Beat genres," he says.

In Vancouver for Music West, Keith and his Wild Band of Indians were on stage with Rick Patterson and Vern CheeChoo at the Aboriginal Friendship Centre. Unfortunately, a small audience didn't ignite the band. A more intimate setting at the Railway Club inspired moments of brilliance showcasing Secola's best material.

ceremonies they would have the serous dancers in front of them, and behind them the sacred clowns would be making fun of the seriousness."

A collection of Keith's work, *Circles*, brings together previous recordings from *Time Fly's Like an Arrow, Fruit Flies Like a Banana* and *Acoustic Aroma*. Secola offers a hybrid of Native influenced rock and traditional Native music. What separates him from other Native artists is a poetic sensibility that allows him to capture pieces of contemporary Native life and turn them into social commentary.

The instrumental, *Wassondale*, performed on electric guitar, has no traditional percussion or woodwinds but captures a mood that is Native in spirit and ambience. The country

Keith has spent time with Robbie Robertson who selected him as one of the artists he wants to work with on a Native documentary he is producing. Though Keith Secola may never achieve mainstream recognition – and that's fine with him – he could use the spotlight to introduce native music to the world.

"When Quinn the Eskimo gets here everybody's gonna jump for joy."

"Yes, I welcome mainstream appeal. It is happening. More and more people are coming for the shows. More success enables me to help our people more, to do God's work," says Secola.

# THE LUBICON GENOCIDE

**Last Stand of the Lubicon Cree**
**By John Goddard**
**Published by Douglas & McIntyre, 1991,**

**Reviewed by Peter Cole**                    **Published September, 1991**

Goddard's book is a comprehensive and easy-to-read chronicle of the Lubicon Lake Cree. It reveals how the governments of Canada and Alberta have subjected the band to genocidal policies and legislation.

After describing the current situation at Little Beaver, Goddard takes us into the history of the Lubicon people and of six other bands in the area. The commissioners responsible for getting signatories for Treaty 8 in the spring and summer of 1899 did not go into this area of the province, so the above-mentioned bands were not part of the agreement. They did not sign away their aboriginal rights to their lands.

These people have lived in their current homeland since the eighteenth century. They have lived traditionally and up until a few decades ago, had not participated in the communications and transportation explosions of the century. The Lubicon Lake people and their neighbors hunted in order to feed and clothe themselves and they trapped in order to allow them to purchase the commercial items that they required.

Today, the author tells us, within a 15-mile radius of Little Buffalo, where the band office is located, there are 400 oil and gas wells. Wildlife in the area has all but vanished. The trap lines have been buried and otherwise sabotaged by oil company employees.

Hundreds of miles of roads criss-cross the traditional lands of the Lubicon Lake people. A third of the band suffers from tuberculosis. A drug and alcohol problem now exists. Violence and family break-ups are common.

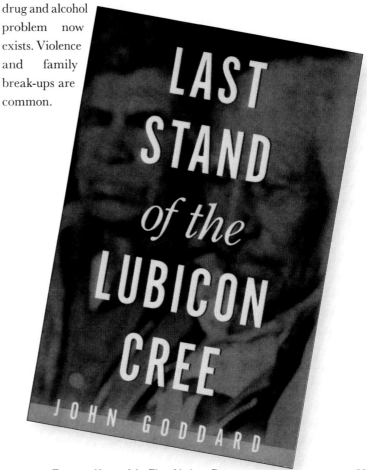

*Once the Lubicon land became the source of revenues of $1.2 million per day for the oil companies and for the provincial government, it became too valuable, we are told, to let the Indians get title to it.*

Today much of the band is on welfare, a kind of parallel development to go along with the (in situ) corporate welfare. Suicide has moved into the area and devastated the young. Civilization has arrived.

We are told about Malcolm McCrimmon, the Presbyterian accountant who worked for Indian Affairs. He created policy as he went along. In 1942 he struck off 640 people from band list in the area. As registrar under a new Indian Act in the early 1950s, he had final and conclusive control over band membership.

When oil was found in Alberta, McCrimmon tried to move the Lubicon people to the Whitefish Lake band lands. He managed to transfer some. It was politically and economically convenient that the Lubicon Lake prairie oasis was now a semi-waste land, a barren outreach, unsuitable for human habitation. Not that he considered Indians to be human. Not that he cared about how they lived, as long as it did not inconvenience the government and its friends.

Goddard describes an incident in 1967 in which 40 buildings were leveled at the nearby community of Marten River under instructions from the Alberta government. Indian people, who couldn't even read, were lied to and kicked out of their homes. Two years later, the adjacent land became the first producing oil field in the area. Says Goddard:

*All that is known for sure is that the people of Marten River attended meetings that they didn't understand, signed papers that they couldn't read, heard promises that were never kept, and had their homes and possessions bulldozed and burned virtually without warning on what soon afterwards became part of a productive oil field.*

We are told about the policies of Indian Affairs Minister Jean Chrétien, about Harold Cardinal's rebuttal to the White Paper, and about the policies and practices of the Lougheed and Getty governments.

Once the Lubicon land became the source of revenues of $1.2 million per day for the oil companies and for the provincial government, it became too valuable, we are told, to let the Indians get title to it. Human rights activists around the world could not believe the measures the Alberta government was willing to take in order to secure land to which it had no right.

People were further outraged when in the middle of a Supreme Court of Alberta case in May, 1977, in which the Lubicon Lake band was trying to put a caveat on its own unceded land, the government of Peter Lougheed changed the wording of Alberta Land Titles Act to prohibit caveats on unpatented Crown land, and the law would be lap-lied retroactively. Some democracy.

Goddard skillfully changes the focus and pace of the book and thereby holds the reader's interest. He allows us to digest information and to put numbers and names into perspective, into some kind of meaningful context. He gives brief biographies of Chief Bernard Ominayak, Fred Lennarson, Harold Cardinal, and James O'Reilly. We see the human element behind the newspaper stories. These chapters also give us a feel for the internal dynamic of the major players of the Lubicon camp, where they came from, what their beliefs are, and why they are involved.

We are told about Ominayak's problems with alcohol in 1978, problems directly related to the disempowerment of his people, the genocidal assault on his band, and the destruction of the traditional economy and lifestyle of the Lubicon Lake people. We are shown Ominayak the man, the human being who is possessed of needs and wants; Ominayak, the leader who knows that although he is in the right, also knows that he is fighting an opponent who changes the rules to suit its battle plans. We see the young Ominayak attending meetings in isolated communities, a man who, though poor, does not take advantage of the transportation expenses available because, "I don't believe in taking money from people who are trying to help me."

Fred Lennarson, the civil rights activist from Chicago, is now Ominayak's main spokesperson. He tells us: "I came intellectually to understand concepts that are important to me yet today….one person's rights are determined by everybody else's right….and if that is true intellectually, what does that mean in terms of action?"

Lennarson, called meywasinkitche ogemow (good big chief) by his Lubicon Lake friends, moved to Edmonton in 1974 because of his association with Native leader Harold Cardinal. He was, up until that time, principally a resource, a behind-the scenes person. When he allied with the Lubicon people in 1979, he began to speak for them because Ominayak wanted to watch and learn from the background.

Of the tragedy at nearby Peerless Lake in March 1986, where six young people died out of 13 who drank photo-copy fluid, Lennarson writes:

*"The tragedy at Peerless Lake is clearly a direct result of social and economic disruption, dislocation and disintegration caused by the Alberta Provincial Government's aboriginal people of their aboriginal land rights."*

In speaking of the boycott of the 1988 Calgary Olympics, he says: "A display of North American Indian artifacts to attract people to the Winter Olympics is being organized by interests who are still actively seeking to destroy Indian people: namely, the Alberta government and its oil-company allies."

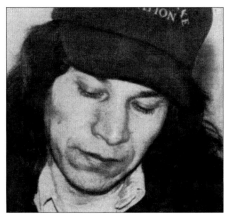

*Chief Bernard Ominayak*          Photo: Unknown

Goddard tells us of the massive support the Lubicon people have from cultural, educational and human rights groups in Europe. Rallies, fund raising events, marches and forums inform the European and Asian public of what the Lubicon people have been going through at the hands of governmental and corporate bureaucracies.

We learn that in October, 1988, the Lubicon people declared its intention to "assert and enforce its aboriginal rights and its sovereign jurisdiction as an independent nation, with its own law-enforcement and court systems…(the band would) no longer participate in any court proceedings in which the Lubicons are presently a party…"

The band put up barricades within the boundaries of the disputed land. The media came. And the Mounties came – with helicopters and automatic weapons. Following the invasion, 27 Lubicon Nations became "POWs."

Goddard tells us that negotiations were made with Alberta's premier, Canada's Minister of Indian Affairs, and *other foreign politicians.*

*In the end, nothing came of the talks except talk. Canada's Minister of Indian Affairs encouraged new bands to form in the area of Lubicon Land and monies were paid to voters in order to encourage them to vote in a certain way.*

In the end, nothing came of the talks except talk. Canada's Minister of Indian Affairs encouraged new bands to form in the area of Lubicon Land and monies were paid to voters in order to encourage them to vote in a certain way. This way the Lubicon Lake band became smaller and smaller. Eventually Ominayak's wife, Louise, unable to stand the pressure and the frustration, left him and took their children with her. So here is another casualty, another theatre in this conflict, the home front – the family.

We are then informed that although the plight of the Lubicon Lake people is now out of the main focus of the public gaze, the band continues to lobby for its aboriginal rights, including its sovereign right to assert its laws within its boundaries of its homeland.

Just as the spirit must be fed and the emotions healed, so too, must the body find appropriate action for its needs. Goddard describes how the Lubicon Lake people and their allies and friends continue to fight oppression and ignorance. They continue to chip away at the inflexible will of the Canadian and Alberta governments and their corporate sponsor.

## AUTHOR CLAIMS HE IS BLACKLISTED

**By Peter Cole**

John Goddard, the author of *Last Stand of the Lubicon*, spoke to a Native Studies class last November, and to an anthropology class and several law classes at the University of Alberta the following day.

He described how Indian Affairs had blacklisted him just days before. He had obtained an internal memo that said the Department of Indian and Northern Development employees were not allowed to speak with him without first contacting certain persons in upper management. Goddard claims this is because of the book about the Lubicon Lake people. Everyone contacted in DIAND denied knowledge of the memo, including the person who had signed it.

Goddard described his early work in the Arctic with the Canadian Press wire service and his assignment with *Equinox* magazine to do a story on the Lubicon issue. He was looking at the news value of his story. A few years later he traveled with the Lubicon Lake group when they went to Europe to publicize their story of neglect and oppression.

Goddard also tells of seeing fifty-dollar cheques being written at polling booths during the Woodland Cree vote for band membership. Goddard claims the size of the Voters List at this same venue kept increasing as the day went on. He claims he was told to leave the venue by "officials."

# A FUNNY THING HAPPENED ON THE WAY TO THE SUPREME COURT OF CANADA

**By Lloyd Dolha**                    **Published September, 1998**

*The Supreme Court of Canada*

*Photo: JD Foy*

In the 1997 Delgamuukw decision the Supreme Court of Canada ruled that aboriginal title exists and is equivalent to fee simple ownership. It must seem ironic to the provincial NDP government that it only has itself to blame for the tremendous policy implications for provincial land use and the subsequent political fallout in the aftermath of this historic decision.

*Seen in this light, the entire judgement stands as a condemnation of provincial and federal policy and practice in treaty negotiations with BC First Nations to date.*

It's important to recall that is was the province that broke off negotiations with the Gitxan in March of 1996, when Gitxan negotiators rejected the provincial policy of the Land Selection Model, in which BC First Nations are expected to choose a few pieces of their traditional territories in which the First Nation would have majority control.

Wet'suwet'ten negotiators would break off negotiations in September.

Both the Gitxan and Wet'suwet'en favour a joint jurisdictional approach to lands and resources.

It's almost as if the province couldn't imagine that the Supreme Court would move from the BC Court of Appeal's finding of aboriginal rights as unextinguished non-exclusive user rights to such an expansive definition of the content of aboriginal title as: a constitutionally protected right; establish a test for proof of its existence; set out a stringent test for the justification of any infringement on established aboriginal title; and, provide for the acceptance of the "aboriginal perspective" in establishing proof of aboriginal title.

Seen in this light, the entire judgement stands as a condemnation of provincial and federal policy and practice in treaty negotiations with BC First Nations to date.

The judgement was recently cited by the federal Reform Party in an emerging national debate in which critics charge that the Supreme Court is exercising too much influence in political affairs in setting public policy.

But the Supreme Court itself noted, in the recent legal reference on the issue of Québec separation, that the court was thrust into this position by the adoption of the Charter of Rights and Freedoms in 1982, which transformed government "from a system of parliamentary supremacy to one of constitutional supremacy."

Similarly, in Delgamuukw, the Supreme Court cuts a great swath into the realm of public policy in treaty negotiations in their function of interpreting decades of aboriginal title and rights cases at common law in terms the recognition of "existing aboriginal rights" as set out in section 35(1) of the Canadian constitution.

Indeed, the legal principles set out in Delgamuukw represent a stern warning to the provincial and federal governments, whatever their political stripes, that negotiations must be conducted in good faith.

In expanding the legal content of aboriginal title and rights, the Supreme Court has forced the provincial and federal governments to drastically re-examine their positions in future treaty negotiations that must be animated by the Delgamuukw principles on what now could be considered a more or less "level playing field.'

And the implications of the judgement are staggering.

No one really knows the full content of aboriginal title. As a burden on federal crown title, what effect does the recognition of aboriginal title have on a provincial government system predicated on complete ownership and control of provincial lands?

Moreover, there is a vast chasm between governments and BC First Nations as to the precise meaning of the judgement. Indeed, there are many who argue that Delgamuukw raises more questions than it answers.

The Federal Treaty Negotiation Office (FTNO), typically applied a minimalist interpretation of the judgement, arguing that the decision did not ultimately find the existence of aboriginal title for the Gitxan or Wet'suwet'en on their traditional territories because the court dismissed the findings of fact and the case was sent back to the BC Supreme Court for re-trial.

Noting that the "crown is under a moral if not a legal duty to enter into and conduct negotiations in good faith," the FTNO suggests the case did not impose a legal duty on the crown to negotiate settlements and suggested negotiation in the "voluntary" treaty negotiation process at hand.

The First Nations Summit, which represents the majority of BC First Nations, contends that aboriginal title is a proprietary interest in the land that continues to exist in full force over all of British Columbia.

Aboriginal title, as recognized by the Supreme Court, confers on BC First Nations the full range of uses to traditional territories and all licenses, leases and permits issued by provincial or federal governments constitute unlawful infringements in which compensation for all past and future infringements must be forthcoming in negotiations.

No one knows the position of the provincial government, through it may be surmised to be largely in sync with the federal position.

*I*ndeed, the legal principles set out in Delgamuukw represent a stern warning to the provincial and federal governments, whatever their political stripes, that negotiations must be conducted in good faith.

Since Delgamuukw was handed down, the province has responded only once with a fixed cash and land package in late May 1998, which would then be the subject of negotiation for distribution.

That offer was rejected out of hand by the First Nations Summit.

Since then, all three parties are working to develop new mandates for negotiations in the post-Delgamuukw era.

With such vastly differing interpretations of the decision and the rising expectations of BC First Nations, it is difficult to conceive a meeting of minds anytime in the near future.

Nevertheless, despite the general and abstract nature of the principles laid down by the Supreme Court concerning the nature of aboriginal title, the reconciliation of the constitutionally protected aboriginal title of BC First Nations and federal crown title remains the ultimate goal.

As so many times in the past, the Supreme Court of Canada has deftly dodged another of the most pressing issues of our time and thrown it back into the hands of the politicians. God help us all.

# CHILLIWACK STUDENT GARNERS PRESTIGIOUS AWARD

**By Lloyd Dolha**                    **Published May, 2004**

Seventeen year-old Robert Kowbel of the Chilliwack Senior Secondary School was one of 50 students in the province to receive a Provincial Excellence Award from the Canadian Millennium Scholarship Foundation this year.

In recognition of his outstanding academic achievement and community service, the Interior Salish native youth will receive a cash award of $4,000 to go towards his post-secondary education.

The Millennium Excellence Award Program recognizes, supports and encourages talented Canadians who make positive and significant contributions to the betterment of their communities, demonstrate a capacity for leadership and academic achievement. The awards provide an incentive for the brightest students to complete their studies here in Canada.

"These students come from vastly different backgrounds, cultural influences and interests, but what they all have in common is the significant contribution they have already made to their communities and the potential to become some of Canada's premier community leaders," said Norman Riddell, the Foundation's executive director and chief executive officer. "Although past achievement is important in our selection process, the excellence awards are primarily an investment in the future achievement of these outstanding citizens."

Robert plans to pursue a career in orthodontics at the University of British Columbia. The cash award is based on his grade point average (Robert attained A honours with a GPA of 3.75), and is renewable for an additional three years to a maximum of $16,000.

In addition to his scholastic achievement, Robert won praise for his volunteerism activities in the community life of Chilliwack.

Robert initiated and ran a drop-in tutorial service for other students of the Chilliwack Senior Secondary with a group of friends, helping fellow students in the scientific disciplines of biology, chemistry and physics.

# WHITE HATE
## THE MURDER OF LEO LACHANCE

**By Len O'Connor**                    **Published June, 1991**

The Northern Pawn and Gun Shop in Prince Albert, Saskatchewan, is owned and managed by Carney Nerland; a white supremacist and leader of the Aryan Nations in Saskatchewan. In September of 1990, Nerland was invited to a gathering of Aryan Nations in Provost, Alberta. The meeting was held on the farm of Ray Bradley, founder of the Brotherhood of Racial Purity.

Photo: Unknown

Protesters against the meeting, which included Harvey Kane, leader of the Jewish Defense League and Sigmund Sobolewski, an Auschwitz survivor, confronted the brotherhood at the gates of Bradley's farm. Nerland, dressed in a Nazi uniform and holding a pistol-handled shotgun, taunted the protesters, directing his verbal abuse at Harvey Kane:

"Why don't you tell me they made f*** soap out of your auntie and luggage out of your uncle? They made luggage out of him. I've got it in the trunk of my car."

Nerland pointed his shotgun at Kane: "A 12-gauge shotgun cuts a person right in half.

It's just great for preventing further Jewish births."

**"***These are not simply misguided eccentrics. They are dedicated Nazis.***"**

**Inquiry Commissioners**

Fortunately the confrontation didn't go beyond the shouting. What it did show was Carney Nerland's total commitment to the twisted revisionist ideology of white supremacists.

Later, the Alberta Human Rights Commission conducted an inquiry into the confrontation. Nerland, along with other Aryan members, was questioned. When asked what Hitler's place was in history, he replied: "Adolf Hitler, as far as I am concerned from my research and what I have read in the Bible, I would consider Adolf Hitler to be Elijah the Prophet, the prophet sent forth by God in the last days."

The inquiry commissioners were not able to lay charges against Nerland but they issued a stern warning that any organization that promoted racial and religious hatred would not be tolerated.

"These are not simply misguided eccentrics. They are dedicated Nazis."

It was shocking news to Canadians everywhere. White hate belonged to American sickos – not Canadians – but here they were in this nation's back yard waving swastikas while drinking Molson Canadian beer.

Carney Nerland returned to Prince Albert. News of the inquiry had made it onto the CBC news hour and even the local paper,

but it didn't surprise Nerland's neighbors nor did it have a negative effect on his business. He never hid his political beliefs. In his gun shop was Nazi paraphernalia and a Klu Klux Klan robe hanging from the wall. He rarely discussed his ties with Aryan Nations with his customers, and few people knew how deep those ties were until they saw him on television waving a shotgun at Jewish protesters. Prince Albert authorities either ignored the danger that Nerland represented or had little understanding of the Aryan Nation's agenda.

The California Church of Jesus Christ Christian Aryan Nations believe that white Americans descendant from British colonists are the chosen people of God. The Jews are the anti-Christ, African Americans and First Nations along with anyone who is non-Caucasian are "mud people" deserving of the same hatred reserved for Jews.

There are many similar white supremacist groups in the United States; while the Klu Klux Klan is best known their membership has decreased during the last decade. The new hate groups are more militant and none are as organized and dangerous as The Aryan Nations.

Under the direction of Richard Butler, the American high priest of the far right, a fortified compound was built in Hayden Lake, Idaho in the mid-seventies, that served as the official headquarters and training centre; recruits are indoctrinated in the theology of hate and trained in arm-to-arm combat as Aryan Nation soldiers.

*I*t was shocking news to Canadians everywhere. White hate belonged to American sickos – not Canadians – but here they were in this nation's back yard waving swastikas while drinking Molson Canadian beer.

In 1984 Allen Berg, a Jewish radio broadcaster, was killed by two members of the compound. Oliver Stone's movie *Talk Radio* was based on this murder. There was also a series of robberies committed by the same duo. It was precisely at this time that Carney Nerland arrived at Hayden Lake for a conference and remained for training. He later went to Louisiana to work for the former national organizer of the KKK.

Nerland returned to Prince Albert where he opened The Northern Pawn and Gun Shop, and became the leader of the Saskatchewan Aryan Nations. Three months after the incident in Provost, Nerland was in his shop with two friends, Russ Yungwirth and Gar Brownbridge, sharing a bottle of rye when a Native man walked in the door.

Leo Lachance, a Cree from the Big River Reserve that is 170 kilometres from Prince Albert, had come to the city with some pelts he wanted to sell to the Katz Bros, a shop on River Street and next door to The Northern Pawn and Gun Shop.

It was after five pm when Leo arrived at the Katz Bros, only to find out that the shop was closed. He entered Nerland's store and after a short discussion with the owner, he left the premises. Nerland was holding a M-56 semiautomatic when Leo talked to him and at some point during the discussion he fired two shots in the floor, which he had the habit of doing to show off the capacity of a rifle.

As Leo walked out the door Nerland fired a third shot in the direction of the door. The bullet hit Lachance in the arm then went through his rib cage but did not exit. He felt

> *Nerland returned to Prince Albert wher he opened The Northern Pawn and Gun Shop, and became the leader of the Saskatchewan Aryan Nations.*

the pain yet still managed to pick up his pelts and walk fifty metres before falling face down in the snow.

Kim Koroll was driving on River Street when he saw Leo, semi-conscious. He stopped to see if he could help. He saw no blood on Leo, who was mumbling perhaps in Cree. It was obvious that he was in serious pain.

Maurice Morin arrived at the scene along with Donald Blunden. Both men tried to comfort Lachance, while Koroll looked for a telephone to call the ambulance. His first stop was Nerland's gun shop. He quickly explained the emergence of the situation and asked if he could use the phone. No, was the immediate response he got from Nerland, who must have realized the reason for an ambulance.

Koroll left the gun shop and two blocks later he called 9-1-1 from the A&W restaurant. The ambulance rushed Leo Lachance to the Holy Family Hospital where the seriousness of the wound was discovered in the emergency ward. He was moved to the Royal University Hospital in Saskatoon for immediate surgery and died the next morning.

The police questioned Nerland who came up with a wild story of two men in his shop who fired a rifle by mistake. He gave a fictitious description of both men, he could not remember a Native man entering his shop. When Yungwirth and Brownbridge were

> *Nerland was holding a M-56 semiautomatic when Leo talked to him… As Leo walked out the door he fired a third shot in the direction of the door.*

questioned in the presence of their lawyers and told the real story, Nerland admitted that he had fired a shot accidentally at the door when Lachance walked out but didn't realize Lachance had been hit.

The police charged Nerland with manslaughter, rather than murder, because intent could not be proven. Why he was not charged with murder would cast a shadow on the police handling the investigation. One of the reasons for the lesser charge surfaced after the hearing. Yungbridge and Brownbridge both worked for the Saskatchewan correctional services, which gave weight to their testimony that was questionable at best. The prosecution accepted their testimony without questioning why they never made an effort confirm whether Lachance was wounded.

*T**he inquiry exposed the fact that Nerland had been a informant for the R.C.M.P. This explained why the police went along with the manslaughter charge...*

Carney Nerland pleaded guilty to manslaughter and was sentenced to a laughable four years. The Native community in Saskatchewan was shocked. Eventually an inquiry was conducted and even more shocking facts surfaced such as the leak from the police that showed how unrepentant Nerland was about killing Leo Lachance.

"If I'm convicted for shootin' that Indian, you'll have to pin a medal on me. I've done you all a favour," Nerland told police guards the day before his sentencing.

The inquiry exposed the fact that Nerland had been an informant for the R.C.M.P. This explained why the police went along with the manslaughter charge but it also cast a shadow on the judicial system in Saskatchewan, and the thin-veiled contempt police have for Natives.

Leo Lachance was shot in the back by a self-admitted racist who was sentenced to four years. If a Native man committed the same crime against a white man, how many years would he be sentenced to? If Carney Nerland shot a Caucasian would he have been charged with manslaughter? Never, never, never.

# BC's Murdered and Missing Native Women

**By Sean Devlin**

**Published April, 1997**

The driver of the giant compactor disposal truck was tired and yawning. It was 7:30 a.m. and his shift was nearly over. In a downtown eastside Vancouver alley he slid the forks of his behemoth into a dumpster filled with construction waste and raised it high. Something fell off the container, landing with a thud beside the truck. The driver yawned again, hugely, and jumped down from his cab. He was expecting to scoop up a chunk of drywall or two-by-four. What he did find was a small duffel bag, stuffed and crammed with the body of a young Native woman, chin crushed into her knees, wrapped in a cotton comforter, her hair pulled up in a ponytail.

# LISA MARIE GRAVELINE'S SHORT AND TRAGIC LIFE

The 20-year-old woman's body was found on May 1. Police confirmed her identity and said she had been a prostitute and a drug user and a drug dealer, roughly in that order. Also known as Lisa Marie Bear Graveline, she had been addicted to heroin and crack cocaine. When found, her body was intact, fully clothed, with no signs of sexual assault.

*Lisa Marie's family had come to Vancouver about eight years ago from a Manitoba reserve. Their lives on the streets of the most impoverished postal code in Canada were not happy.*

Lisa Marie's childhood was troubled. One month before her 13th birthday, she was arrested for theft under $5,000. Before she was 14, she was arrested twice more, for theft and possession of a weapon. At the age of 16, she was put on probation after being convicted of robbery and assault. In November 1998, Graveline was first charged as an adult, for trafficking in cocaine. She was a known prostitute, according to police, but had lately been involved exclusively in the drug trade.

The founder of one drug rehabilitation facility Lisa Marie had resorted to said: "You could see a little girl inside her who was desperately crying out for help. But the window of opportunity is so small. They do want the help. Yet the minute they see the drug they run right back to it."

Lisa Marie's family had come to Vancouver about eight years ago from a Manitoba reserve. Their lives on the streets of the most impoverished postal code in Canada were not happy. In the fall of 1998, Lisa Marie's two brothers and her mother overdosed in separate locations in the city. They all wound up in St. Paul's hospital at the same time. Her brother Oswald died.

Then in June 1999, her mother was found dead of an overdose behind a strip joint, the No. 5 Orange at Powell and Main. Her father had died four years previously from addiction related problems.

"They all loved each other, you could see that," said Jean-Claude, a close friend of the family. "But it was just so sad to see them on the street."

A worker in an east-end social agency, who didn't want to be named, said Lisa Marie's story is familiar.

"This happens to a lot of Native families down here," he said. "You get whole families who are in an addictive cycle."

On the wall of a drop-in centre for drug-dependent women in the downtown eaastside, a poem in blue marker on a large sheet of white drawing paper says good-bye to Lisa Marie:

*My friend, the times you set my temper afire*
*Are less than the shine of your generous smile!*
*You were too good to go out gangland style!*

The death of Lisa Marie Graveline had one unexpected consequence. Police rapidly caught up with her alleged killer. On June 15 Thong Thanh Huynh, 34, was arrested in a car in the 2800 block east Hastings Street on an outstanding immigration warrant concerning deportation proceedings. On June 19, Thong was charged with Second Degree murder. The alleged killer is a resident of Vancouver, well-known to police and loosely associated with the drug trade. He came to Canada in 1980 from Vietnam; he holds Landed Immigrant status. He has been in Vancouver for three years and is unemployed.

Graveline is believed to have been stabbed to death at a drug house. Her body was then put in the duffel bag and placed in the dumpster.

## UNSOLVED MURDERS

The thing that makes Graveline's murder unusual is that the police arrested a suspect very quickly. This in contrast to the 40 plus known murders of Vancouver area prostitutes, whose bodies have been found in the past 15 years. Most of these murders are still unsolved.

The statistics of violence against the working women of the Downtown Eastside are horrendous. No one knows more about this than John Lowman, professor of criminology at Simon Fraser University; he is Canada's leading expert on prostitution. His research shows that prostitutes are 60 to 120 times more likely to be murdered than other Canadian women. A fierce critic of current policy toward prostitution, Lowman accuses the Vancouver police and fearful civic politicians of complicity through inaction in the murders and, more frightening, the unexplained disappearances of 31 skid-row area women – all prostitutes, all drug addicts, all almost certainly murdered, most in the past five years.

## MISSING EQUALS NATIVE

Professor John : "The police and the politicians actively created the problem they are now trying to fix. The rhetoric of the '80s and early '90s was: 'We'll get rid of the prostitutes.' The idea of eliminating prostitution in Vancouver has translated tragically into *REALLY* getting rid of prostitutes. We chase them from one area to another. They find themselves in dark streets in defenceless situations. They get into strangers' cars. There are no eyes there. But there *ARE* men who get off on violence. They see the women's vulnerability."

Based on the number of deaths and recent disappearances, Lowman suspects there are three or four serial killers who have been operating in Vancouver over the past 15 years. And they have become very good at hiding the bodies.

## A SISTERHOOD IN FEAR

For the devastated women of the Downtown Eastside, desperate and driven by the demon of drug abuse, there is a haven they can go to – the Womens Information and Safe House (WISH). They come by Skytrain from as far away as New Westminster and Surrey, seeking a temporary refuge. At WISH they can share

*Seventy per cent of the women in the Downtown Eastside are native. More than 60 per cent of the participants at WISH (Womens' Information and Safe House) are First Nations people.*

a meal and gossip; exchange information and warn one another about the "bad dates" they have had.

Program Director Karen Duddy: "Our women are very worried about their missing sisters. There is a great sense of fear out there."

Seventy per cent of the women in the Downtown Eastside are Native. More than 60 per cent of the participants at WISH are First Nations people. The sense of menace and the fear that stalks these women has encouraged them to seek both solace and help in sisterhood.

*As one 31 year veteran of the Vancouver Police put it, the maliciousness and viciousness of some of the sexual assaults and murders is "beyond belief."*

The number of them participating in WISH has doubled in the past year; there are now between 70 and 90 women in attendance each evening.

Karen Duddy: "Both Lisa Marie Graveline and her mother were participants in our program. Both of them were victims of drug abuse and were emotionally disturbed as a result.

"The majority of our women suffer from Fetal Alcohol Syndrome, especially Native women. They are women who come from situations of extreme incestual and sexual abuse. The tragedy of the residential schools also plays a role in the situation of these women. They are multi-barriered, really in a difficult spot."

Duddy explained that Native women become "urbanized" after they have spent time in the city. Their rural reserves no longer want to have anything to do with them. Roughly 80 per cent of them suffer from Hepatitis C; roughly 35 per cent are HIV positive and a great proportion of that number suffer from AIDS.

"These women speak openly about feeling like the 'throwaways' of society," said Duddy. "Nobody gives a damn about them. They genuinely feel terror around the issue of the missing women. But they are caught up in the extreme addiction problem."

While the estimated 500 "hookers" in the skid-row area may have boyfriends with whom they share money and/or drugs, they are not "pimped" in the traditional sense. John Lowman: "Once the price of a habit-forming, mind-altering substance is driven up by criminal prohibition, a drug like heroin or cocaine can be as demanding a pimp as any man."

Because of their addiction, women on the Downtown Eastside are generally not as discriminating about clients as their higher-priced, non-addicted counterparts. This makes them even more vulnerable to the continuum of misogynist violence inherent in our culture.

As one 31-year veteran of the Vancouver Police put it, the maliciousness and viciousness of some of the sexual assaults and murders is "beyond belief." He described the behaviour of many of the men who assault prostitutes as "very physical...very intimate...and designed to hurt."

# POLICE INACTION

John Lowman believes that police have waited far too long to react to the ever-growing number of vanished women, dismissing the appeals of friends and families of the prostitutes by saying, in effect: "They're drug addicts. They're transients. They'll come back." Yet 40 some deaths, 31 missing women – the pattern surely cannot be random. The situation can be compared to the famous unsolved case of 49 Seattle-area prostitutes who went missing or whose bodies were found along Washington State's Green River in the early '80s. No other Canadian city has a similar pattern of disappearances. Yet it is known that ten American cities are facing the same diabolical problem.

Police Media Liaison Officer Anne Drennan defends her force against accusations that they were slow to react and often insensitive to complaints. She points out that if 31 university coeds were to go missing, their friends and relatives would report it immediately and the details of their recent whereabouts would be known. With street prostitutes...Drennan lets her hands fall open, upward and empty.

In many cases, police often only have access to the body dump site, not the murder scene, which one homicide detective said yields an estimated 75 per cent of useful evidence. Police also cited the anonymity of the suspect and victim. People tend to notice what is out of place but street prostitutes are not noticed when they climb into a vehicle. The most common crime scene is a vehicle, but in very few cases are witnesses able to identify it. The offender has total control of the crime scene and he takes it with him, usually without much trace, after he has dumped the body.

# FEDS AND CITY AT FAULT

The quasi-legal status of prostitution also hampers police effectiveness. Prostitution is not illegal. However, it is unlawful to communicate with another person for the purpose of buying or selling sexual services. This alienates prostitutes from the protective powers of the police. For a prostitute to report an assault or robbery might entail that they were committing an offence (communicating), or violating a bail or probation area restriction. Why have anything at all to do with the police?

Criminal law sanctions have institutionalized an adversarial relationship between prostitutes and police. This can lead to a mindset in which police brutality or negligence is "acceptable." Karen Duddy tells of a young Native woman being "taken down" in the WISH safe house parking lot because she was wanted under two warrants for solicitation. "It took seven cops and a police dog in her face to arrest one small woman. It was just the most unreasonable use of force."

In another case, a Native woman was held down and raped by two men, nearly strangled by the chain they wrapped around her throat. She managed to escape and flee to the police to

*I*n many cases, police often only have access to the body dump site, not the murder scene, which one homicide detective said yields an estimated 75 per cent of useful evidence. Police also cited the anonymity of the suspect and victim.

*Prostitution is not illegal. However, it is unlawful to communicate with another person for the purpose of buying or selling sexual services. This alienates prostitutes from the protective powers of the police.*

report the incident, only to be arrested on an outstanding warrant for solicitation. Nobody would listen to her complaint. Only when she threw herself at the feet of a WISH worker in the jail and begged for help was anything done. The two men were later arrested.

"This was no joke," Karen Duddy said. "Women do not fantasize about being raped. Yet she was completely ignored. It happens time and time again."

Only after the well-known "America's Most Wanted" TV show came to town and did a program on the missing women were the city of Vancouver and the province shamed into posting a $100,000 reward.

John Lowman has labeled the city as the "biggest pimp on the street." The 1985 communication law and police harassment

forced prostitutes into darker and more dangerous places to do their business.

That made them targets for misogynistic and predatory men.

The City of Vancouver makes a great deal of money licencing the 100 or so high-end body-rub parlours and escort agencies while, at the same time, hounding street prostitutes.

The city licence fee for body-rub parlours can be nearly $7,000, compared to $175 for a therapeutic massage parlour.

"They are up to their necks in facilitating prostitution on the one hand while condemning it on the other," Lowman said. "They are a bunch of hypocrites."

Vancouver's bylaw defines a body rub as "the manipulating, touching or stimulating, by any means, of a person's body or part thereof but does not include medical, therapeutic or cosmetic massage treatment."

"It's the only thing they're allowed to do, according to the city's own bylaw," Lowman said. "Body-rub parlours are by definition brothels."

"*They [the City of Vancouver] are up to their necks in facilitating prostitution on the one hand while condemning it on the other. They are a bunch of hypocrites.*" **John Lowman**

# TOBACCO ROAD REVISITED
## A WOUNDED MOHAWK NATION

### TRADITIONAL MOHAWK PEOPLE STRUGGLE TO DEFEND THEIR WAY OF LIFE THROUGH THE IROQUOIS CONFEDERACY'S GOOD MIND

**By Dr. John Bacher**   Assistant Research: Danny Beaton      **Published June-July, 2003**

The terrible way of organized crime disguised by the rhetoric of the Warrior's Society, which peaked in the late 1980s and early 1990s in Iroquois country, had its roots in the assault on the lands held sacred by Native people through the construction of the St. Lawrence Seaway during the 1950s.

*Illustration: Bernard Low*

This was a decade in which basic political rights, such as the vote, were denied to Native Canadians. This crippled their voices to protest the assault suddenly unleashed on their ancestral lands.

The assault on the Seaway was combined with the other invasion of other Iroquois lands. This included the preliminary Oka golf course and the construction of dams, which flooded much of the New York State reservations of the Tuscarora and Seneca; including the Cold Spring Longhouse from which emerged the sacred message of the peace prophet, Handsome Lake.

*An abundance of marine life had nourished Mohawk communities along the St. Lawrence for more than a thousand years, since the valley had been part of Iroquois territory from time immemorial.*

The assaults on the earth in the homeland of the Iroquois launched a complex and complimentary toxic brew of hatred, deadly chemicals, polluted waters, violence, racism, corruption and despair. Once again, war and terror came to a land that had not seen violent political conflict since the Saskatchewan Metis Rebellion of the 1880s.

Turning the turbulent St. Lawrence into a canalized channel for ocean commerce was pushed forward by right wing Republicans prominent in the presidential administration of Dwight Eisenhower. Similar business tycoons influential today in the U.S. presidential administration of George Bush are trying to further expand the Seaway to accommodate larger ships for the same narrow interests of the polluting coal, automobile and steel industries. They remain blind to the widespread contamination this would cause through the introduction of more exotic marine species and the destruction of islands and shoals by dredging and explosions.

The 1950s Seaway scheme was born out of another tragic episode: the ecocidal invasion of the Innu homeland, Nitasssinan. Until this decade, the homeland of the Innu of Québec and Labrador remained pristine wild lands where these people were able to continue to live through a traditional subsistence economy, respectful of the vast herds of caribou that teemed their land.

Then an industrial assault suddenly appeared in a virulent form through iron ore mines, since abandoned, in the interior of Québec and Labrador. These were serviced through a new train line to the port of Sept Isles blasted through old growth boreal forests. The main reason for the construction of the Seaway was to get iron – marginally cheaply for a few decades – from Sept Isles to steel refineries in Ohio.

For short-term steel industry profits, enormous harm was done to the earth during an era when Native Canadians could not vote and environmental assessment legislation did not exist. The greed of a few well-placed plutocrats in the Republican Eisenhower Administration devastated the traditional Native subsistence economy based on fishing.

An abundance of marine life had nourished Mohawk communities along the St. Lawrence for more than a thousand years; the valley had been part of Iroquois territory from time immemorial. When Jacques Cartier arrived at what is now Québec City he found a large Iroquois community numbering in the thousands. The plagues brought about by Europeans compelled the Mohawks to retreat to the central New York area until they had regained sufficient population to return to their ancestral territories.

## ORGANIZED CRIME LAYS ROOTS

One of the leading and courageous foes of the drift to organized crime is Kanentiio, a Mohawk journalist and author more widely known as Doug George, who for many years braved the gunfire of the Warrior's Society and their organized crime allies. Despite bearing the brunt of considerable hostility from these elements, involving serious threats on his life, and a period of imprisonment from a trumped up charge manipulated by the Québec government's dam building maniac, Robert Bourassa, George has no hesitation in tracing their origins to the greedy devastation of the St. Lawrence for the Seaway's construction.

In his book *Iroquois Culture and Commentary*, published by Clear Light Press in 2000, George describes the great bounty of the St. Lawrence before the coming of the Seaway. Before its completion on the dark day of April 25, 1959, he recalls:

"A family could do well on the river. Like the lifeblood of our mother, it provided all one needed to survive. The rapids scoured the water clean so that when the river finally slowed at Akwesasne, it was a shimmering green. The turbulence brought a rush of rich oxygen into the waters. Species of fish such as sturgeon, walleye, northern pike, trout and salmon took to the rich beds with excitement. When the ice surrendered in defiant, crashing roars in the

*Photo: Danny Beaton*

**❝***Powerful, arrogant and flush with cash, companies such as Reynolds Aluminum, the Aluminum Company of America, Domtar, Courtland Textiles, and General Motors built new factories or expanded old ones along the St. Lawrence.***❞**
**Doug George**

spring, the fish began to run, spawning by the millions. A family working together with gill nets and spears could catch enough bullheads in two weeks to take care of their financial needs for a year."

George stresses that the problems caused by the drowning of the St. Lawrence rapids causing former fish breeding ground to be choked with weeds, were compounded by the toxic contamination unleashed by new industries which were located in the region to take advantage of cheap hydro power.

"Powerful, arrogant and flush with cash, companies such as Reynolds Aluminum, the Aluminum Company of America, Domtar, Courtland Textiles, and General Motors built new factories or expanded old ones along the St. Lawrence. Employing thousands of workers in upstate New York, they became virtual lords of the St. Lawrence."

Fluoride contamination from an aluminum refinery in Massena, New York, resulted in the demise of cattle farming. After Mohawk fish consumption was reduced by pollution, the rate of adult-diabetes began to soar. Captured fish became too toxic to use for garden fertilizer.

The slow process of environmental litigation and cleanup eventually revealed some of the scope of corporate abuse of the St. Lawrence. The Alcoa refinery eventually received a $3.75 million fine for a hazardous waste violation, the largest

criminal penalty ever assessed in the history of the United States. A foundry of General Motors in Massesna was convicted of illegally dumping 31,000 tons of PCB contaminated waste.

## POLLUTED ENVIRONMENT LEADS TO WARRIOR SOCIETY

The various forms of environmental disruption caused by the Seaway would sow the seeds of the Warriors Society in complex ways. It both undermined the traditional subsistence economy and faith in the integrity of the Canadian justice system. An image emerged of Iroquois people having to use violent methods to escape their polluted environment, a belief that first emerged in Kahnawake.

The Mohawk community of Kahnawake, surrounded by the suburbs of Montreal, was also devastated by the Seaway. Here 1,260 acres were lost through the construction of a new canal channel, although for an expense of an additional $2 million, these lands guaranteed by sacred treaties could have been avoided through constructing a canal away from the shore.

One of the Kahnawake leaders who worked the hardest to defeat the Seaway's assault on Kahnawake was artist and writer Louis Hall. He worked closely in courtroom battles wit able Jewish lawyer Omar Z. Ghobashy, a prominent Egyptian civil servant before the Nasserist revolution.

Ghobashy persuaded Hall to adopt the fighting model of Israel, where a relatively few well armed committed zealots could form an army. They successfully returned to the Jewish nation some of their ancestral lands that had

*An image emerged of Iroquois people having to use violent methods to escape their polluted environment, a belief that first emerged in Kahnawake.*

been seized in the past, despite being heavily outnumbered.

Hall dreamed of creating a Native Warrior Society. He hoped to use armed might to return to earth-respecting Native Americans some of their land stolen by whites who built such monstrous projects as the Seaway.

Hall was like many in Kahnawake, disillusioned with the Canadian justice system and its inability to protect their community from the destruction of the Seaway. He mocked and ridiculed the peace orientated confederacy elders who had been able to stop through nonviolent methods such assults on their lands as the Kinzua dam, which flooded away the Cold Spring Longhouse.

At the same time Hall was planning the formation of the Warriors Society in nearby Montreal the FLQ was demonstrating the explosive impact of terrorism to get publicity for various injustices faced by French Canadians.

On August 22, 1973 an FLQ bomb exploded near Kahanwake on a nearby CPR railway bridge closing Seaway traffic for several hours. A huge FLQ proclamation was painted in red overlooking Kahanwake. Hall would mimic the Québec separatists in their fierce determination to regard those who disagreed with his aims as "traitors."

Hall's was determined to build an armed Warrior Society, which would wrest territory for a homeland for Native Americans like the exiled European Jews. This group had carved Israel out of predominately Arab Palestine, and was in keeping with fashionable justifications for armed conflict in the 1960s and 1970s among much of the political extreme left in North America and Europe.

*H*all dreamed of creating a native Warrior Society. He mocked and ridiculed the peace orientated confederacy elders...

Since the Seaway encouraged many to believe in armed struggle to obtain land in a clean environment away from polluting industries, many Native Americans from around the continent flocked to his cause to join the Warrior Society after it was formed in 1971.

## NATIVES FLOCK TO WARRIOR SOCIETY

One important figure in the early Warrior Society was a Shawnee Native from Oklahoma named Richard "Cartoon" Alford, a veteran of the occupation of Wounded Knee as well as the co-founder of the Oklahoma chapter of the American Indian Movement. AIM was founded in 1969 and was an expression of the struggle for social justice manifested in the civil rights movement.

Cartoon was a direct descendent of the famed Shawnee leader Tecumseh. When he was asked to go to Kahnawake in the fall of 1973 to assist in the training of the young men, he did so without hesitation. In time, he would be asked to accept Mohawk citizenship while carrying the Turtle Clan name Tronnekwe.

While other armed struggle movements for social justice in North America such as the Black Panthers, the Weathermen and the FLQ made little headway, for more than a decade Hall's Warriors were able to achieve some of their goals.

*A major victory took place on May 13, 1974, when the Warrior Society seized at gunpoint a 612-acre site in Adirondack State Park in New York…*

A major victory took place on May 13, 1974, when the Warrior Society seized at gunpoint a 612-acre site in Adirondack State Park in New York at Moss Lake, previously a girl's scout camp on Moss Lake. The camp was renamed as the Mohawk community of Ganiekeh or "place of the people of the flint."

Cartoon successfully organized Ganiehkeh's defense against New York state police. More than 300 Natives from across North America journeyed to the camp, some well equipped with weapons. Such armed strength resulted in a 1977 agreement between the Warriors and New York State (negotiated by Mario Cuomo, then New York's Secretary of State) to move Gainekeh to the more northerly Altona corner of the Adirondacks, a few miles south of the Canadian border.

Community relations were smoothed by Christian ministers who viewed the Mohawks as similar to the Jews, returning to their sacred ancestral lands. Under an agreement with New York State the community was given control over a 698-acre settlement site, and the 5,000 acre Macomb Reforestation area was dedicated to their use for subsistence use.

*Ganiehkeh was able to come so close to Iroquoian ideals of being a drug and alcohol free community that it became for several years a cherished place for native Americans to undergo rehabilitation for substance abuse.*

## NEW COMMUNITY PROSPERS

Under leaders such as Cartoon, Ganiehkeh was able to prosper. It was able to come so close to Iroquoian ideals of being a drug and alcohol free community that it became for several years a cherished place for Native Americans to undergo rehabilitation for substance abuse. The community kept cattle and chickens, raised and sold rabbits and operated a small sawmill.

In 1981 a craft store was opened. Under an agreement with the Miner Center of New York State, a program of maple syrup production was developed. Although such subsistence activities were commonly combined with ironwork for employment, this pattern had long been customary in Iroquois communities.

Ganienkeh also provided an important point to many young Iroquois; that the direct assertion of aboriginal land claims and treaty rights could force New York to concede criminal, civil and administrative victory over Native people. This victory would have some unexpected consequences. Originally conceived for the high ideals of living in a clean environment, it would unexpectedly open the door to commercial gambling, cross border smuggling, and the rise of an "entrepreneurial" class among the Iroquois that would in time, seek to undermine the authority of each and every Native government.

*T he brave Oneida journalist and police investigator, Jim Moses, has traced the major shift in the nature of the Warrior Society, to the Racquette Point incident of 1980 describing it as: "The last time the Mohawk Warrior's Society acted from a purely altruistic motive before the movement corrupted itself."*

## SOCIETY CORRUPTS ITSELF

In the early 1980s Ganienkeh had realized some of Hall's dreams for the creation of a drug and pollution free haven for the Iroquois in the relatively clean environment of New York's Adirondacks. It was soon destined however to change into a center for organized crime, causing its founder Cartoon, to eventually lead a Mohawk police action against the remaining Warriors he'd formerly commanded at a critical standoff at Akwesasne.

The brave Oneida journalist and police investigator, Jim Moses, has traced the major shift in the nature of the Warrior Society to the Racquette Point incident of 1980 describing it as: "The last time the Mohawk Warrior's Society acted from a purely altruistic motive before the movement corrupted itself."

The Mohawk Nation Council (the Longhouse people) refused to permit the formation of a "warrior society" at Akwesasne even if there were individuals who referred to themselves as such.

The Racquette Point incident (an almost year long armed standoff) created a law enforcement vacuum, which presented a few opportunistic Mohawks with the chance of a lifetime. The international border was open for business. The resulting smuggling activities would draw the Warriors Society into the destructive vortex of organized crime. It would also result in a conflict with the traditional adherents of the Longhouse and the Confederacy that originally had been sympathetic to it. The most important factor was that the incident promoted a need for guns, which would be exploited by criminals associated with organized crime.

During the Raquette point siege, individuals connected to organized crime offered weapons to the Warriors. Moses found these gunrunners, with as much experience as mob connected thugs, had "extensive connections to the underworld in Chicago and Detroit" and had "very sinister" reputations.

## SHADY ALLIANCES FORM

The new organized crime connections would be exacerbated in their dangers by other new developments, most critically in 1982 after a close vote of 325 to 307 conducted by the U.S. St. Regis Tribal Council, after the successful nonviolent resolution of the Racquette Point incident. The close vote resulted in the dissolution of the American Mohawk police force. This situation would last 15 years, until it

*W hat made the border situation so explosive for the corruption of the Warrior Society were new sinister and cynical political developments by right wing political forces in the United States…*

*A key architect of the destructive, cynical policy to use Native governance to facilitate organized crime in the early 1980s was the late Stephen Henntington Whidden.*

was finally remedied as part of the coordinated approach to the problem of organized crime long advocated in vain by courageous voices like Jim Moses.

Four Mohawk communities were now straddled near the Canadian-U.S. border; the two American communities of St. Regis and Ganienkeh being no- police zones. These communities are only within a half hour drive of each other. The Warrior's birthplace, Kahnawake, surrounded by Montreal, provides a good location to sell such contraband goods as tax-free cigarettes, alcohol and illegal drugs on a massive scale.

What made the border situation so explosive for the corruption of the Warrior Society were new sinister and cynical political developments by right wing political forces in the United States, hostile to the earth protecting agendas of the allied environmental and Native movements.

These forces consciously sought to cut federal expenditures on Native programs, have Native communities fund their economies through gambling and exploit Native governance as a weak link to undercut public efforts to curb organized crime.

Since the alliance between greens and Natives promised a new form of people's power,

threatening to big polluting corporations, corrupt conservative strategists in the Regan and Nixon administrations forged an alliance between opportunistic Native entrepreneurs, who were environmental outlaws, and organized crime.

A key architect of the destructive, cynical policy to use Native governance to facilitate organized crime in the early 1980s was the late Stephen Henntington Whidden, who had earlier served as legal counsel in the corrupt Presidential administration of Richard Nixon. Whidden, a Harvard University trained lawyer in 1979, was serving as solicitor for a Seminole nation when it clashed with state authorities over the installation of poker and video slot machines in a bingo hall in Hollywood, near Fort Lauderdale

Whidden aggressively encouraged the Seminole nation to seek commercial advantages by undertaking various activities, including gambling, which were prohibited by Florida state law. Investigations by the California Department of Justice would reveal that Whidden's schemes with the Seminoles were part of an effort financed by such pillars of organized crime as the Genoveses, the family of Sebastian Larocca in Pittsburgh and the key financial wizard of Mafia gangs, Meyer Lansky.

More than a few Iroquois watched the Florida events closely so when the Seminoles won their legal fight against the state to operate commercial bingo halls, similar ventures sprouted up in Akwesasne, Oneida, Cattaraugus and Gagienkeh. Each gambling venture was based on the assertion of Iroquois sovereignty extracted from the 1973 Moss Lake

*Whidden's schemes with the Seminoles were part of an effort financed by such pillars of organized crime as the Genoveses...*

occupation; only this time the issue would be economic rather than territorial.

Illegal gambling, as defined by the traditional leaders of the Confederacy, would appear in Iroquois soon after the Racquette Point incident in Ganienkeh. Here, the community would follow the Seminoles and ignore state law regarding gambling, which established limits of $1,000 a prize for bingo.

This resulted in the establishment of the Sunrise Stakes Bingo Hall. Ganiekeh would soon pioneer in another activity unregulated by state law. This would be the establishment of gasoline stations that did not charge state tax. The economic capitalists exploited the sovereignty struggles of the Confederacy in ways that defied the very laws the leadership was seeking to preserve, and without any tangible benefit to those aboriginal governments that were entrusted with the task of defending the collective rights of the people.

## LOOPHOLES ENABLE GAS AND GAMBLING COMMERCE

The commercialization of Warrior activities to defend gasoline stations and gambling halls, resulted in criticism of the Warriors, from their former allies at the Racquette Point standoff, who adhered to the traditional Iroquois Confederacy, most notably, Doug George. He viewed the proliferation of gasoline stations in various Iroquois communities, which were not subject to the same environmental controls imposed on similar off reserve enterprises, as a dangerous blight.

George deplores how to this day on a single mile stretch of U.S. Route 37 through

Akwesasne, "there are seventeen large gasoline stations dispensing millions of gallons of fuel each month. Very few of them have effective environmental controls, follow any kind of spillage guidelines, or are prepared to clean up the frequent overflows that have polluted the wells of many homes. The profit motive is supreme. The fuel-station owners treat any mention of natural law and its consequences as the whining of unrealistic Iroquois dwelling 'in the mythical past'."

In speaking to Tom Porter, a highly respected Mohawk elder and spiritual leader, he pointed out there is only one Iroquois community where the blight of cut rate cigarette stores, gasoline stations and other opportunistic commercial activities, which seek to exploit

*Tom Porter Mohawk elder and spiritual leader*

> *" The fuel-station owners treat any mention of natural law and its consequences as the whining of unrealistic Iroquois dwelling 'in the mythical past'. "*
>
> **Doug George**

*A*fter Hill's gas station was shut down, it was discovered that its leaky pumps left a thick layer of gas stretching for 80,000 square feet. These 10,000 gallons of leaded fuel contaminated an aquifer that provided Onondaga residents with drinking water.

loopholes to avoid regulation and taxation has been halted. This is the traditional Iroquois capital of Onondaga, seat of the Confederacy government.

Onondaga has the strongest confederacy government of any Iroquois community, not faced like other communities by a rival body imposed by U.S. or Canadian law. Its investigations into the past activities of Warrior businesses which were expelled from the community, indicate there is likely a chain of toxic time bombs around various Warrior-protected businesses throughout Iroquoia.

It was very difficult for the Onondaga government to close down the Warrior allied business that refused to recognize the authority of the Confederacy council. Conflict

centered around a gas station operated by Oliver Hill, who was organizer of the Iroquois Businessman's Association. Hill's establishment was subject to long blockades organized by traditional Onondaga clan mothers.

Eventually, Hill's gas station was demolished by the authority of the Confederacy council. This action was unfortunately denounced by the Canadian Alliance in Solidarity With Native People's (CASNIP), which until its end in 1998, would continually endorse the most outrageous actions associated with the Warriors Society.

It tragically just repeated the justifications made by Louis Hall in his influential publication The Crisis, until his death, disorienting much of the Native leadership across Canada about

*Judy Swamp, Mohawk Clan Mother*

Photos: Danny Beaton

*Ann Jock, Mohawk Clan Mother*

*D*espite massive protests, the bars that became a vehicle of recruitment into the worlds of Warrior activity and organized crime, remained open.

the dangers posed by the dual problems of the Warriors and organized crime.

After Hill's gas station was shut down, it was discovered that its leaky pumps left a thick layer of gas stretching for 80,000 square feet. These 10,000 gallons of leaded fuel contaminated an aquifer that provided Onondaga residents with drinking water.

Warrior rhetoric became a device whereby any Iroquois businessman could attempt to escape community regulation through manipulating arguments around sovereignty which, instead of being vested in the institutions of Iroquois governments, were used to justify a variety of antisocial actions.

While such justifications had some basis in critiquing the actions of imposed band councils, they were also applied to the traditional confederacy – Louis Hall at one point even denouncing all of these revered spiritual leaders as "traitors" and condemning them to death. This problem of disrespect for any legal authority was especially troublesome in Akwesasne since it disrupted attempts to regulate bars, which could not be enforced in the absence of a police force on the American side of the community.

## SPEAKEASIES RECRUIT; CAUSE DEATHS

Unregulated bars by the mid-1980s became seen as responsible for deaths resulting from high speed driving. The owners refused to close despite referendums held by councils on both

sides of the border; one by a margin of 665 to 151. One march to close the speakeasies resulted in a demonstration of 2,000 persons in a community of only 8,000 residents.

Despite massive protests the bars, which had become a vehicle of recruitment into the worlds of Warrior activity and organized crime, remained open. An undercover police investigator, Carl Broeker, whose activities briefly lead him to be imprisoned on a makeshift smuggling island prison on St. Lawrence River island, spent some time in one such facility. He described it in Paul William Roberts and Norman Snider's recent book *Smokescreen*, as a "dingy, desperate place, the kind of hard drinking sty where alcohol pours like gasoline on fire…Fathers and sons, brothers, friends and acquaintances knifed each other over a hostile word or a dubious look."

In the decade between 1985 and 1995, the peak of the blight of the Warriors and organized crime, some 75 tribal members in Akwesasne would die violently or disappear. Most of these deaths involved conflict between criminal groups or accidents involving smuggling.

Violence however, was also involved in efforts to intimidate opponents of organized crime and the Warriors. Two newspapers edited by Doug George, *Indian Times* and *Akwesasne Notes*, would have their offices destroyed by arson in 1988 and 1989. Here they were housed in a fortress like concrete block structure on the Canadian side of Akwesasne close to the police station. The Mohawk Radio station CKON

*T*he peak of power for the Warriors and their allied organized crime supporters took place between 1988 and 1994 when they controlled the St. Regis Tribal council.

was also targeted. Its broadcasting cable was later cut to sabotage its broadcasts.

Social corrosion was caused by the explosion of unregulated gambling casinos, cut rate cigarette stores, gas stations, and the smuggling of various contraband items such as drugs, alcohol, guns and tobacco. This was accompanied by a variety of other criminal activities such as counterfeiting and money laundering. Eventually it resulted in the souring of many former Warrior leaders, most notably Cartoon.

He told investigators working with Jim Moses that his turning point came when he realized the Warriors were drug dealing and using "cocaine and high balls", a potent mixture of cocaine and heroin. This led to his departure from Ganiekeh, in a manner akin to Christ's angry reaction "among the moneychangers in the temple."

The peak of power for the Warriors and their allied organized crime supporters took place between 1988 and 1994 when they controlled the St. Regis Tribal council. Critical to the control of the council was Chief Leo David Jacobs who signed a gambling pact with New York State. It was eventually ruled illegal by the courts in May 2002. He would ultimately be convicted by the Federal Racketeer Influenced Corrupt Organization (RICO) statute for running the St. Regis Tribal Council as a criminal enterprise.

Among those convicted with Jacobs was former New York State trooper, John Fountain, a typical example of the corrosive impact of the corruption of law enforcement, which contributed to the toleration of the Warriors by governments on both sides of the border for many years.

After his arrest Jacobs admitted to taking kickbacks from Larry Miller, a Las Vegas-based businessman who had a slot machine business and extensive connections with organized crime.

Miller was a partner with Robert Tavano, former chair of the Niagara Falls New York Republican Party, who was convicted of stealing $400,000 from the county government. As a result of a subsequent gambling investigation, it was revealed that Tavano had close connections with major Mafia czars such as local godfather Stefano Magaddiono, and Hamilton crime boss Johnny Papalia.

## BLOCKADES FORM

Papalia acquired alcohol smuggled into Canada via Akwesasne with Warrior aid from out-of-state locations as far away as California and Oregon. In 1994 this amounted to 600,000 cases generating profits of $7.8 million, which were used to acquire casino sites. Jacobs confessed to taking $3,000 in kickbacks for every tractor trailer load of illegal goods Miller moved through Aksesasne.

Opponents of the Warrior protected businesses in Akwesasne resorted to blockades of roads leading to casinos. This was after their repeated requests for the stationing of a Canadian-American police force had been rejected in a racist manner by the surrounding governments, especially that of New York State. The blockades were established on March 23, 1990, with the support of the Canadian Mohawk police force and tribal council.

Gambling supporters tried to destroy the blockades even as they were being built. The resistance held, however. Women baked bread, cakes and pies to feed two hundred people who rotated in shifts around the clock. One leading gambling foe, Brian Cole, a prominent Mohawk environmentalist, withstood two beatings by gambling supporters on the blockade.

By late April 1990, faced with the loss of millions in revenues, the Warriors began to escalate their violence. On April 23, the North American Indian College was set on fire. Gas bombs were fired at blockades. A live hand grenade was tossed into a crowd in front of the Canadian Mohawk police station, as 15 Warriors lined up their cars. Several private homes were damaged by firebombs. The police station was later hit with 200 rounds of fire from unidentified men carrying AK-47 assault rifles.

During the evening of April 24, 1990 the blockades ended in an explosion of gunfire. Hundreds of rounds of automatic weapon fire were poured, parallel to the ground, on the blockades. Warriors at the time of this offensive were staggering and howling, apparently drunk and high on cocaine. Twenty cars of gambling foes were torched. The American side of Akwesasne became a no man's land, rent by bursts of weapons fire.

On April 26, 1990 the Canadian Mohawk council prepared a mass evacuation. Within a few days some 2,667 of the 3,920 people on the Canadian side had fled, along with 1,000

of the 4,000 American residents. Nearly 2,000 refugees were sheltered in public facilities of the Transport Canada Training Institute in Cornwall. The gun battles at Akwesasne were the most intense since the Metis rebellion over a century ago.

As their foes fled, Warriors embarked on a reign of terror. Brian Cole was beaten with baseball bats and forced to hide in the woods for 24 hours, until being able to escape to a hospital. The sons of three sub-chiefs of the Confederacy council were beaten when they went to Cole's aid. Automatic weapon fire was aimed at the home of traditional sub-chief Jake Swamp, and gambling foes Barbara and Barry Montour, the son of Art Montour, a key leader of the Warrior Society.

An action was taken by the Canadian Mohawk police force to prevent a Warrior takeover of Akwesasne in April 1990. Despite the pleas of Mohawk cops they were abandoned by every Canadian police agency leaving them no choice but to leave the reservation. The only resistance to the complete takeover of Akwesasne-and subsequent control of the Mohawk nation itself was led by a small group of 12 men defending the home of a Mohawk man in the Snye district of Akwesasne.

---

*An action was taken by the Canadian Mohawk police force to prevent a Warrior takeover of Akwesasne in April 1990. Despite the pleas of Mohawk cops, they were abandoned by every Canadian police agency leaving them no choice but to leave the reservation.*

---

## CONTINUOUS GUNFIRE

That home was the residence of Dave George, Jr. the brother of Doug George. From April 27 to April 30, the small band forced back repeated attempts by the heavily armed Warriors to overrun their position. On the evening of April 30 they were joined by two Canadian journalists who would witness 12 hours of almost continuous gunfire.

Providing tactical leadership was Cartoon (now Doug's brother-in-law) and Ron Lazore, a former U.S. Marine and member of the Akwesasne Mohawk Police. George later recalled how "Cartoon and Ron kept us going, because they were steady and knew what they were doing. We could not have survived without them."

George said they were outnumbered 10-1 with gunshots coming at them from all four directions including the St. Lawrence River, making retreat impossible. He and Cartoon later compiled a list of the Warriors who were at the scene. They identified Warriors from Akwesasne, Ganienkeh, Kahnawake and Oneida (they were also joined by a number of white and black men connected with gambling and smuggling operations. All organized for what they thought would be an easy victory.)

Instead, the Mohawk men at the George residence received critical assistance on May 1, which enabled them to launch a frontal attack on the Warrior positions compelling that group to break and run. The victory was however, soon completely overshadowed by the subsequent revelations of two deaths that had taken place sometime after the April 29 barricade assault. The victims were two Mohawks. Matthew Pyke, a long time anti-gambling activist was shot in his back at 6:30 pm on his way to join the George group. Earlier that morning JR Edwards, an apolitical resident, was shot when walking to his uncle's home. Both deaths remained unsolved by the American and Canadian criminal justice systems.

No charges were ever laid in the death of Matthew Pyke. A friend, Bruce Roundpoint, helped to get Pyke to a hospital but was stopped at a Warrior roadblock, causing a critical delay in Pyke receiving medical aid. He would die of his wounds a few hours later.

Evidence later gathered as a result of charges laid in connection with JR Edwards' death points to efforts to manipulate an accidental death from massive rounds of gunfire. It was later revealed by pathology that Edwards' body had been moved after his death. He originally fell forward on impact, rather than lying on his back (photographed by the press).

Following the two deaths the Akwesasne reservation was finally occupied by the Canadian Army, the Ontario Provincial Police, the New York State Police and the Sûreté du Québec. This occupation by 500 police stopped the gunfire and encouraged refugees to return home.

Despite the massive police intervention, no charges were laid against any Warriors for

*D*espite the massive police intervention, no charges were laid against any Warriors for the numerous extreme acts of violence they carried out in the past two years.

the numerous extreme acts of violence they had carried out in the past two years. Aware of their continued impunity, the Warriors harassed even the occupying police.

On June 16 Québec police officers were forced to take cover after twenty shots were fired at one of their roadblocks. Two days later, New York state troopers narrowly escaped injury when a speeding van rammed two of their roadblocks. Warriors drove back and forth in front of the home of the late Matthew Pyke's parents screaming profanities. The homes of Jake Swamp and Doug George also became targets of random gunshots. No charges were laid in connection with any of these incidents.

Rather than charging Warriors for anything, Québec police charged Doug George with the murder of JR Edwards – a move compared by Jim Moses to a pedestrian being charged after being struck by a drunk driver on the basis of accusations made by equally intoxicated passengers.

While the arrest fit a pattern of a cowardly refusal to challenge a still numerically superior combined Canadian-U.S. security force, it also points to the Québec government's long standing conflict with the environmental activist, Doug George. He was flown to Montreal for his incarceration in the personal plane of Premier Robert Bourassa.

# FINGER POINTING AND INTIMIDATION

An investigative reporter, who earlier was distinguished by being the only editor daring to publish through his newspaper, *Indian Times,* the secret subsidized contracts between Hydro Québec and major industries, Doug George

> *While Québec police declined to take any Warriors into custody for questioning, George, his brother Dave, Ken Lazore and two Mohawk police officers… were intensely interrogated for 12 hours and denied counsel despite repeated requests.*

was long a thorn in the side of the Québec government. His information was used by the Cree of northern Québec as part of their campaign. The absurd and contemptible charges put one of Bourassa's most effective environmental critics behind bars.

While Québec police declined to take any Warriors into custody for questioning, George, his brother Dave, Ken Lazore and two Mohawk police officers, Steve Lazore and Roger Mitchell, were intensely interrogated for 12 hours and denied counsel despite repeated requests. This detention caused the entire Mohawk police force to resign their commissions with the Sûreté du Québec, although retaining their Ontario credentials. Following the interrogation, Doug George was arrested and charged with second-degree murder. He was imprisoned for ten days and released on $10,000 bail.

George was arrested on the basis of testimony by Ken Lazore, which he later recanted after three and a half months. Then he indicated that his statements had been read by Québec police officers who pressured him into signing it. He also revealed that Québec police had threatened him during the 12 hour interrogation and denied his request for legal counsel eight times.

They told Lazore that he would never see his children again and would face a 25-year sentence unless he implicated George. Considerable pressure was also brought on Lazore by the Warriors to recant. On October 23, 1990, an unknown gunman in a passing car fired at least 18 rounds of ammunition at his home from a machine gun.

The prosecution's case collapsed on the third day of a preliminary hearing in Valleyfield, Québec, which was held to determine if there was sufficient evidence to hold a trial. In addition to Lazore's repudiation of his statement, a ballistics expert testified that the bullets that killed Edwards could not be linked to rifles used by Lazore or George.

On November 1, 1990, Québec judge, Pierre LaBerge, indicated that after reading the file the previous evening, he concluded that the evidence against George wouldn't stand up in court. He ordered that since the case was so lacking in merit, George should be released immediately.

A few months following the two deaths from gunfire in Akwesasne, another death from a firefight, involving a Québec policeman, Marcel Lemay, took place in the Mohawk community of Kanehsatake. Unlike the disputes over the activities of organized crime in Akwesasne, this involved the community's attempt to protect a sacred pine forest and burial ground. An unarmed blockade against the golf course had been put in place on March 11, 1990, and had been established with the advice of the Alliance for Nonviolent Action, a Canadian peace group.

Doug George maintains the incident at Oka was in direct response to the Akwesasne crisis. He says the Warriors had lost tremendous face at Akwesasne as a result of their defeat and arrived at Oka in July 1990, uninvited by the community with their vehicles stocked with firearms and looking for a way to assert their power.

Such an action, George argues, was certain to provoke the Sûreté, which was angry over accusations of cowardice rising from its refusal to aide the Akwesasne Police. George says officer Lemay, who was to die at Oka after being shot by a Warrior, had been at Akwesasne.

Following the two deaths at Akwesasne, Warriors began to show up at the blockade in late June. On July 11, 1990 100 outgunned Sûreté officers unleashed tear gas against the Warriors. The Sûreté quickly retreated after they encountered an unexpected barrage of bullets from the Warriors at the blockade, which lasted less than 30 seconds but left one police officer dead.

The violence at Oka resulted in sympathy blockades at Kahnawake, the most significant of which blocked the Mercier bridge, a major Montreal traffic artery.

*The Warriors had lost tremendous face at Akwesasne as a result of their defeat and arrived at Oka in July 1990, uninvited by the community with their vehicles stocked with firearms and looking for a way to assert their power.*

*C*aught up in their own rhetoric, the press refused to investigate the criminal backgrounds of the Warriors despite pleas by the Mohawk people.

# THE OKA CRISIS

Aware of the Oka crisis' potential to spread violence across Canada, the federal government moved swiftly to buy the disputed land on generous terms, spending $5.2 million for 39 hectares by early September. Then all but 300 of Kanesatake's 1,500 residents had become the second wave in 1990 to flee from Warrior terror.

Warriors in Kanesatake openly manipulated the prolonged armed standoff to legitimate organized crime activities. Not present during the fatal shooting, Akwesasne Warrior leader and casino operator, Loran Thompson, showed up the next day and made a rousing speech in a community gym.

Following the purchase of disputed land on July 27 Thompson again persuaded those taking part in the blockades to maintain them at high risk. Thompson knew if his various criminal activities were to continue he would need the cloak of sovereignty and the threat of violence.

An unexpected ally of the Warriors were members of the press, both domestic and foreign, who put aside their journalistic objectivity in a mad rush to label the outlaw group as "freedom fighters" waging war against an oppressive government.

Caught up in their own rhetoric, the press refused to investigate the criminal backgrounds of the Warriors despite pleas by the Mohawk people. The result was "Oka" became synonymous with legitimate aboriginal struggle rather than the genesis of a criminal enterprise that would come to dominate, and contaminate, the Iroquois for the next 13 years.

Investigative reporter Jim Moses developed a concept known as "silks" to describe the entrepreneurs who used the Warriors to build a fortune. One of the worst cases of such tactics took place in Tuscarora, New York in July, 1990. Shortly after the Oka crisis erupted, Warrior critic Harold Printup was shot in the head and fell into a coma. Two gunmen piled debris around the shooting site with pro-Oka slogans to disguise their motives.

# WARRIOR SOCIETY FALLS

Cresting by the fall of 1990, the Warrior Society would be in deep decline as a political force five years later, but its work had been accomplished. The threat of brute force had convinced both the United States and Canada to retreat from overseeing Iroquois affairs; while the Iroquois governments, which lacked adequate physical or economic resources, were swamped by a criminal elite.

Much of the tribute for the decline of the Warriors as an organization is due simply to the dogged persistence of Jim Moses, who badgered reluctant security services to perform their duties. While accompanying Jim Moses on one of his daring investigations, I remember strongly his words to me as he went to report on his activities to the London office of the RCMP. He repeated a saying that he learned from Doug George, that one of the most effective political actions that can be undertaken is to simply pressure a police officer into doing his job.

In addition to working with law enforcement, Moses cooperated with a strategic studies think tank, The Mackenzie Institute. The publicity generated by their report Sin Tax Failure played a major role in reducing cigarette taxes in Canada, a determined move taken by the newly elected government of Prime Minister Jean Chrétien in February 1994, through a drastic cut of $1.17 a pack.

This single action dried up an estimated $1 billion in Warrior controlled smuggling activities. Before this action 60 per cent of the retail tobacco market in Québec and 35 per cent in Ontario was supplied by the black market. Moses at the time personally appealed to the Prime Minister to lower the tax because of the problem of organized crime terrorizing Native communities.

Cutting the tax eroded what Moses called the "aura of fear" in Native communities. The lowered tax was a dramatic shock to hundreds of smugglers and smoke shop owners. Band council police, who had previously been impotent in the face of openly criminal elements, became more respected in their law enforcement efforts.

## LOWER TAX LEADS TO BREAKTHROUGHS

In addition to getting the tax lowered, Moses also successfully pressured police agencies to cooperate. As a result, a Cornwall Regional Task Force was established between the RCMP, Canada Customs and American agencies. New multi-border blitzes were developed. Databases were shared. Combined resources allowed enforcement agencies to collectively target larger smuggling groups.

In March 1996, such efforts resulted in a major breakthrough when the RCMP made 170 arrests, including Warriors, members of a Montreal area chapter of Hell's Angels, and organized Vietnamese criminals. A year later a joint task force cracked a bigger crime ring, leading to the arrest and conviction of Jacobs, Miller and casino czar Tony Laughing.

The arrest of the Warrior crime lords caused them to reveal some of their corporate collaborators. The U.S. subsidiary of RJR-Macdonald, the third largest tobacco company in Canada, was forced to pay $15 million in penalties. Two of the largest cigarette traffickers from Kahnawake received individual fines of $25 million and $20 million.

Most of the credit for the collapse of the Warrior crime empire, which threatened to make much of the country a war zone like Columbia, is largely due to a handful of brave Iroquois traditionalists. In addition to those already mentioned, they include Longhouse reader, Huron Miller, who worked closely with Jim Moses, Onondaga chief Oren Lyons, the Confederacy Tadodaho, the late Leon Shenandoah, the Six Nations Cofederacy Chief Deskaeh, Harvey Longboat, the reciter of the Great Law, Jake Thomas and the Iroquois diplomat, Leaman Gibson.

All of these spiritual leaders put the principles of the good man and concern for the earth above the sensationalism and greed exploited by the Warrior Society. They have all been active in promoting earth respecting efforts at environmental restoration.

Racism, greed, bribery, environmental destruction and corruption played major roles in why the Warrior problem grew to such dangerous proportions. To prevent such a plague ever happening again in Canada, the lessons of the good mind need to be applied. The earth should be protected and restored so that the blessings of nature can again provide healthy food from clean rivers. The rule of law needs to be vigorously and fairly enforced.

While some major victories have been won against organized crime, the challenges are enormous. Tobacco smuggling, although linked increasingly to funding terrorism, is not an important issue in North American politics. Rather than contemplating a bigger Seaway, as the Bush Administration is doing, we need to correct some of the mistakes of the first folly. The dark decade from 1985 to 1995 when the Warrior Society held many Native communities in a grip of terror, is a powerful image of the urgent need to protect the earth and human rights.

*Most of the credit for the collapse of the Warrior crime empire which threatened to make much of the country a war zone like Columbia, is largely due to a handful of brave Iroquois traditionalists.*

*Traditional Chief Oren Lyons, Turtle Clan, Onondaga Nation*
*Photo: Danny Beaton*

# FEDERAL COURT OF APPEAL REVERSES TAX IMMUNITY DECISION

**By Lloyd Dolha**                                   **Published July, 2003**

The Federal Court of Appeal overturned a major ruling in the *Benoit v. the Queen*, on June 11, 2003, the decision that granted over 15,000 Dene and Cree peoples absolute tax-free status "at any time for any reason," regardless where they reside in Canada.

On March 7, 2002, the trial judge, Justice Douglas Campbell, ruled that because of a misunderstanding during the negotiation of Treaty 8, in 1899, the decendants of Treaty 8 Indians do not have to pay taxes at any time for any reason.

In dismissing the trial judge's ruling, Justice M. Nadon of the appeal court found that the trial judge gave preferential treatment to the oral history evidence of three Dene elders and found that the Treaty 8 First Nations of Alberta did not establish that the aboriginal signatories of Treaty 8 understood that the Treaty Commissioners of the day had made a promise exempting them from taxation. Nadon said that the evidence was "sparse, doubtful and equivocal."

"Since there is nothing in the record which can reasonably support the conclusion reached by the Trial Judge, I am compelled to find he made a palpable and overriding error. The Trial Judge appears to have failed to consider a sizeable portion of the evidence and to have misapprehended material evidence," wrote Justice Nadon.

The Canadian Taxpayers Federation – interveners in the case – applauded the substantive reversal.

Calling the trial judge's ruling "divisive and destructive, Tanis Fiss, the director of the federation's Centre for Aboriginal Policy Change, said, "This is a great victory for all taxpayers, knowing that they will be treated equally regardless of race or ancestry."

AFN national chief Mathew Coon Come expressed disappointment with the ruling, noting that previous case law at the Supreme Court of Canada level have stated that treaty and aboriginal rights have to be determined by taking into account both First Nations and Crown perspectives and law.

"I am hopeful that the Supreme Court will look at this differently and find favour with the original ruling," said Coon Come.

The Treaty 8 First Nations of Alberta have announced that they will apply for leave to appeal the decision to the Supreme Court of Canada.

"We were very disappointed with the ruling, but not surprised. Our clients were prepared for the fact that they may lose at some level and hope that the Supreme Court will hear their case," said Karen Buff, lawyer for the Treaty 8 First Nations.

# BUFFY SAINTE-MARIE: VERSATILE ARTIST COVERS ALL BASES

**By Rick Littlechild**                    **Published April, 1998**

Buffy Sainte-Marie received her Ph.D. in Fine Arts from the University of Massachusetts and also holds degrees in philosophy and teaching. These combined interests are clearly evident in her music, her visual art works, her writing and her life.

*Buffy Sainte-Marie's recent CD* Up Where We Belong *features fifteen recordings including some of Buffy's most beloved classics:* Universal Soldier, Until It's Time for You to Go, The Piney Wood Hills, Soldier Blue, God is Alive, Eagle Man, *and* Indian Cowboy, *as well as her own version of* Up Where We Belong.

She won an Academy Award for writing the song *Up Where We Belong* (from *An Officer and a Gentleman*), and worked in the film industry. She ducked bullets, raised a son, and spent five years on *Sesame Street* teaching little kids and their caretakers that "Indians still exist."

Her electronic paintings on her Macintosh computer have been exhibited in both museums and galleries as well as online. In March she was inducted into the Canadian music industry's Juno Hall of Fame. The versatility in her work is a reflection of her life and is best described as extremely varied, both universal and unique.

As a college student in the early sixties Buffy Sainte-Marie became known as a writer of protest and love songs. Her songs have been performed by hundreds of artists including Elvis Presley, Indigo girls, Barbara Streisand, Quicksilver Messenger Service, Chet Atkins, Bobby Darin,

Donovan, Glen Campbell, The Highwaymen, Roberta Flack, Neil Diamond, the Boston Pops Orchestra, and Janis Joplin.

The folk-scene in those Greenwich Village days was a mixture of preservationists and originals. Buffy was of the latter group and a loner. Having written *Universal Soldier*, which became an anthem for the sixties' peace movement, she was still absent from the mass protest marches in favour of shedding her unique light on Indian rights and environmental issues. She continues to do so today, "…because nobody's covering those bases."

Her musicianship is a reflection of her curiosity about sound. Even in the beginning she strung and tuned her guitar in all sorts of unusual ways and played a mouth bow, which relies on harmonics and a remarkable ear.

But what Buffy Sainte-Marie is best known for is song writing. From her first record to the present time her songs have been meaningful to other artists and to audiences as well, making sense to both the head and the heart. She is a real original.

## LOVE, COUNTRY AND PROTEST

The songs she wrote were varied. Some music lovers might think of her as a writer of country protest songs, but her big financial successes (which allowed her to remain an artist instead of having to work in some other field) were her love songs; particularly *Until It's Time for You to Go* and *Up Where We Belong*.

She had a string of country hits as well, including *The Piney Wood Hills*, *I'm Gonna Be a Country Girl Again*, and *He's an Indian Cowboy*

> *B*uffy Sainte-Marie's songs have been performed by hundreds of artists including Elvis Presley, Indigo girls, Barbara Streisand, Quicksilver Messenger Service, Chet Atkins, Bobby Darin, Donovan, Glen Campbell, The Highwaymen, Roberta Flack, Neil Diamond, the Boston Pops Orchestra, and Janis Joplin.

*in the Rodeo.* The protest songs she's written are scathing and pointed. There is no counter argument that holds up against *Universal Soldier, Now That the Buffalos' Gone*, or *Bury My Heart at Wounded Knee.*

Buffy went from Greenwich Village to Europe, Canada, Australia, Hong Kong, and Japan, and had a unique career outside of the United States. She appeared in movies, wrote essays, worked with early computers, presented a colloquium to Europe's philosophers, established a scholarship foundation to fund Native studies, painted huge pictures, spent time with indigenous people in far away countries, received a medal from Queen Elizabeth II, and won an Academy Award.

In 1976, when her son was born, she quit professional recording to become a mother and an artist. For the next five years she was a cast member of *Sesame Street* and she continued to be a student of experimental music for the next sixteen years.

In 1966, Buffy made the first ever electronic quadraphonic vocal album. In the seventies she used a Boucla synthesizer and later a Serge, creating electronic soundtracks for songs and movies. During the same period she made rare appearances at huge European music festivals, using the early Roland MIDI guitar. In the later seventies and early eighties, she worked at home with a Fairlight and a Synclavier. When the Macintosh computer came out in 1984, Buffy was at the head of the line.

Today her digital home studio is as personal and hands-on for her as a guitar was in the sixties. Her come-back CD, *Coincidence*

> *Today Buffy teaches at colleges and lectures in a variety of fields including digital art, philosophy, film scoring, electronic music, song writing, Indian issues and the Native genius for governments.*

*and Likely Stories*, was made at home in 1991. Using her Macintosh as a recording instrument she played most of the parts herself. When it was just the way she wanted it she dialed the number of her co-producer in London, England, and sent the music down the phone lines via modem, bounced it off the satellite, and it went onto tape in London.

Upon the release of that album, France named her Best International Artist and presented her with the Grand Prix Charles de Gaulle Award. In Ottawa newspapers reviewed her performance with the 85-piece electronic band for 20,000 people last summer at Big Sky in Alberta, as well as at tiny Reserves and fly-in communities across Canada.

Today Buffy teaches at colleges and lectures in a variety of fields including digital art, philosophy, film scoring, electronic music, song writing, Indian issues and the Native genius for governments.

Most importantly, Buffy teaches us to remain positive

amidst tough human realities. Her digital paintings vary in style as do her songs, speeches, classes and essays, each reflecting her lifelong wish to empower creative people's multifaceted potentials "because we need fresh alterNative ideas from every direction...students, artists, women, and indigenous people."

Her latest single and video *Darling Don't Cry* is a "Pow-Wow love song." It was released in 1996 followed by another CD, *Up Where We Belong*. The album features fifteen recordings including some of Buffy's most beloved classics: *Universal Soldier, Until It's Time for You to Go, The Piney Wood Hills, Soldier Blue, God is Alive, Eagle Man,* and *Indian Cowboy,* as well as her own version of *Up Where We Belong.* Chris Birkett, who co-produced *Coincidence and Likely Stories* is once again her co-producer for *Up Where We Belong.*

*Shown are the covers of some of the 19 albums released by Buffy Sainte-Marie*

# From "Smoke Signals" to Hollywood Stardom

**By Peg Hill**                    **Published July, 2002**

## A BRILLIANT STAR IS RISING IN CANADA AND HIS NAME IS ADAM BEACH.

After shining in *Smoke Signals* two years ago, he's about to enter a new orbit of fame and accomplishment. In August he starts filming with Nicolas Cage in *Windtalkers*, a $100-million movie directed by John Woo, who was behind the camera of Mission: Impossible II. "The craze from it," he says, "is going to be insane."

*Promtional still from the movie* Windtalkers *showing Beach playing a Navajo code talker in the Second World War*

**"***I am Indian. I am Saulteaux. I'm Native. I am aboriginal, whatever word they have. That's who I am and I'm not letting anybody use that in a negative way.***"**

Beach plays a Navajo code talker in the World War II who becomes friends with his bodyguard (Cage). He says getting the part happened quickly. A call came, he flew to Los Angeles, read for the producer and three days later met with Woo. "That was it."

Although he speaks Saulteaux, he learned Navajo for the part. And on the set he was getting lessons from an acting coach. He was told not to smile so much, but it's hard to hide his happy nature. It's the first formal training he's had since he started in the business at age 16. He learned on the job and relied on instinct to give his comic and touching performance in *Smoke Signals* and for his powerful roles in *The Last Stop*, and *Dance Me Outside*.

## ORPHANED AT AGE 7

Beach's journey toward stardom has been awesome. A Saulteaux born on the Dog Creek Reserve north of Lake Winnipeg, Beach, 27, was orphaned at age seven when his mother was killed by a drunk driver and his father drowned two months later. He was taken in by an uncle and aunt for the next five years, then moved in with another uncle and aunt, who adopted him and raised him in Winnipeg.

Now living in Ottawa with his wife and two sons, aged 4 and 2, Beach talks openly about the hardships of his childhood. "I will always have that reflection to the past: the hurt and pain and anger. But I've learned to overcome it with love for people, love of myself and to achieve my goal of being the greatest actor I can be — not the greatest — but within myself to become a good actor."

"Now I'm in the position to ask 'What mountain am I climbing now?'"

## "THERE'S NO STEREO-TYPE. I AM WHO I AM."

Along with *Windtalkers*, Beach starred in a comedy with David Spade and Christopher Walken. *In The Adventures of Joe Dirt*, Spade plays "a young, white trash guy" who wants to find out whether his parents really died or whether they abandoned him as a baby. Beach is enlisted by Spade as his Indian tracker. Beach says his character tries to make a living by selling fireworks but they're cheap fireworks and he and Spade blow up a lot of stuff.

Beach talks head-on about the perception by some people that he might end up playing stereotyped Native roles.

"I am Indian. I am Saulteaux. I'm Native. I am aboriginal, whatever word they have. That's who I am and I'm not letting anybody use that in a negative way. When people say, 'Adam, do you feel you're stereotyped in film?' I say, 'No, because I am Indian. I am proud of who I am.' When I'm doing an Indian running in the woods, I am proud of doing that because that is a part of our life. When I'm playing an Indian cop trying to solve a murder, I am an Indian cop and I'm proud of who I am. So stereotype to me? There's no stereotype. I am who I am."

While on the edge of potential international stardom, Beach already has mapped out his retirement. He says he'll act another 20 years and then get into politics. For now, he goes into schools to speak to Native children, trying to show them by example that dreams can be achieved.

## NATIVE YOUTH DON'T GIVE A DAMN ABOUT LAND CLAIMS

Beach's dream is to take the small organizations across Canada that are trying to create a positive awareness for Native people, especially the youth, and gather them under an umbrella group to make them stronger. They've been taught to fight for the biggest piece of pie among themselves, he says passionately, with growing frustration in his voice, and he wants to create an environment in which they would share resources and power more equitably.

He's disgusted with both the federal government and Native leadership, but he's particularly impatient with the Assembly

> **"***About 70 per cent of the Native population is under 25 years of age and nobody is doing anything to support that.***"**

of First Nations (AFN) for not paying more attention to aboriginal youth. "About 70 per cent of the Native population is under 25 years of age and nobody is doing anything to support that . ... They're attempting to keep the younger generation under control. ... There's the whole structure that's been built over the years, of land claims, that just doesn't work anymore."

He says the young Native generation doesn't give a damn about land claims. He thinks it would be better to delay settling because when the younger people come of age they "will be 50 times more educated" than their elders and could get better deals.

In the next few years, Beach wants to work on his own education — he quit school while in Grade 11 to act — and get a degree in political science. He is at times poetic in his speech, with moments of lightning clarity and away from a tape recorder he is a natural speaker. But when he talks in a situation where he thinks what he's saying counts, as in an interview, he knows he sometimes struggles to find the right word. He's bothered by that, by what he sees as a limitation, and is determined to learn how to express himself better.

"I want to be, not a grand chief, but I want to be able to be a guy with a voice, which I already have with the (Native) youth across Canada." He wants to use the voice fame has given him to push for change from

> **"***I want to be able to be a guy with a voice, which I already have with the (Native) youth across Canada.***"**

the "old-school" thinking of organizations like the AFN.

"I feel I'm destined for something, and it's greater than the acting because acting is an occupation. ... I want to push farther and a lot of that pushing is going to be going against the grain."

## READY FOR CHANGE

*Below: Promotional still of Nicholas Cage and Adam Beach in a scene from Windtalkers*

But before he walks away from acting he wants to get on a television series to fight negative images of Natives. It would be American "of course" because that would expose him to a wider audience. Canadian shows, such as North of 60 which Beach appeared on, limit themselves, he says. Asked what they need most to improve, he bursts out laughing and answers quickly: "A budget."

Beach is being told that after the Woo movie comes out, that's it, he's a star. He says he's made his career by not falling into the "I can't" way of thinking that holds people back from making their lives happier and more complete. In this next phase of his life, he will likely journey well through the changes he faces by doing what he believes in: "Just following my heart."

# THOMAS KING
## CANADA'S CELEBRATED AUTHOR SHARES HIS INSPIRATION

**By Natasha Netschay Davies**                    **Published September, 2003**

*"If you can live your life without writing then do so -- it will be a lot easier that way. But if you're desperate to write because it is so much a part of you, forget about having any sort of personal life."*

This advice comes straight from someone who knows all about writing, its challenges and rewards – Thomas King, Canada's celebrated Native author.

"When people ask me what they have to do to become a writer I say, 'Don't get involved with anyone, don't get married, don't have any children, learn to live on as little as possible, and then see if you could afford to try to be a writer.' But of course no one takes that advice," King explains, in his deep and calm voice.

King hasn't exactly followed all of his own advice either. He began writing "seriously" at the age of 40, to impress a very special woman, his wife. Before that he was busy working at regular jobs in order to raise his family.

Born in 1943 to a Cherokee father and a mother of Greek and German descent, King grew up in Northern California, received his PhD in English literature at the University of Utah, and worked for a number of years at the University of Minnesota as Chair of their American Indian Studies program. A Canadian citizen, he returned home in 1980 to accept a position as Professor of Native Studies at the University of Lethbridge.

Photo: Dean Palmer

*"Basically you still see that cliché Indian character pop up in books. You would think by now, non-Natives or Natives would be able to get around that..."*

# FINDING INSPIRATION

As a young reader, King found himself inspired by N. Scott Momaday, author of *House Made of Dawn*, which won the Pulitzer Prize in 1969. The book received a lot of attention and brought even more attention to Native writers, both literary and oral. At the time, there were few published Native writers. However, it led King to think "If they bought one book about Indians, maybe they'd buy another one."

With that thought in the back of his mind, King believed writing would one day be a real possibility for him. In the 1980s King's creative and critical writing were widely published: his articles, stories, and poems of appeared in many journals, including *World Literature Written in English*, the *Hungry Mind Review*, and the *Journal of American Folklore*.

He has also edited a book entitled *The Native in Literature* (1987) and a special issue of *Canadian Fiction Magazine* (1988) devoted to short fiction by Canadian Native writers.

His first novel, *Medicine River*, published in 1990, was turned into a television movie that starred Graham Greene and Tom Jackson. Other books included *Green Grass, Running Water*, which was nominated for the Governor General's Award in 1993; *One Good Story, That One*; and *Truth and Bright Water*. He has also written books for children, and a popular CBC radio series, *The Dead Dog Café Comedy Hour*. His latest book is *Dreadful Water Shows Up*.

# COWBOYS AND INDIANS

One of the biggest obstacles for Native writers is that North Americans have grown up on a particular kind of Indian in literature.

"You never know how big a market there's going to be in non-Native North America for novels about Indians, especially if you're trying to do something different than the old cowboy and Indian routine or the historical western stuff," says King.

"There are many non-Natives who have written about Indians, so you have this backdrop against which you have to write. If you move away from that backdrop, as a lot of Native writers try to do, than it puts you on the fringe because people aren't used to seeing Indians in those roles; they're not used to seeing some of these narrative strategies."

King notes that the stereotypical Indian gets repeated over and over again in different ways and varieties.

"Basically you still see that cliché Indian character pop up in books. You would think by now, non-Natives or Natives would be able to get around that but those images are pretty well burned into our minds," says King, citing the stoic and innocent, loner type; or the savage Indian type.

"It's disheartening in this day and age to have it repeated," says King. "The fact of the matter is publishing houses are only going to publish so many books a year by Native writers that deal with Native issues."

For aspiring writers seeking an audience King suggests contacting Native publishing houses that may "look kindly" at their work. Another option is to solicit literary journals, Native and non-Native.

"Of course the other thing that may happen is that you'll have Native writers doing non-Native material, and that's legitimate. Just because a person is Native doesn't mean they have to write about Native issues," says King.

"It's a slow process. Don't wait until 40 like I did," advises King, with a soft chuckle.

## NATIVE STYLE

There's a difference of narrative strategies between Native and non-Native writers, observes King. Non-Natives who write about Indians usually write about the historical Indian; their books are set in the past.

"But when Natives write about Native material, for the most part we write about the present. I'm not sure why that is, but it seems to be the case," says King.

A good example is a new book entitled Porcupines and China Dolls, by Robert Alexie. A terrific book, King says, that deals with present day concerns. "Its narrative strategy is one that North American readers aren't going to be used to – they may even find a little bit on the laboured side. But for Native readers, what they'll hear is some of the overtones of oral literature and oral story telling."

## NEW BOOK, NEW DIRECTION

King's latest book takes him from his usual "serious, adult writing" to a more fun style of writing. Thumps DreadfulWater, is a Cherokee photographer living in Chinook. An ex-cop, he gets to play detective when a computer programmer is found dead in the band's new resort and casino just before its grand opening. Writing under the pseudonymous Hartley GoodWeather, Thomas King plans on making DreadfulWater a series of detective books.

"This book will get to more Native readers than Green Grass, Running Water, which is more complex." Green Grass is currently scheduled to go into filming next spring.

How does King find motivation and ideas for his writing today?

"To be able to hear a good story well told is a wonderful thing," says King.

"At this point in my career I guess I have to look to myself for inspiration. I have friends who are writers who are kind to me and say nice things to me when they read my work, which is encouraging. I also hang out with all sorts of weird Native people. They tell their stories, and sometimes bits of those stories become bits of my prose. I keep my ears open."

Currently, King is a professor at the University of Guelph where he teaches Native literature and Creative Writing. He will appear at the Vancouver International Writers Festival at Doing Canada Proud, an event that takes place on Wednesday, October 23 at 8:30 pm at Performance Works on Granville Island. For more information, visit the Festival's web site at www.writersfest. bc.ca.

*Below: The cover of Thomas King's latest book*

# A Business Bro

**By Bernie Bates** from the "Bee In The Bonnet" series     **Published September, 1999**

What's the meaning of life?  The bottom line, the cost, the value, an assigned worth- that's it!  Anything and everything, on this planet, has a tag.  Even an entire race of people has a price!  Hell, I know where you can get Jesus for sale.... $9.95 on cassette or $12.99 on CD!

*Cartoon by Bernie Bates*

**Beads & Trinkets Inc.**

The Native man that sold Manhattan for a few beads, is, and will forever be thought of as a fool.  But let's take a closer look at this first attempt at business by a Native person.

First, ask yourself this:  If some fool walked up to you and said in a broken language- *"Hello, Indian person.  How much would you charge me for that moon, up there in the sky?  Will a million dollars in cash be enough?"*  Now be an honest Injun, would you take the cash?  Or would you take the time to learn the man's language and then explain to him, that it's impossible for a person to own the moon?  Think about it.... a million dollars in cash, no joke, no hidden cameras, no strings attached.  What would you do?

I can only imagine that's what it must have been like for that poor Manhattan Bro.  Back in the days of buckskin underwear and tepees, it was accepted as common knowledge – that a human, could no more own the dirt that he stood on, than he could own the wind.  So, why not take the beads and trinkets?

To our first Native realtor, he must have thought to himself:  *"This has to be my lucky day!"*  Because, who in their right mind, would give away such beautiful beads, for something that has been here long before he was born and will be here long after he's dead?  And in the mean time....  *"Me got'um pretty beads! Hum, I wonder if this pilgrim, would be interested in some swamp land that I have in Florida?"*

Business is a very old concept, it's even older than the oldest profession known to mankind.  Did you know that the caveman who invented the wheel, was murdered for the rights to his invention, by the caveman that invented the spear?  He was overheard to have said "Hey, it's only business!"  I'm only teasing, I was just trying to make a point (no pun intended).

The point being – in business, only the sharp ones survive (pun intended)!  Which brings me to another point – we Natives had better get busy in business or we too, will go the way of the caveman.

Like any group or person that is intent on starting a business, they should first: analyze available data concerning the variables of a proposed enterprise. In plain language – the pluses and minuses. If you're going to start a business, you'd better get used to understanding documents that read like a completely different language altogether.

Let's take a look at the plus side of owning a business on indigenous terra firma. The first plus that comes to mind is the land doesn't have a mortgage held against it. Other pluses include: Government grants, rent free and let's not forget the tax advantages. The only thing standing between us and financial independence, is our own imaginations and a little hard work!

Now to one of the minuses of being a "Businessbro." Do you remember the children's fable, about a chicken that asks the other animals in the barn yard to help her grow some wheat to make bread? To make a long story short, she asks them to help with the planting, harvesting and the baking and they all refuse to lift a finger. But, when it came time to eat the tasty bread.... well! I don't want to give away the ending, but, when the bread comes out of the oven, is, I think, the best part of the story. It's the part where she gets to tell them… Oh, never mind, you'll enjoy it more if you experience it for yourself!

Which brings me to yet another point: are Natives "communist bastards" or "heartless capitalists?" Is every business on a reservation "our business?" Or, is a "Rez biz" their biz and none of your biz? Is it one for all? Or all for one? I'm sorry but I just don't know the answer – I must've been out of town when that memo got passed around.

For instance, if I were to build a bakery on the Rez and no one came to help me.... would I be honor bound, by some unwritten tribal law, to provide them all with free bread? Or, could I be more like the old hen in the children's fable and just tell them *"Ah, go cluck yourself!"*

## REZ RAZZER BY-3B

*Cartoon by Bernie Bates*

# 2002, A NEW YEAR?

**By Bernie Bates** from the "Bee In The Bonnet" series

**Published January, 2002**

*Another year older and deeper in debt — so goes life! Where does all the money go? Rent, food, doctors, lawyers and Indian chiefs?*

*Cartoon by Bernie Bates*

I'm a Native that lives off Rez, and I've been getting packages and packages of mail from my old stomping grounds, telling me of the on-going treaty process. Have you ever read any of these seemingly endless pages of legal mumbo jumbo? I hope and pray that some smart Native is. Because, after the first few pages, my eyes crossed, my mind went blank and I'm not sure, but I think I went into some sort of a trance!

I think I smell a conspiracy here! Has the government found a new way of keeping the Native down and out on the Rez? Many, many moons ago the "white devils" discovered they could control the "Injuns" by killing off their food supply. That's the reason you'll never have to worry about stepping in a fresh buffalo pie any time soon. Then came the addictions of firewater, drugs and welfare. Is boring us to death with endless paperwork their next diabolical trick?

I've been hearing for years and years now: that every last Native is supposed to get some big wampum! Yeah, right! If you believe that piece of buffalo pie, I've got some swamp land in Florida for.... oh! Never mind, that piece of land was signed away, in the last round of treaties. Speaking of buffalo, I wonder if the old adage of: "Getting Buffaloed," came from that sad era in our history?

If you have a computer, "click" onto the government statistics concerning the huge amounts of money, intended to help the poor indigenous people of this great land (go ahead, I'll wait).

Yeah, "WOW" is right! And I'll bet the next thing you exclaim after the words: "HOLY SHIT!" Is: "Where the hell is my share?"

Well, let me tell you a little story that I experienced first hand. It just may shed a little light on where all that money goes.

I was trying to get a government grant to help me pursue my dreams of getting a book published. Well, I applied year after year and from one branch of the government to another, with no positive results. I had to ask myself: what was I doing wrong? I filled out all of their Q's, I crossed all the T's and dotted all of the I's. So I started to ask a few Q's of my own!

I phoned one of the places that I had

unsuccessfully tried to procure a grant from, and I asked them why I was turned down time after time? I was told that it was the decision of the board. She proudly went on to proclaim that their office had "nine" successful applicants that year! To which I responded: "And just how many people work in your office?" After a moment of silence she said that she couldn't give out that information, with that, she curtly said, "Good-bye!"

Later that day I called again, but this time I purposely called during the lunch hour and asked for Mrs. X (Sorry, no names, no how, no way. I may want to re-apply... again!). The young lady that answered the phone said, "I'm sorry she's at lunch, may I help you?" Luckily, she couldn't hear me smiling, as I told her – "I'm sure you can."

"I'm Jess Razzin, I'm a manager from the department of statistics, concerning office space projections for the coming quarter." (And, yes, I wrote and rehearsed that little white lie). "I was wondering how many desks you have and are there any empty ones?" I

REZ RAZZER BY-3B
*Cartoon by Bernie Bates*

could hear her counting, then she said, "We have twelve, but we sometimes hire up to three temps and then we're always a little short of desks then." I asked her a few more "official questions" and then hung up.

Please allow me to do the math for you; one government office, twelve full time people, working (ha, ha) eight hours a day, week in and week out. Not to mention the money spent on; three part time workers, supplies, computers, travel etc.

All that time and expense just to grant nine Natives grants. Count'um- NINE! You wouldn't even need all of your fingers to count that high. You'd still have one finger left over, and if I had my way, I'd show them just which finger was left over! Now, you have some idea where all that grant money went.

Education, I feel, is our best weapon in this day and age. And the most powerful bang for the buck (pun intended) is the almighty computer! Mastering it will do more to

help our people than anything I can think of. If there's anything the terrorist attacks of September the eleventh should have taught us, is that, "Ignorance kills!"

I sincerely hope that I'll never have to report that some Native shot another human being at a roadblock, while protesting some injustice perpetrated against the first nations people.

It's said that if we don't learn from the past, history will repeat itself. And, what goes around comes around. How about this one- "Stupid is as stupid does!" Let's not forget my all-time favorite quotation, by B. H. Bates: "Never bring bows and arrows to a gun fight!"

Now that I'm done with my quote-fest, did you get anything from it? Did it ring any bells with you? I guess all I'm trying to convey are my hopes that the next treaties we sign are thought of as "wise" by future generations of the brown bottomed club.

## REZ RAZZER BY-3B

*Cartoon by Bernie Bates*

# BOOOO-ZZZZ

**By Bernie Bates** from the "Bee In The Bonnet" series          **Published November, 1997**

Gather close to the campfires, my children and let me tell you the story of the "HAIR OF THE DOG!" But be warned.... it is said, that all who hear this tail of woe, will forever be changed!

'Twas a bright and shining day, when from a tent climbed four bedeviled souls, each sicker than the last. Eyes half closed, hair a-muss with cottoned mouths they declared: "NEVER AGAIN, NEVER AGAIN!"

The pain they felt was self-imposed. The way they felt; was theirs to blame. The eagle that flew the night before, was now home to roost. "But why did it have to crap in my mouth, they groaned and moaned and moaned and groaned. "NEVER AGAIN, NEVER AGAIN!"

Do you have coin? One inquired of the others. The pockets that once were full, from hard earned toil, only the night before, now had little or none to offer. My life! My life is over, cried one. What shall I tell my daughter, my son, my wife? Oh, Great Spirit.... "NEVER AGAIN, NEVER AGAIN!"

To each other they looked for comfort and pity. Why? Said one: "Do we feel so dammed dirty and gritty, when mere hours ago we stood so tall? We could kill a bear with our own hands. Oh, why? Oh, Great Spirit, why? Why do you torture your children so? They cried to the skies, "NEVER AGAIN, NEVER AGAIN!"

What shall we do? What choice do we have? If we intend to live, we must find a way not to die. Let's turn to Mother Nature for

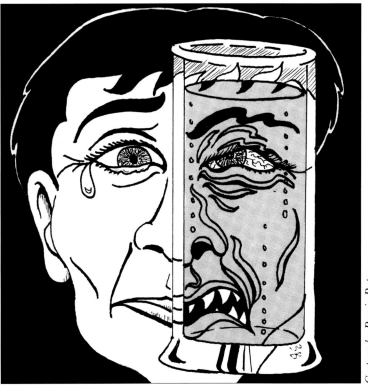

*Cartoon by Bernie Bates*

our relief. She's sure to help us once again. Oh, the pain.... "NEVER AGAIN, NEVER AGAIN!"

By the river one man sat and drank and drank, until his nose bled. But it was not the cure for the pounding in his head. Another took to gobbling grass, but alas, he mumbled, this stuff's made for the long-eared ass! Oh, yuck! "NEVER AGAIN, NEVER AGAIN!"

Then the third Bro jumped from a cliff. For him that was it! He never again felt pain. Then again, he never again felt a soft summer's rain, or laughed at a silly joke. For him and his kin, that really was it. "NEVER AGAIN, NEVER AGAIN!"

The fourth Native lad was indeed sad, at his friends demise. But he thought: "Hey, that's not it! That's not for me." The rest were quick to agree. Now, that we are only three, we must all try even harder to beat this demon, BOOO-ZZZZ! Or next, it could be me you'll lose, they all agreed.... "NEVER AGAIN, NEVER AGAIN!"

We must concoct a brew, a brew that'll beat and defeat this scourge called BOOO-ZZZ! They chopped and burned and ate and stirred all the plants of their world. That is, until one ate a flower of poison. His lips turned a purple-ish blue. By the next morn, there

was only two, to curse.... "NEVER AGAIN, NEVER AGAIN!"

Tears and fears tore at their hearts, then from the sky, came a ray. One turned to the other to say: "Can you hear? Can you hear?" Then with his eyes a blur, he dropped to his knees and said, "Yes, yes, oh lord, I hear your words!" With that, the man ran into the woods, never to be seen again. All the while, he screamed: "NEVER AGAIN, NEVER AGAIN!"

Then there was one! Alone he walked, until from the shadows came three more Bros, with bottles in hand. "Here!" Said one, as he raised his glass to the sky. "Drink, drink, drink my friend, for tomorrow will never die! Here, drink the hair of the dog!" As the Bro put that glass to his lips, a tear formed in his eye. He stopped and turned away and said.... "NO! NEVER AGAIN, NEVER AGAIN!"

## REZ RAZZER BY-3B

*Cartoon by Bernie Bates*

# A Tribute to Bill Reid 1920-1998

**By Lloyd Dolha**

Photos by Angie Smith

**Published April, 1998**

Bill Reid, Canada's most noted and influential Northwest Coast artist passed away on March 13, 1998, following a 30 year struggle with Parkinson's disease. He was 78. While he is most widely recognized as a carver, Reid was also a writer, broadcaster, jeweler and accomplished artist working in many mediums to convey his vision.

*"The Raven and the First Men"*
*Completed 1980*
*University of British Columbia,*
*Museum of Anthropology*

Two services were held to honour Reid. The first was in the Great Hall of the University of British Columbia's Museum of Anthropology, just steps away from the Haida village he helped create in 1959. This project was the first of a series that won him global recognition.

On the evening of March 24, with a service that lasted over eight hours, more than 1,000 people came to pay their last respects to Reid. First Nations leaders, elders, fellow artists, family, friends and mainstream politicians attended. Notables include Miles Richardson, a hereditary chief of Reid's Native clan; Alfred Scow, a retired Native judge of the BC provincial court; Dr. George MacDonald, president of the Canadian Museum of Civilization in Québec; David Suzuki, broadcaster; Aurthur Erikson, architect; Philip Owen, mayor of Vancouver; Ian Waddell, BC's Minister of Culture; and artists and writers George Rammell, Robert Bringhurst, Don Yeamons, Doris Shadbolt (Reid's biographer), and Bill Holm.

Micheal Audain, president of the Vancouver Art Gallery, described Reid as one of the most important sculptors of the 20th century. "His work, installed in public places, captures the attention of hundreds of people every day," said Audain.

"Whether a teacher, writer, jeweller, or carver, through his work, he gave us a different insight into art," said Arthur Erikson, who designed the Museum of Anthropology that houses the majority of Reid's work. According to a former director at the museum, Reid was the only person to have 24-hour access to the site.

Reid was diagnosed with Parkinson's, a chronic neurodegenerative condition that causes tremors in the hands and stiffness of the limbs, in the early 1970s. As the disease progressed, he was less and less able to create with his own hands and increasingly relied on assistants.

Perhaps no other Northwest coast artist was as widely recognized as Reid. He brought about a change in the way northwest coast Native art was viewed by the Western world – whereby Native art came to be seen as fine art rather than handicraft. At the height of his career, Reid earned more than any other Native artist in existence. In the early 1990s, tiny gold replicas of the *Raven and the First Men* – a sculpture based on the creation myth of the Haida people – were fetching $125, 000 each. In 1995, the Vancouver International Airport Authority paid Reid $3 million for a second version of the *Spirit of Haida Gwaii*. This was an unheard of commission for a First Nations artist. Reid recreated the *Spirit of Haida Gwaii* with a green patina, calling it the *Jade Canoe*. . The *Spirit of Haida Gwaii* resides at the Canadian Embassy in Washington, D.C. and the *Raven and the First Men*, at UBC.

While Reid's most famous creations were large scale carvings such as these, Reid saw himself primarily as a maker of fine jewelry.

William Ronald Reid was the son of Sophie, a Haida from Skidegate and Billy Reid,

*P*erhaps no other Northwest coast artist was as widely recognized as Reid. He brought about a change in the way northwest coast native art was viewed by the Western world.

an American of German and Scottish descent. By all accounts, the relationship between Reid's parents was strained, with Sophie and the children living in Victoria and travelling frequently to Hyder, a small community on the BC/Alaska border where Billy Reid owned and operated several hotels.

Following their marriage in 1919, Sophie Reid distanced herself from her Haida roots, knowing that children of mixed blood were less acceptable to the early 1900s Victorian culture. However, though she adopted an Anglo way of life, Sophie kept close contact

> *Throughout the 1960s and 70s, Reid executed a number of commissioned works for the University of British Columbia and Expo '67.*

with her family, often taking her children to Skidegate where Reid was first exposed to Haida art. When Bill Reid was 13, he moved back to Victoria for the final time and never saw his father again. Five years later, at the age of 18, he began his career as a radio broadcaster at CBC.

In 1943, at the age of 23, he returned to Skidegate, where he met his maternal

*The Jade Canoe,*
*Vancouver*
*International Airport*

grandfather, Charles Gladstone. At the time, Gladstone was one of the few remaining Haida artists producing silver and argillite work using traditional Haida motifs. During his visit, the young Reid spent his time watching his grandfather make silver bracelets and argillite carvings. Just as Gladstone had learned to carve and mold from his uncle, the great Charles Edenshaw, Reid learned the basics of his craft from his grandfather.

Reid continued at CBC, working in BC, Québec and Ontario, before joining the Toronto team in 1948. During that same year, he began to study jewelry making at the Ryerson Institute of Technology. He studied there until 1950, working in gold and silver. During this time, Reid also studied the Northwest coast art form through visits to museums such as the Royal Ontario Museum and through books. He began incorporating what he learned into his work. As his jewelry-making and sculptural skills progressed, and his appreciation for Northwest coast art grew, Reid slowly transformed from

a radio broadcaster who made jewelry, into a world class Haida artist.

In 1951, Reid returned to Vancouver where he opened a jewelery workshop in a tiny basement. There, he utilized European jewelry making techniques in the casting of Haida designs. While in Vancouver, Reid participated in a number of projects that focussed on Haida art and culture. He was, for instance, part of a Provincial Museum team that salvaged totem poles from the historic village sites on Haida Gwaii. In 1957, Reid carved his first totem pole under the direction of master carver, Mungo Martin.

Throughout the 1960s and 70s, Reid executed a number of commissioned works for the University of British Columbia and Expo '67. In 1978, for the Skidegate Band office, he carved a 57-foot red cedar totem pole.

The second ceremony took place at Skidegate, where a feast was held in Reid's honour. At his request, Reid's ashes were interred near Skidegate, at T'annu, a deserted village and birthplace of his grandmother.

# MOHAWK BRINGS ENVIRONMENTAL MESSAGE TO UNITED KINGDOM

**By Danny Beaton, Turtle Clan Mohawk Nation**
**Photos by Andy Paradise**

**Published March, 2005**

*Iraquois Sunrise Ceremany by Danny Beaton, Mohawk, London England*

The Living Rainforest in England invited me to participate in discussions and presentations for ten days to promote the protection of our sacred Mother Earth from a Native American perspective. My old elders instructed me to go to England and help the people heal. They said I could do no wrong, that I would be welcomed and respected for what I would do to help their situation. Offer their ancestors tobacco for a gift and make sure to ask their permission to speak on their homeland. Sing when you are tired, my teacher Robertjohn Knapp told me. Sing when you are not sure of yourself, sing when you are hurt. Sing when you need peace. I put tobacco down whenever I could to the spirits of England, for the people of Stonehenge, to the ancestors of the stone. I honoured them and asked for their permission to speak out. And I asked for their protection, wisdom and guidance.

Throughout my talks in England and at the Living Rainforest, sharing teachings and songs, I stressed that I was told to honour their ancestors, and I would remind people that Stonehenge was one of the seven wonders of the world. And that their ancestors were like ours, honouring their grandfathers, the stone people, and the natural world, and all our relations. There is a powerful movement in England that aims at educating children and society of the beauty and importance of protecting our sacred Mother Earth, and the need for society to return to spiritual values. There is also an intellectual movement in England for solving the problems of autism. The British Empire has intellectualized its ideas of religion, philosophy, humanities, economics, law, geography, and education and exported them to the world for generations.

The descendants of the British colonial experience in superiority in India, Africa, Canada, Ireland, and other countries around the world are trying to solve problems created by Western thinking/ ideology and centuries of exploitation. Many academics and intellectuals are using the struggles of indigenous peoples and environmental destruction around the world to portray themselves as leaders in the fight against injustice.

But in fact, the result of their rhetoric is the denial of leadership of the original people on their territories and their way of life. People with financial status or academic or political status have no right to put themselves above the peasant or indigenous peoples. Nor do non-indigenous peoples have the right to make laws or set standards for indigenous nations to live by or under. True leaders and educators do not seek to gain status from people. But true leaders have compassion and work for spiritual leaders of the land.

"In the final analysis, the survival of Native America is fundamentally about the collective survival of all human beings. The question of who gets to determine the destiny of the land, and of the people who live on it – those with the money or those who pray on the land – is a question that is alive throughout society." (Winona Laduke).

faithkeepers, and do everything possible to bring honour, respect and restoration to the indigenous cultures that have been assaulted by Western domination.

There are non-native educators who are struggling to find ways of learning, who have a reverence for the ones who have maintained a way of life with the natural world and laws

*"Our songs honour the life giving forces and the Spirits of our Ancestors."*

## COMMON GOAL WITH NO PLAN

Many academics are completely sincere in their concerns for justice, equality, peace and harmony. Many academics and intellectuals will sincerely honour our true leaders, chiefs, clan mothers, healers, singers, firekeepers,

by traditional native ceremonies. There are non-native people around who will voice their stand with us, and do everything possible to honour our way of life on our territories, which we call Turtle Island, and who will admit to the failings of their ancestors. There are some people with outstanding values who will struggle with keeping the facts and truth alive

*The great work before us, the task of moving modern industrial civilization from its present devastating influence on the Earth to a more benign, healing presence, is not a role that we have chosen. It is a role given to us, beyond any consultation with ourselves.*

by denouncing broken treaties and stolen land in North America.

Peter Matthiessen wrote Indian Country, one of the greatest books I ever read about the state of Indian affairs and struggles since the white man set foot on American land. Our white brother has viewed the wilderness as something other, as a hostile or beckoning landscape he could shape to his own ends. But the American Indians view this very differently. In Indian country, the land is sacred and man is at one with it.

Environmental desecration in the name of progress and spiritual transgression are the same thing and will invite the same eventual destruction. The Indian cannot love the Creator and desecrate the Earth. The Indian existence is not separable from Indian culture, which is not separable from the natural world. By seeking to dominate it, non-natives set themselves in opposition to a vital healing force of which they were a part, and thereby mislaid a whole dimension of existence. Respect for nature is reverence for the Creator and it is also self-respecting since man and nature, though not the same thing, are not different.

Father Thomas Berry, a true elder of non-natives who has participated in native justice, said Christians should listen to native elders for the next hundred years and put away our bibles if we were to learn anything at all from history. The great work before us, the task of moving modern industrial civilization from its present devastating influence on the Earth to a more benign, healing presence, is not a role that we have chosen. It is a role given to us, beyond any consultation with ourselves.

We did not choose. We were chosen by some power beyond ourselves for this historical task. We do not choose the moment of our birth, our particular culture, or the historical moment when we will be born. We do not choose the social status or spiritual insight or political or economic conditions that will be the context of our lives. We are, as it were, thrown into existence with a challenge and a role that is beyond any personal choice. The nobility of our lives, however, depends upon the manner in which we come to understand and perform our assigned role.

The crusaders might be considered the beginning of the historical drive that has led European peoples in their quest for religious, cultural, political and economic conquest of the world. This movement was continued through the period of discovery and control of the planet into our own times when the western presence dominates politically in the United Nations and economically in such establishments as the World Bank, International Monetary Fund, the World Trade Organization, and the World Business Council for Sustainable Development. We might even interpret this western drive toward limitless domination in all its forms as leading eventually to the drive towards human domination over the natural world.

# WOUNDED NEED TO HEAL

The struggle to solve problems and to heal is of the utmost importance. We must be ready to admit that we are wounded, and learn to heal ourselves and protect ourselves the same way for our sacred Mother Earth. Life cannot survive with the continual minimalization and marginalization, abuse and exploitation of indigenous wisdom, culture, resources and territories. England is no different from the Americas, and the Americas are no different from anywhere else in the world. We are all wounded. But in America, natives are the first to admit that we are wounded and for native peoples we have our sacred ceremonies to heal ourselves.

People need to join forces and strengths together and support the native elders, indigenous wisdom-keepers of the world, spiritual leaders of the world, and give them their voice, let them have their power with the universe. Let their wisdom be heard. They cannot be told how they're supposed to live and how things are going to be. The ceremonial elders have an insight into the problems that western society has created. Native people of the Americas are the leaders of their own country, even after colonization.

We are not living on universal land where we are subservient to people of financial, educational or political status. Indigenous peoples did not create the world's problems. There is a great beauty when non-native people do everything they can to create justice and respect for our elders, for indigenous elders and cultures who have survived five hundred years of culture shock.

*The peoples of England are suffering like most countries of the world. In America and Canada, there are still many native peoples with traditional culture and ceremonies to heal from. I truly believe England has lost their healing ceremonies.*

As Chief Oren Lyons states, "devastation on a scale of unimaginable injustice. I'm amazed at how tolerant our people are of history. And how we think of your children, not just our own, how we talk about the future, the Seventh Generation, we don't just talk about Onondaga children or Six Nation children, we talk about all children. Our instructions are that every man is an uncle and every woman is an aunt or a mother to every child. And any child that asks a question must be respected and answered as a human being."

Elder Ted Strong says, "This enslavement and impoverishment of nature is no more tolerable or sensible than enslavement and impoverishment of other human beings."

# ENGLAND NO DIFFERENT THAN AMERICAS

The peoples of England are suffering like most countries of the world. In America and Canada, there are still many native peoples with traditional culture and ceremonies to heal from. I truly believe England has lost their healing ceremonies. One of my greatest experiences that I had when I was in the UK was my chance to meet and speak to hundreds and hundreds of elementary schoolchildren who opened their hearts and minds to native culture. They were filled with excitement when they heard the sun was their brother and that he made things grow and that without our brother we could not see each other as we travel about, that our brother keeps us warm throughout the day.

children the leader of the birds was the eagle because he flew the highest and he would warn of danger when danger was near. The leader of the forest was the deer, I told them, because he could run the fastest and warn all other life of danger when danger was present. I told

I told them that our elders were our wisdom-keepers and that we were the protectors of our Sacred Mother the Earth, and that our mother gives us her sacred nourishment and all her beauty for us to see. I mentioned that the moon was our Grandmother and the night sun. Our grandmother is a special lady – she controls all the great oceans and tides. The flowers are our sisters, the animals our brothers. I shared with the children all that we are taught by our old elders. I told the

the children that we were no better than the animals, and our elders taught us the natural laws and we belong to the natural world just like their ancestors used to live.

I brought along my turtle rattle, drum and native flutes and shared songs that some old elders had shared with me. This to me was amazing, singing and drumming and planting the songs into their little minds, being able to plant seeds of our knowledge into their little minds. It felt good knowing at least one of us, of my people, was able to remind them of the sacred, and that we must respect all of life with our actions and thoughts. I shared with them that our elders teach us to work with the life-giving forces, that our old elders teach us to honour and be thankful to the air, the waters, the fire, and our Mother the Earth. That we were taught to talk to Creation, animals, birds, insects, fish, plants, and that we all have duties and responsibilities.

When I showed my film *The Iroquois Speak Out for Mother Earth* at Oxford University, I realized then that there were no native studies programs in the UK for the students to learn about our way of life, of thanksgiving and respect. A life with a spiritual foundation, with ceremonies to communicate with the natural world, and healing ourselves with the sacred fire, water, air and earth. North American native people have influenced most aspects of education and justice here in Canada.

Our elders teach us that our ceremonies are not for ourselves but for all Creation, and for everyone's benefit and safety. In Canada and the United States, native peoples still maintain sacred ceremonies to honour and give thanks to the life-giving forces and the natural world. Our old elders say that our ceremonies are for honouring and maintaining peace and harmony. My heart is sad because I see the people in England that want to heal and need ceremonies. I feel they are a wounded nation.

In Canada, we know we are wounded. We are hurt inside. Our minds and our spirits, even our bodies, are hurt from colonization and dominant forces. We need to heal together.

> **"My greatest hope is that organizations like the Living Rainforest will continue to maintain a working relationship with indigenous peoples in Canada and the world. "**

We need to put our forces together so that all of life benefits. So that life ceases to suffer. Our way of life must be honoured and respected, not forgotten or hidden in some agenda. In America, our old elders are the true lamas and cardinals of our continent.

Our ancestors were disrespected and raped. But we must continue the struggle for truth, justice, Mother Earth, and our children's future. Our way of life is to share. We have never stopped sharing. We have always shared, we have always been respectful to our brothers and sisters across the great waters.

## HOPE FOR THE FUTURE

I told the children, we have a way of life with all the animals, birds, insects, fish. We talk directly to the rivers and plants, and that the cosmos is our family. We are connected to all of life and we understand Creation has a right to be happy.

I am honoured to work with my elders, and I am honoured to work for our people. The way we are taught and we do not just pray for ourselves, we pray for everyone. To all of life, so life continues.

The director of the Living Rainforest is my brother Karl Hansen, and I travelled to the Amazonia with him fifteen years ago. Part of the mandate for the Living Rainforest is

*"Our minds, body and spirit need to be connected to a way of life that responds and respects Creation and our sacred Mother Earth, and that we become one mind, one force, one smile. In the spirit of our ancestors, and our sacred Mother Earth."*

to give indigenous peoples the same respect that the plants and animals receive. Our old elders agree that the lungs of Mother Earth is the Living Rainforest.

My greatest hope is that organizations like the Living Rainforest will continue to maintain a working relationship with indigenous peoples in Canada and the world. My journey to the UK was amazing because the people who came to hear me were England's most beautiful for their love, compassion and interest in native people and culture and their concern for a better world.

In this world, we have moments of awakening, in this life we have moments of deep thought, sometimes by pain and sometimes by beauty. We have chances to do great deeds with action that has a direct connection to all the life-giving forces and forms, the spirit world. Overwhelming destruction is threatening the elements of life on our sacred Mother Earth.

Here in Indian country, we have ceremonies to bring balance and respect to everything that moves from the four directions. Our truth is the way with the natural world, not the unnatural. Our minds, body and spirit need to be connected to a way of life that responds and respects Creation and our sacred Mother Earth, and that we become one mind, one force, one smile. In the spirit of our ancestors, and our sacred Mother Earth.

# A Cree Woman in Defense of Mother Earth

**By Dr. John Bacher**

Photos by Danny Beaton

**Published May, 2003**

The massive wilds of Québec and Labrador, which are largely road-less lands that support herds of one million caribou, are today threatened by an industrial assault, which to understand, we must go to centuries past. A helpful analogy is the sudden and devastating onslaught on the great plains of the 19th century.

*"Native people must speak out now in order to create a balance for harmony to continue."*

*Today in 2003, in the forests of the eastern tundra and taiga humanity is at a potentially similar devastating turning point for the health of the biosphere as that which faced the great plains in 1864.*

The wild prairies of what is now Canada and the United States, in 1800 contained an estimated 60 million buffalo. There, vast roaming provided an environmentally appropriate basis for a dazzling array of native cultures such as the Lakota, Mandan, Assiniboine, Cheyenne, Omaha, Blackfoot, Ponca, Pawnee and Plains Cree nations.

Their horse-buffalo culture, provided for a magnificent way of life based on reverence for the earth, characterized by a magnificent rich ceremonial life, full of spectacular pageantry based on earth's thanksgiving rituals.

Despite various incursions onto fringes of the Great Plains, this grassland dominated ecosystem essentially remained ecologically intact. It could still support the millions of free roaming buffalo that provided subsistence to native peoples, until transcontinental railways cut up migration routes after conclusion of the U.S. Civil War in 1864.

Today, in 2003, in the forests of the eastern tundra and taiga, humanity is at a potentially similar devastating turning point for the health of the biosphere that the Great Plains was at in. Now the northeastern wilds, as the prairies in the days of Custer and Crazy Horse, are faced with a sudden invasion, which may bring widespread ecological devastation in a twinkling of an eye.

There have been relatively minor incursions on the taiga and tundra of the northeastern continent, going back to the 1950s, and the now abandoned iron mines and the infamous Churchill Falls dam.

This drowned many of the best hunting lands of the Innu nation in the artificial, now mercury poisoned waters of Lake Smallwood, which bends the earth's crust- threatening devastation by earthquakes. To this industrial blight in the 1970s was added the infamous James Bay One Project. It dried up the once mighty Eastmain River, diverting its once pristine waters into the poisoned, artificial reservoirs of La Grande.

## NATIVES BLOCK DEVELOPMENT PLANS

Empowered by brave leaders, Natives of the northeast have been able to resist some of the craziest schemes for the industrial devastation of their lands. The Innu halted schemes for a NATO bombing base in the interior of Labrador. The Cree of Québec blocked a second wave of dam building in Québec in the 1990s.

Suddenly however, a once inspiring northern native leadership has crumbled, buying into a series of deals with the nickel mining giant, INCO, over the proposed Voisey Bay mine, and a new series of mega dams and diversions planned by Hydro-Québec. Innu Chief Peter Penashue now states that he has learned to "love Inco" while Cree Grand Chief Ted Moses grumbles that the Rupert River is worth only $80,000 to the Cree people.

Scientists have estimated that the currently one million strong caribou populations of the northeast would likely be a herd enhanced by another 250,000 free roaming mammals, were it not for the flooding of the James Bay project.

This pattern illustrates how the future of the ecological keystone of the north is more seriously threatened by a new round of ecocidal projects, comparable to the railways, which sliced up the plains as a prelude to industrial exploitation. It would turn the now mighty caribou herds of the north east to an endangered, fragmented relic population, struggling to survive in ghostly wanderings between mines, roads, power lines and reservoirs.

## AN ECOCIDAL INVASION

A critical stage in the planned new ecocidal invasion was the final signing of an agreement between the Cree Nation and the government of Québec on February 7, 2002, in a pact called, "The Peace of the Braves".

This agreement gave Hydro Québec authority to divert the now free flowing Rupert River into the contaminated reservoirs of the La Grande complex.  It also established new incentives to remove its opposition to logging and mineral exploitation through revenue sharing and joint corporations.

The Peace of the Braves was soon followed by a similar deal reached with the Québec Inuit on April 11. It opened up vast vistas for industrial exploitation. Under a $457 million comprehensive agreement, Québec begins joint studies with the Inuit of an array of

*A critical stage in the planned new ecocidal invasion was the final signing of an agreement between the Cree Nation and the government of Québec on February 7, 2002, in a pact called "The Peace of the Braves."*

northern rivers for future hydro projects to be undertaken on their traditional homeland of Nunavik.

Hydro Québec has paid $50 million to the Inuit owned corporation Makivik, to conduct plans for massive hydro development in Nunavik. Through revenue sharing projections, based on paying Inuit upfront 1.25 per cent on the sale of electricity, some $400 million a year is projected to flow to the native residents of Nunavik.

Nunavik is an enormous road free area, which comprises almost half of the land base of Québec. This Inuit homeland, until the surprise signing of the deal between Nunavik and Québec was believed by the United Nations Environment Program, to be the Arctic area the most likely to escape what it terms the "insidious ways" that roads play in "breaking down ecosystems".

When the Nunavik deal was announced, Hydro-Québec President Andre Caille rejoiced that, "This agreement opens up a whole new world." The agreement also promotes the study of a railway or road link to Kuujjaq and a road to Kuujjuarappik.

In two years a massive tearing up of Nunavik may be unleashed for a multitude of dams and roads.  If only one of the proposed projects go ahead, Québec has promised the Inuit $28 million a year in new revenues.

*UNEP cautions that populations of significant bird species in the Arctic can crash as much as 44 per cent up to 1.5 kilometers from a new road.*

Virtually the whole of the massive Ungava peninsula, which comprises Nunavik may, within four years, be laced with dams, roads and transmission lines. Studies are underway for hydro development on the George, Caniapiscau, Little Whale and Nastapoksa (Payne River). These projects extend from the base of the watersheds now impacted by the La Grande project, all the way to the tip of northern Québec, traversed by the Nastapoksa River.

## UNITED NATIONS WARNS OF ENVIRONMENTAL RUIN

Under the proposed blanket of dams, the vast wild area of Nunavik, much of it fragile tundra, would be torn up by roads, providing the basis for a destructive wave of poaching activity and new incentives for mining development.

The road onslaught ignores warnings outlined in a recently released report by the United Nations Environment Program (UNEP) that stresses how new roads in the Arctic lead to environmental ruin.

Lars Kellerud, UNEP polar program manager, warns that, "You bring in a whole chain reaction when you bring in a road."

*Increasingly the warnings of scientists sound like the cautionary prophecies of native elders about the sickness forced on Mother Earth by human abuse.*

The UNEP reports warn that caribou are one of the most sensitive species to road building, often reducing the use of grazing ground by 50 to 90% within three to ten kilometers of roads, power lines and resorts. Native animals are threatened with collision with vehicles, disruption by the chemical environment, and the introduction of exotic species caused by the invasion of highways in the Arctic tundra.

UNEP cautions that populations of significant bird species in the Arctic can crash as much as 44 per cent up to 1.5 kilometers from a new road, being impacted negatively by noise from traffic and the disruption of drainage.

Vegetation is affected up to 10 kilometers away from an Arctic road by changes to permafrost and water levels. Large carnivores such as wolves abandon areas where roads are built.

Increasingly the warnings of scientists sound like the cautionary prophecies of native elders about the sickness forced on Mother Earth by human abuse. In the Arctic areas with permafrost, road building may lead, they warn, to changes in hydrology and habitats several kilometers away.

Such changes in the hydrology of the tundra may result in putting the world's climate into a dangerous tailspin, accelerating global warning. This threat is spelled out in the words of a recent GLOBIO report commissioned by UNEP, that there is a disastrous possibility of the release of massive amounts of greenhouse gasses from Arctic road construction, these frozen lands "hold some of the world's largest carbon reserves."

## NATIVES GATHER IN MONTREAL

Just as such spiritual leaders such as Crazy Horse and Sitting Bull resisted the invasion of their prairie homeland, so do native people connected to the spirits of the earth today oppose the industrial invasion of Nunavit, the Cree homeland of Eeyoo Istchee. This is why opponents of the diversion of the Rupert River and the assault on Nunavit gathered together in Montreal on February 7, 2003.

Participants mourned the anniversary of the Peace of the Braves and unveiled their strategy for protecting the threatened rivers of northern Québec. Their Action Plan seeks to end what Rupert Reverence co-chair, Eric Gagnon, has termed the attempted "James Bay and Nunavik massacre."

The press conference, organized by Rupert Reverence at the offices of Réseau Québécois des Groupes Ecologistes, which supported the event, was a reverential gathering of good minds.

Unlike the 19th century plains Natives, isolated from their era's Euro-American ecologists, environmental organizations from around the world have rallied to help Rupert Reverence. Those taking part in the press conference included Movement Au courant, Opération Adoptez une rivière, Comité Baie James, Fondation Rivières.

## INTERNATIONAL OPPOSITION

Although they were not in attendance, many other environmental groups have come to the aid of the Rupert River. These include Greenpeace, Earthwild International, the Sierra Club, Société pour vaincre pollution, International River Network, the National Resources Defense Council (a New York City group that helped defeat James Bay Two), Ottertooth, the Fédération québécoise de canot et de kayak and several recreational outfitting businesses.

One native environmentalist who journeyed the farthest to mourn the anniversary of the Peace of the Braves, is a Mohawk activist/film maker and frequent runner for elders of the Six Nations Iroquois Confederacy, Ronkwetason, (Spirit Man), better known as Danny Beaton.

Aware of the devastation to the Mohawks of the St. Lawrence River caused by the Seaway, which destroyed fish habitat and subsequently was contaminated by a wave of polluting industrial development, Beaton journeyed from his home in Toronto to meet with those struggling to save northern rivers.

Beaton said:

"It was a great honour to be at the press conference in Montreal because the Cree woman from James Bay, Diane Reid, spoke of the north and its power in a way that epitomizes the spirituality with Mother Earth many native people still have, but many can't remember now because of the effects of Western colonization.

"It was a great day for Mother Earth when Diane spoke for the remaining voices of native people trying to continue and restore values that keep in harmony with Creation. The plea and cry for Québec's rivers was echoed in a peaceful, intelligent way by what I'd call one of the last strong, natural, beautiful and potent voices for traditional native American justice.

*If the Earth and her children are to solve the problems we all face it will be through voices like Diane Reid's...*

> **"*Native people must speak out now in order to create a balance for harmony to continue.*"**

"If the Earth and her children are to solve the problems we all face it will be through voices like Diane Reid's and her willingness to defend what she describes as the "Power of the North".

"I urge environmentalists, human rights activists, educators, the government of Canada and the general public to support Reid's call to stop the destruction of Rupert River and the further development of roads and power dams in the north before nothing is left of the natural world.

"The Cree Nation should be proud to have a real spiritual leader among them that has been successful in defending their real culture and homeland for future generations. In these times of chaos, strife, unrest, greed and stupidity of the U.S. and Middle East, native women should be taken seriously in their voice for what should be the most important thing in our minds and hearts -- our Sacred Mother Earth and her life-giving blood, rivers, lakes, streams and oceans.

"It seems the priorities of some of our so called leaders today have been put aside for profit, power, control and shortsightedness for lack of spiritual teachings. I now say thank you for this sacred day, for all the gifts the great mystery has allowed us, to wander around in peace and harmony in a good way, for all my relations and for the spirit of our ancestors, elders, chiefs and clan mothers.

> **"*The dominant culture here will soon see and feel the devastating effects of destroying Mother Earth more than ever.*"**

"Through our songs, dances, ceremonies, actions and activities, we as human beings can heal ourselves, bring true strength to our families and enhance the life-giving forces and cycles of life on our Sacred Mother Earth with all our relations.

"Native people must speak out now in order to create a balance for harmony to continue. The old elders are trying to maintain our culture but are not receiving the support they need to achieve success. The dominant culture here will soon see and feel the devastating effects of destroying Mother Earth more than ever, so we must continue our spiritual ways our traditional ways of oneness with the universe and cosmos. Our children are crying inside from the abuse to creation and our inability to create harmony. All spiritual people must continue their struggle with the natural world as their wisdom and beauty."

## CREE WOMAN DENOUNCES GREEDY DEALS

At the Montreal press conference Diane Reid, denounced the Peace of the Braves as "an agreement signed exclusively by men blinded by money and power."

This insight was developed by the veteran Cree journalist and broadcaster, Diane Reid. Wearing a traditional Cree dress, Reid related in three languages the concern of her people for the past sacrifice of the Eastmain, and planned destruction of the Rupert River.

She then sang a moving prayer, with her traditional drum, in honour of her late grandfather, whose trap line encompassed both shores of a segment of the Rupert River. Her song urged the "sacred waters" to "come into my heart."

Reid, who played a major role in stopping both James Bay Two and dams on the Arun River in Nepal, began her journalism career with CBC North in 1974. In her position with the National Aboriginal Communications Society from 1979 to 1989, she played a major role in establishing 11 native radio stations in Québec and also fostered aboriginal broadcasting in South America, Australia and New Zealand. As the official representative of the Cree Nation, her campaign against James Bay Two took her to 20 countries.

For Reid, the anniversary of the Peace of the Braves, although described by Cree leaders Ted Moses and Matthew Coon Come, as "a great accomplishment" is not "a cause for celebration", since it was accompanied, "by the destruction of rivers".

Reid lamented how:

"The Peace of the Braves created the first major difference of opinion in modern times in the history of the Cree Nation. We had for many decades shown a unity of strength and strong determination to protect the earth. This united commitment to defend our ancestral lands gave us a major impact. It was shown in Québec, Canada and on the international stage, although we are a nation of only 12,000 people.

"In the election for Grand Chief this summer, almost 50% of the Crees voted for a candidate in opposition to Ted Moses, Matthew Mukash, who ran largely in opposition to the diversion. Ted Moses was only elected by 28 votes. Now even families are divided.

"What do you do when you oppose half your nation? I ask myself that question many times. I do it because I have a conscience. I do it because of my responsibilities to my ancestors and to the spirits of the water, which have called me to defend it.

"People may say that I am an urban Cree. But that doesn't change my responsibility to the air and the water...The only thing I have is prayer, for my people, for the rivers, the land and for their protection."

## CALL FOR WOMEN

Reid sees the Peace of the Braves as a monstrosity signed by men. None of the Cree chiefs who signed the deal after three weeks of secret talks were women- nor were any of the

> *"What do you do when you oppose half your nation? I ask myself that question many times. I do it because I have a conscience. I do it because of my responsibilities to my ancestors and to the spirits of the water which have called me to defend it."*

signatories from Québec. She called upon "all the women of the world, since the women in our community, in our tradition are the water carriers, who carry it in a sacred manner. All women around the world should rise up and take responsibility for water."

There is already some sign that Reid's call for women to take actions to save the threatened rivers of the wild northeast is having an impact. The National Council of Women,

one Canada's oldest national women's groups, with a distinguished record of protecting the environment going back well over a century, is considering at its upcoming convention an important resolution. It resolves that, "mega dams should not be built in Canada's north as sources of electricity."

Both Reid and the National Council of Women have condemned the inadequacy of environmental assessment processes by the federal and provincial governments, which are being used to review the Rupert River diversion.

Reid explains how misunderstanding among the Cree about the fairness of the environmental assessment procedures, which would be used to review the proposed Rupert River diversion, contributed to the acceptance of the agreement with Québec in a referendum held in late January and February last year.

"The vote in favour of the agreement was obtained under the understanding that there would be a fair environmental evaluation process to review the Rupert River diversion that the Cree people voted to accept the new agreement with the Québec government. This is not the case. The Minister of the Environment is now saying that the review doesn't matter."

"The process will not fully evaluate the desirability of the undertaking. They are just talking about mitigative measures that are taking place to reduce the impact of the diversion. It is not examining the bigger question if the project itself is acceptable. Is that any acceptable evaluation process?

"All these assessments, studies and hearings are only leading to recommendations. There is no obligation to follow the recommendations. These processes are not legally binding. Under the terms of the James Bay and Northern Québec Agreement the Ministry of Environment can simply issue a certification order."

Gagnon shares Reid's contempt for Québec's environmental assessment process. He does not see the assessments underway as the means to killing the Rupert diversion, noting that "In Québec there is no history of power dams being defeated by formal consultative processes and hearings. What has proven effective, as shown recently in the minipower dams, which were defeated in southern Québec by groups such as artists who were dedicated to protecting the streams of their communities, which they adopted, is independent, creative, citizen actions. We support all such heart touching, common sense actions which will educate people as to what is happening in northern Québec."

For Gagnon, Québec's environmental assessment process produces results "similar to health studies on the impacts of smoking funded by tobacco companies. What is missing from the assessment process is any funding for independent studies of likely environmental impacts."

## WEAK ENVIRONMENTAL LAWS MAY HELP

The weakness of Québec and Canadian environmental assessment laws, in comparison with those of the United States, may turn out to be the key factor, paradoxically, to kill Hydro Québec's plans to divert the Rupert River and assault Nunavik. A growing coalition of the business sponsors of alternative energy, such as solar and wind power, and environmentalists, is sponsoring a growing list of draft laws, which would restrict and penalize Québec power exports.

This would be done on the grounds that the facilities that produce them are not regulated by environmental assessment and are not as strict as those that protect the environment in the United States. Québec power, therefore, would be barred or restricted on the grounds that it is dirty electricity, generated under conditions made possible only by substandard environmental regulations.

As pointed out in *Restructured Rivers*, a study prepared by Philip Raphals of the Helios Centre and published by the International Rivers Network and distributed by Gagnon at the Peace of the Braves commemoration, the outrage of U.S. environmentalists over low Canadian environmental assessment standards may well save northern Québec's rivers.

*For Gagnon, Québec's environmental assessment process produces results "similar to health studies on the impacts of smoking funded by tobacco companies."*

This was contained in draft legislation introduced in the U.S. Congress by the late Democratic congressman William Hoyt, together with Republican Senator, Frantz Leichter. This bill, intended to aid opposition to James Bay Two, sought to prohibit US power imports unless the generating facility that produced them had undergone environmental assessment substantially equivalent to what would be required for a similar project in the U.S.

Stronger versions of the Hoyt-Leichter legislation are advocated by American environmental law experts. One would require that the U.S. Congress amend the Federal Power Act to require authorization of power imports. Such authorization would only be permitted if the power did not create unacceptable environmental impacts.

## AMERICANS BLOCK HYDRO MARKETING

American environmentalists are also attempting to block efforts by Hydro Québec to market its electrical exports in the U.S. as a form of green power. Legislation in New Jersey would only permit this if the facilities

*American environmentalists are also attempting to block efforts by Hydro Québec to market its electrical exports in the US as a form of green power.*

*Much of the momentum for Rupert Reverence's campaign comes from the successful opposition, spearheaded by artists, to save the rivers of southern Québec...*

have "the highest environmental standards and minimizes any impacts for the environment and local communities."

This law is being challenged by Hydro-Québec and their arguments have been repeated by the then Canadian Ambassador to the United States, Raymond Chrétien (brother of the Canadian Prime Minister). Chrétien claims that this law and similar proposals are "inconsistent with the NAFTA investment chapter and the WTO agreement on trade-related investment measures."

Gagnon notes that Hydro Québec has also failed to emulate the planning and regulatory measures that are common to publicly owned utilities in the United States. At the February 7 press conference, he notes that commercial objectives for Hydro Québec has caused the utility to abandon a 1996 regulatory body, the Régie de l'énergie.

It had sought to take social environmental concerns into decisions regarding new energy generation. Under Bill 116, the regulatory body was stripped of its role in approving dam construction, which was given back to Hydro Québec.

Much of the momentum for Rupert Reverence's campaign comes from the successful opposition, spearheaded by artists, to save the rivers of southern Québec from further destruction by hydro development. This was announced on November 26 2002, when the Québec government announced

its cancellation of plans, originally made in response to demands for large power purchases made by U.S. President George Bush, to dam southern rivers.

To protect these southern Québec streams from Bush's attempted power grab, some 33 watershed management associations were created. No such protected measures were applied to the majority of the province's water in northern Québec.

Rupert Reverence is advocating a clear strategy to stop Hydro Québec's assault on the northern wilds through the use of river corridors as the basis of meeting Québec's stated goals of protecting 8 per cent of its land base in all ecological zones. Under this approach, the Rupert River would be given a protected area status from its headwaters in Lake Mistassini to its James Bay mouth, for a width of 17 kilometers on both sides.

It is also advocates that "all Northern rivers be given the protected area status". This status would prohibit dams, mines and logging, while respecting traditional Cree economic pursuits.

The concept of protected areas, advanced by the International Union for the Conservation of Nature, (IUCN), is based on the notion of excluding certain predominantly natural areas from industrial exploitation. This approach is in keeping with respecting traditional native land tenure where native people are custodians of the land.

This concept was ridiculed by Grand Chief Ted Moses – the most outspoken Cree defender of the Rupert destruction. "We are not mere "janitors", but rather real "owners" of the land," Moses said.

The IUCN developed the concept of protected areas, as opposed to past definitions of designated parks, in order to protect traditional native controlled and sustainable subsistence uses of the earth, while also excluding industrial exploitation. Especially in the past, many formally designated parks excluded native people, despite the reality that they had been the actual custodians of creation for thousands of years on these lands, protecting a richness of biodiversity poorly understood by recently arrived Euro-Canadians.

## QUÉBEC NEEDS GREEN MAKEOVER

While the IUCN targets a minimum 12 per cent protected areas for every nation, in each of is representative ecological zones, Québec is one of the areas of the democratic world which have fallen most behind its target. Although well below the IUCN goals, which have been achieved in other Canadian provinces, notably British Columbia during its recent eco-activist New Democratic Party government, the eight per cent goal if achieved, would represent a major green leap for Québec.

While Québec, after a doubling of its protected areas network last year, claims to have safeguarded 2.8 percent of the province, environmentalists dispute this figure, believing it has only achieved half of this goal. Accepting the province's claims however, it would still mean that Québec would have to almost triple its current protected designations within three years to meet its own targets.

This increase moreover, would largely have to come in northern Québec areas proposed for hydro development. There are currently no areas in northern Québec that

*Mining corporations, along with Hydro-Québec, have been the chief villains in the failure of the Québec government to meet its own targets for the creation of protected areas.*

meet ICUN standards for protected areas. All of these lands are in the southerly watersheds of the St. Lawrence.

In its battles to secure protected area designations in northern Québec along free flowing rivers, Rupert Reverence is battling not only Hydro-Québec, but major corporations in the logging and mining industries. Mining corporations, along with Hydro-Québec, have been the chief villains in the failure of the Québec government to meet its own targets for the creation of protected areas.

The northern area where Québec has come closest to establishing a protected area, which would exclude power dams and mines, is the area around the Pingualuit Crater, created 1.4 million years ago from a meteorite crash. Its waters are considered to be among the purest on earth.

Inuit residents of the community of Kanqiqusujuaq, have been lobbying the Québec government to create a protected area around the Pingualuit Crater since 1974, which they want designated as a provincial park.

These designations they hope will promote ecotourism from activities that celebrate

*Inuit residents of the community of Kanqiqusujuaq, have been lobbying the Québec government to create a protected area around the Pingualuit Crater since 1974, which they want designated as a provincial park.*

*I*n the early 1990s, Québec actually suggested that park boundary studies be financed by two of the impacted corporations – Hydro-Québec and Falconbridge.

Inuit culture such as dog sledding and living in igloos. To meet IUCN standards for the protection of an ecological zone, in this case a representative part of the Ungava Plateau region, it is necessary to go beyond the narrow perimeter of the Crater, to include other environmentally significant features, notably the Puvirnituq River Canyon, a refuge for gyrfalcons and peregrine falcons.

Since the Pingualuit park is close to Falconbridge's Raglan nickel mine, which opened in 1995 after a payout of $75 million to the Inuit, it is considered to be within a rich mineral zone. This has caused a delay in the proclamation of protected area status, arising out of a dispute between the Inuit and the Québec government over the park's boundaries.

The local Inuit community, like Rupert Reverence, is seeking to protect watersheds. Québec has so far refused to agree to their request for a one-kilometer buffer around the Puvirniuq River, delaying the final proclamation of the park's boundaries. In the early 1990s, Québec actually suggested that park boundary studies be financed by two of the impacted corporations- Hydro-Québec and Falconbridge.

*O*nly through public education efforts of the type that Rupert Reverence is undertaking, will the dream of protecting this area, which stretches back to unrealized visions of Pierre Trudeau, actually become a reality.

Over the next five years Québec has committed to improve its knowledge about wildlife at four other potential park sites within Nunavik. While these studies proceed however, Hydro-Québec and mining corporations continue to survey and explore these areas for possible industrial exploitation in the other four areas of the Parc des Monts-Torngat-et-de-la-Rivière-Korpoc, Parc du Lac Guillaume-Delisle de L'Eau-Claire and Cap Wolsteholme.

## OTHER NORTHEAST THREATS

Currently Nunavik is flooded with mining corporations undertaking staking and exploration activities, many of whose activities would be stopped if Rupert Reverence were able to achieve its proposed river based network of protected areas for Québec. The Twin Gold has discovered gem-quality diamonds in the Torngat Mountains, and 10 other corporations are staking under 28 new permits in this region.

The Torngat region, which straddles the northern border of Québec and Labrador, are a significant caribou habitat, which has been studied for a national park since the 1970s. It is a key region under consideration for designation under Québec's protected area strategy. Only through public education efforts of the type that Rupert Reverence is undertaking, will the dream of protecting this area, which stretches back to unrealized visions of Pierre Trudeau, actually become a reality.

In order to build support for their vision of the protection of the last northeast wilds on our continent, Rupert Reverence is organizing a 21-day expedition this summer beginning in

**❝** *[May] the Power from the North be no longer needed, and may the true Power from the North be understood.* **❞**
                                                                    **Rupert Reverence**

mid-July and continuing to mid August.

It seeks to educate more people about the dangers of Hydro-Québec's past and future activities. This is divided into three week long expeditions, each of which will continue elements of enhancing appreciation of Cree culture, the environment, together with the adventure of canoeing or kayaking on wild rivers. Among the sites to be visited is the former site of old Nemaska, a community that had to be relocated because of the plans of Hydro-Québec.

A critical aspect of the expedition will be to illustrate the folly of Québec's approach to hydro electric development, which has been termed by Raphals as the "Bypassed reaches", which he notes can have "catastrophic" "local ecological impacts."

One of the most catastrophic would have been the Great Whale project, which would have dried up 40 miles of the stream right above its current James Bay estuary.

In addition to touring the threatened Rupert, the expedition will examine the now dead zone of the Eastmain River. The Eastmain lost 92% of its flow to La Grande, more than doubling its flows from pre-project levels.

It is suspected that a freshwater plume under the sea ice created by the dramatically increased winter flows of La Grande is adversely affecting the eelgrass beds along the James Bay Coast, which provide a crucial food resource for waterfowl such as geese, especially Brant Geese during their northward spring migration and breeding season.

With its campaigns it is hoped that Rupert Reverence wakes people up to what Cree elder, Matthew Robbie, has termed the true, "Power From the North", in contrast to the ecocidal dreams of the late Québec Premier, Robert Bourassa. In his words, "The Power from the North be no longer needed, and may the true Power from the North be understood."

# POWER FROM THE NORTH

Poem Sung by Diane Reid at Peace of the Braves Requiem

O Great Spirit
We, the Nisaka Nation, the Goose People,
Who truly represent the Power from the
    North
Wish to express our appreciation for the
    rivers, lakes and mountains
And for the beautiful, green and golden
    forest
With it's animal life
We are grateful for your abundant
Kindness, Patience and Understanding

O Great Spirit
Unite our Nation as one
Stand with us during our struggle
Comfort us in our sorrow for the loss
Of land of future generations
Only you can correct our mistake
And heal our pain

O Great Spirit
We are so small in number
Hear our voice
Hear our concerns against the world
    destroying
Greed which calls itself progress
Instruct those who will access the Power from
    the North
Do not let them use the Power from the
    North
Against the will of our children and their
    generation

O Great Spirit
The Power from the North can do serious
Damage to civilization on this planet
See that the Power from the North is not used
To make war weapons to harm mankind
Prevent the Power from the North from
    being sold

O Great Spirit
Protect the Sacred Circle of Mankind
With Peace, Harmony, Dignity and Courage
May we all accept our responsibilities
As Peacemakers and Earth Healers
To empower Mother Earth to balance herself
And prevent massive destruction

O Great Spirit
Today, foreign laws are forced upon us and
    our children
Laws that we do not understand
These laws, we are told, will benefit us
For self-determination

We pray one day
Our Traditional Law
And Customary Laws will be
Respected and understood again

O Great Spirit
Guide our youth into the future
May our elders and ancestors
Provide the Wisdom, Knowledge and
    Guidance

Bless our Leaders, Guide them with
Wisdom, Knowledge, Patience and Love
Bless, Guide and Strengthen our Nation
With all your power from above

O Great Spirit
May our lands be no longer submerged
May the Spirit of the Whale rise up
To Sound the Message that the land
Can no longer be destroyed
And that in the future, may the Power from
    the
North be no longer needed
And may the true Power from the North be
    understood

O Great Spirit
These are our true and heartfelt feelings of
    the
Power from the North
And we thank you with all our hearts for
    your guidance
For our children and the future generations
    to come

# THERESA DUCHARME: GLOBALIZING NATIVE CULTURE

**By Len O'Connor**                                    **Published June, 1994**

Photos courtesy of Theresa Ducharme

Robert Davidson takes credit for drawing public attention to Native art, and Kashtin for spotlighting Native music; but Theresa Ducharme stakes her claim by helping to globalize Native culture. Within the last few years she and a Native dance troupe from Alberta have performed in Japan, China, Mongolia, Australia, Bolivia, Israel, France and Spain; including a special performance for the Dalai Lama.

The first performance was for Alberta's Days held in Tokyo in 1991. Theresa learnt that the Alberta government was sponsoring a presentation of their heritage to raise awareness of the province in Japan. Unfortunately, there was no invitation to the Native community. "The presence of Native culture is an integral part of Alberta," argued Theresa, who eventually won a spot for a Native presentation.

*Theresa Ducharme (above) and with her troupe dancing in China (left)*

> **"***We were the first Native performers to be on a stage in China. We were making history. I can't tell you the feeling.***"**

Along with Alberta's Eagle Drum Dancers and a grant from Native Services, Theresa was able to introduce Native dance to Japan and used the opportunity to help promote Native culture.

"I was out there hustling, promoting Native art, Native culture, Native models, and Native business acumen," recounts Theresa.

Tokyo was a success and it led to an invitation to China for the Folk Festivals of Xian and Beijing, the latter televised to 350 million viewers. "We were the first Native performers to be on a stage in China. We were making history. I can't tell you the feeling."

The dancers performed twice daily, and the live audience included the Chinese premier and the Canadian ambassador. The next date on the tour was for the Dalai Lama who was so impressed by the performance he gave a private audience to Theresa and the dancers.

The sense of determination and a "never say die" attitude, is characteristic of Theresa. She started modeling in Winnipeg in her teens, was very successful, and moved to Edmonton to open her own agency. She established Mystique Models, the first agency in Alberta for Native models. The agency had a different premise than others. "I wanted to help instill self-esteem in Native women. Modeling helps that way and even if you don't want to be a model it can help in the work place," Theresa explains.

She went the extra mile by going to reservations and making modeling available to girls who would normally never get that chance. Eventually she coordinated her services with a drug councilor and a nutritionist. She organized fashion shows for the girls to get a feel of what the fashion world was like and to inspire them to follow their dreams.

"Theresa likes to do positive things. She has a 'Let's make it happen attitude,'"

*Theresa in Korea (above) and with Frank Eagle (right)*

> **"**I wanted to help instill self-esteem in Native women. Modeling helps that way and even if you don't want to be a model it can help in the work place.**"**

remembers Melaine McCallum, a coordinator at Alberta Days.

Now residing in Vancouver, Theresa has opened the Wild Horse Talent and Model Agency, which is similar to her company in Edmonton, but with the expanded agenda of finding roles in television and movies for Native actors. With the success of Dances With Wolves and North of 60, doors are opening for Native actors and producers.

"There's a demand for Native talent and since I've developed a lot of good contacts, I think I can help."

Theresa, a stunning brunette with a ton of charm, could easily work in front of the camera. She's already booked for a Robbie Robertson music video and will do a voice over in the Disney remake of Pocohantas.

"I will do whatever it takes to get to know the business of film, but I would like to eventually develop Native scripts and produce documentaries. The time has come for Native writers and actors to make their presence felt, we have stories that can only be told by own people and finally we have the chance make that statement. The opportunity is here and now and I hope to contribute in every way I can," says Theresa.

One of her first clients is Leonard George, who will follow his father's footsteps when he steps in front of the cameras this summer for his first movie role. There are rumors that Leonard is also developing a script based on the life of the late Chief Dan George, this would be a project that would do more to validate Native cinema than anything Hollywood has ever produced, with all due respect of Kevin Costner and Walt Disney. It is also the kind of situation that Theresa's input will be pivotal as it is her special talent to understand creative potential and find a way to make it happen. By doing so she helps to expand the borders of Native culture and art.

*Theresa between Terry David Mulligan (left) and Robbie Robertson (right).*

# BARB CRANMER: MESSENGER OF CELLULOID STORIES

**By Sean Devlin**     **Published June, 1997**

*" The strong point of my films is that they are telling you the straight goods; they are telling you the truth. These people are speaking from what is inside them and that is a very, very strong voice. "*

*Photo: National Film Board of Canada*

The woman is short, stocky; compact. She has a face wide and mobile, a sun-filled smile. She speaks in a voice of brightness and enthusiasm, secure in her self-confidence. She appears filled with an intense and compacted energy, lightly reined, distinctly directed. The woman is of the 'Namgis First Nation of Alert Bay, of the Kwakwaka'wakw Nation of British Columbia. The woman is Barb Cranmer, a documentary filmmaker of note. Her film, *T'Lina: The Rendering of Wealth*, has just won the award for Best Short Documentary at the 1999 American Indian Film Festival in San Francisco.

As with all her work, *T'Lina* shares an intimate view of the power of community and the strength of tradition among the 14 groups speaking the Kwak'wala language, who live in a territory that reaches from Port Hardy on Northern Vancouver Island, then south to the Campbell River area.

"I myself am living my own history through the films that I am making," says Cranmer.

> **"***I have wanted to do this film for at least six years. It became urgent because many of our old people were dying and important knowledge and history were close to disappearing with them.***"**

"The strength, for me, in doing this work, comes from my family, comes from my community. I'm basically working in a non-native world, working and fundraising in Vancouver. The films I direct and co-produce are big-budget documentaries; when I feel I have to be strong, it is the strength of the family and the community that I come from, the community I'm representing, that allows me to carry on. That's critical. Because I have a strong sense of identity, I feel. Both sides of my family still potlatch, still carry on the tradition that's been passed on to us." company

Her visage is earnest, sincere and intense.

"That's what drives my work. I give voice to the community, the Native community at large."

The woman is also possessed of a becoming modesty, an attractive reticence about herself. Interviewed in advance of the film festival at which *T'Lina* was recognized for excellence, she forbore from mentioning that she is no stranger to such recognition.

Cranmer produced, wrote and directed Qutuwas: People Gathering Together, about the rebirth of the northwest coast canoe culture. This film won the first Telefilm Canada/TV Northern Canada Award, Best Documentary at the American Indian Film Festival, and was invited to the 1997 Sundance Film Festival.

"I have wanted to do this film for at least six years," says Cranmer. "It became urgent because many of our old people were dying

and important knowledge and history were close to disappearing with them. When I made a research trip with my family to Dzawadi in 1996, we witnessed a sharp decline in the eulachon run."

While the economic impact of declines in commercial fisheries has garnered national attention – where the local harvesting of a tiny fish known as the eulachon is concerned, it is the potential cultural loss that is important to the 'Namgis community of Alert Bay. In the Kwak'wala language t'lina (pronounced "gleetna") is the name of the precious oil rendered from the fish. This oil is a symbol of cultural wealth, a valuable trade item and important food staple. The oil is rich in vitamins, minerals and essential fatty acids.

Historically, it has been traded on "grease trails" throughout the northwest. For thousands of years, the Alert Bay community has made its way by boat each spring to a remote mainland inlet known as Dzawadi (Knight Inlet). Here the eulachon are harvested and rendered after spawning. Habitat loss and commercial over-fishing now imperil this traditional fishery.

The tiny fish are not used commercially, but have suffered from indiscriminate over-fishing as part of the industry's unwanted "by-catch" – fish that are dumped in pursuit of more saleable species. Habitat destruction from logging is also a major concern.

"It was important to do the story right now," says Cranmer. "In ten years we might not be going up there. The eulachon may be extinct."

> **❝** *This film offers a rare opportunity to share these moments in our community's way of life – for the benefit of audience today, and for future generations. I believe this film will inspire not only First Nations people, but the general public as well.* **❞**

In Kwakwaka'wakw society, the highest honour a Chief can bestow is to give away, or potlatch, the t'lina. In the t'linagila ceremony, families dance with huge carved feast spoons and bowls, symbolizing the pouring of the oil. Hundreds of bottles of t'lina are distributed to guests who have come to witness the potlatch.

"The families who travel annually to Dzawadi are strengthened by the experience," Cranmer says. "Each year brings something new. It is amazing that in these modern times our people are fortunate enough to be able to go to a place where we can still practice a traditional way of life. It is like travelling back in time as we reaffirm our connection to our traditional territory. We have discovered old house posts, which supported many big houses in the Dzawadi area. We can only imagine what it must have been like to live two hundred years ago in this same area.

"This film offers a rare opportunity to share these moments in our community's way of life – for the benefit of audience today, and for future generations. I believe this film will inspire not only First Nations people, but the general public as well. This film is a tribute to our grandmothers and grandfathers. My only regret is not being able to make the trip to Dzawadi years ago, when more elders were still alive."

The film, co-produced by Cari Green of Vancouver-based Nimpkish Wind Productions and the National Film Board, was made with $275,000 from the Canadian Television Fund.

# EXPOSED

Barb Cranmer was born and raised in Alert Bay. When she was 19, she moved to Vancouver to take courses in administration at Capilano College. She then returned home to work for her band in economic development.

In 1980, fortune – in the form of an educational camera crew from Chicago – found her and Cranmer found her life's work.

The quick video course that the visiting crew offered allowed Cranmer and others to learn how to edit on a basic level. What resulted was a library of some 200 tapes; which were oral histories presented by the band elders, many of whom have since died.

"I was really lucky, getting exposed to the film medium," says Cranmer, her face alive and her eyes sparkling with intelligence. "Since then, everything I've done has been a natural progression. I am definitely a self-driven personality."

Returning to Vancouver and Capilano College in 1988, she enrolled in an intensive, ten-month media arts course, sponsored by the Chief Dan George Foundation.

"I got right into the idea of film right away, being on the video crew at home," said Cranmer. "I knew this was something I was very interested in – with the whole idea that I was tired of seeing negative images of ourselves and I wanted to change that in some way. I wanted to make some sort of career out of it and so far I've been successful."

*B*arb *Cranmer creates stories in film; some folk would call this an art form. She also takes care to go deeply into the background of her stories; some folk would call this history.*

Initially, she worked on other's films as a researcher, project manager and production manager, until she felt ready to go out on her own. She made her first film in 1993.

"I felt strong enough to make my own films a long time before that but the people who fund these things were not willing to take a risk on me as a first-time filmmaker. I had to spend some years networking and establishing contacts."

Eventually, she found her funding and made such potent documentaries as The Washing of Tears and Lazwesa Wa: Strength of the River, both about the reclamation of Native land and culture.

Cranmer regards her work as educational. She complains that native voices are never really heard in Canada: "It's not very often our voices get heard and when they do it is in the mainstream media, which has its own twisted take on everything. You never really hear from First Nations people in that sense."

## HERE TO STAY

"For me, film is a valuable tool, to be able to have access to this, because it reaches such a broad audience. Much more so than if it were a book because everyone has TV at home and can plug it into a VCR, or they see it at a film festival or on television.

"And it was important for me to get the truth out there, from our own perspective, and do it with the respect and integrity that comes from our community. That's been a driving force for me."

She pauses. She begins to speak. Her voice has dropped a half tone; her delivery has slowed. Each word is enunciated clearly, precisely. She wants to be taken seriously. And she is.

"For our people, it has been a constant, constant struggle to just be here on this earth. My work is based on the fact that, despite the things that have happened to our people, we are still here. All the powers that be have tried to change who we were, and who we are, and they did not succeed. And I think that is all I have to say on that. I feel strongly about that."

Barb Cranmer creates stories in film; some folk would call this an art form. She also takes care to go deeply into the background of her stories; some folk would call this history.

Cranmer insists she is neither artist or historian.

"I see myself as a kind of messenger of stories. Basically, the way I see it is that I can look at these films twenty years from now and know that I've helped in maintaining the history and the culture of our people."

It seems appropriate, in light of her commitments to promoting the expression of aboriginal voices, that her 'Namgis name is Laxalogwa (pronounced Lak-wa-lo-gwa), which means "yelling for the people to come to feast with her."

She is adamant. Her work is not mainstream. To use a narrator would be nonsense.

"My work definitely has its own feel to it, in terms of being right up front with the people that are speaking, from the voice of the community. I don't have the voice of God in there, with a narrator leading us down the garden path, because I feel our voices are strong enough, that they can speak for themselves."

"The strong point of my films is that they are telling you the straight goods; they are telling you the truth. These people are speaking from what is inside them and that is a very, very strong voice."

Cranmer has been told that her body of work has been successful in educating Canadians about native people.

"Another one of my goals is to educate people to the fact that we have existed along the coast here forever," Cranmer said. "Governments are asking us to prove that we have been here for 10,000 years. But we did not just land here from Mars yesterday; our people have been here forever.

"There are so many more stories to tell. I have my whole lifetime of work in front of me, telling stories from a First Nations perspective. I'd like to try directing a dramatic film at some point; I like drama. But that won't be tomorrow; that's still some time in the future."

> **"***Governments are asking us to prove that we have been here for 10,000 years. But we did not just land here from Mars yesterday; our people have been here forever.***"**

All of Cranmer's future stories will emerge through the vehicle of Nimpkish Wind Productions, a company she formed in 1994 with producer Cari Green, following their successful collaboration on the documentary *The Washing of Tears*. The company, now an established force in the Canadian television scene, is venturing into multimedia, with a CD-ROM series mixing local fishing lore and ongoing political issues.

Barb describes herself as, "a 39-year-old, wise beyond my years, kind of person." She laughs adding that she's teasing.

Teasing or not, the point has been made and the point has been taken. Barb Cranmer is, indeed, a "messenger of stories."

# ABORIGINAL ACHIEVEMENT AWARD WINNER

# SOPHIE PIERRE

## PUBLIC SERVICE

**Reprinted with permission from the NAAF**

At the St. Eugene Mission School the culture of the Kootenay Indian people was nearly taken away. Thanks to St. Mary's Chief, Sophie Pierre and her dream, drive and vision, that very building is where a people,s ancient ways will again burst forth and triumph. After a decade of planning and negotiating, the St. Eugene Mission Resort ^ worth more than $40 million ^ is now, a reality. By any standard, it,s quite a feat ^ a first-class 125 room resort hotel with conference and meeting facilities set amidst a breath-taking B.C. landscape. But the project is about more than that, so much

more. Designed with a proud Ktunaxa theme, the resort also includes a Ktunaxa Interpretive Centre, traditional Ktunaxa Teepee Camp and the Ktunaxa Arts and Crafts Centre. The future is bright and the tide has turned under Chief Pierre's watch. She has led her people for more than 20 years and is one of the most accomplished Aboriginal leaders in all Canada. With Chief Pierre at the helm, the Ktunaxa/Kinbasket Tribal Council is now known far and wide for its wide range of successes. Pierre has fought for Aboriginal control over education, co-chaired the First Nations Summit, excelled in business and improved her community's life in fields such as sport, recreation, the place of women and support for the elderly. Growing up, she wasn't looking for a career in politics. "I never really thought about being Chief," she says. "I actually thought in high school I would be an airline hostess and fly all over the world." Today, so many are thankful that's one plane she missed.

# SHOWDOWN AT GUSTAFSEN LAKE

**By Cam Schmierer**                    **Published September, 1996**

The Sundancers of Gustafsen Lake are suffering an injustice. They have been mistreated throughout the standoff by the RCMP and by the media. They have been presented as having violent intentions when they are simply engaging in a cultural tradition. Are we still being persecuted for our beliefs?

In early 1995, Faith Keeper Percy Rosette decided that the Gustafsen Lake would be the Sundance site. He built a shelter and began to prepare the site for the Sundance. Other members of the Ts'Peten tribe came to the site to prepare it for the Sundance. They erected a fence to keep cattle out, and to discourage trespassing on the sacred ground. By spring, a small community had developed. Everything was going as planned and the Ts'Peten eagerly awaited the Sundance. But, on the morning of June 13, a bad omen came to the Sundance camp.

Lyle James, a cattle rancher who had grazing rights for the Sundance site, entered the camp and served an eviction notice. While twelve of his men stood around him with their weapons drawn, he read the notice aloud, and then affixed it to the sacred staff.

The Sundancers knew that they had a right to be where they were so they were not afraid of Lyle James and his friends. Eventually he returned, and was even more threatening. He and his men strode around with their rifles, and made threatening comments: "This is a good day to string up some red niggers."

Photo: Noel Martin

*Lyle James and his men strode around with their rifles, and made threatening comments: "This is a good day to string up some red niggers."*

They stole the door from Percy Rosette's shelter, and took the wood stove from inside. They left saying they planned to burn the council lodge, and that the RCMP planned to remove them from the camp if they did not leave voluntarily.

At first the Sundancers only had to contend with the intimidation of Lyle James. But, if the RCMP was involved, who could they appeal to if Lyle James made good on his threats?

Officer Woods, an Oneida, tried to be a liaison between the Sundancers and the RCMP. He asked to be part of the Sundance and also assured the Sundancers that the RCMP would "do their best to keep aggravators away from the grounds during the Sundance."

As a precautionary measure, the Sundancers sought the legal assistance of Dr. Bruce Clark. He confirmed that the Sundancers were acting "within [their] existing legal rights by resisting the invasion [of the RCMP]."

The Sundance was held, and went without intervention. The Sundancers began to feel assured that they would be left undisturbed for the rest of their stay at the site.

*Attorney General Ujjal Dosanjh labeled the camp members as "terrorists" and he displayed the rifles seized by the fisheries officers as evidence of the need for a more proactive response to this "threat."*

## PANIC SETS IN

On August 11, an incident involving fisheries officers and two members of the camp (David Pena and Ernie Archie), caused an air of panic to surround the Gustafsen conflict.

The fisheries officers accused Pena and Archie of fishing illegally in the Fraser River. The two men disagreed with the officers' ruling claiming that they were gathering food for their families. One of the officers pulled his gun. Their vehicles were searched and hunting rifles were discovered, a common occurrence in the rural area of Gustafsen Lake. This seemingly innocent event was misconstrued by the RCMP and they began to suspect that the Sundancers planned on holding their ground with violent force.

On August 18, members of the Gustafsen Sundancers noticed seven camouflaged men in the bushes. Initially the RCMP denied affiliation with these men, but they reissued their statement at a press conference claiming their side of the Gustafsen events. Attorney General Ujjal Dosanjh labeled the camp members as "terrorists" and he displayed the rifles seized by the fisheries officers as evidence of the need for a more proactive response to this "threat." At the press conference the RCMP assured listeners that they were "ready to move and disperse" the Sundancers.

The comments made by the Attorney-General and the RCMP vilified the Sundancers in the eyes of the media. The media projection of the conflict was so one-sided that even AFN leader Ovide Mecredi referred to the RCMP's account of the events as truth in his interviews.

Events began to escalate at the camp, or so the media portrayed. On August 27, shots were fired at a RCMP vehicle, apparently hitting officers and nearly killing them. The RCMP reported that the vehicle was "riddled with bullet holes." It was removed from the scene with a tarp covering it "to preserve the evidence." The car was released several days later, and was shown to have bullet holes in it.

The bullet proof vests that both officers wore were also investigated and were found intact, with no bullet holes. Most news organizations supported the RCMP version of the alleged "shoot out"; although some questioned the validity of their accusations.

If there was indeed a "hail of bullets" as the officers described, certainly something more than the car would have been hit, either a camp member or an RCMP officer. Four days after the alleged shooting, Dr. Bruce Clark entered the camp, counseled the camp members and emerged in the evening with bullet casings he had found. He also had a sworn affidavit by journalists that proved that the RCMP had instigated the shoot out, and that much of the damage to the police vehicle had been done by police ammunition.

## MILITARY APPEARS

Regardless of the questionable circumstances surrounding the shooting on August 27, the apparent violent action against the RCMP prompted military intervention. Military involvement on home soil is not an easy thing to bring about. Certain measures have to be taken so that, in the event that the decision to bring increased force was a mistake, responsibility will be taken by someone. Unfortunately, the RCMP seems to have anticipated the possibility of their failure to resolve this confrontation without force.

Although the RCMP portrayed the Sundancers as "terrorists" to the media, they downplayed that image in their request for military assistance. The RCMP sought to use a Memorandum of Understanding that is "designed to move along agendas where there is little or no reason for elected officials to have to take political responsibility for what is being done." This way, as an unsigned memo puts it: "If anything goes wrong, we will not be seen as failing." Despite repeated inquiries, the RCMP denies military involvement.

The military brought in large armored personnel carriers and continued hidden surveillance of the camp. Vehicles were marked as police, rather than military. This is a clear indication of the deceit that both the RCMP and the military engaged in. The fewer people that knew of the military involvement, the less they

> *Unfortunately, the RCMP seems to have anticipated the possibility of their failure to resolve this confrontation without force.*

would have to explain, and then no one would realize that they were essentially doing this on their own, without any higher authorization.

On September 11, two camp members and their dog were en route to get water from the lake. Their truck hit something that caused a small explosion, which disabled it. Later it was discovered that the military had laid land mines, and that was what the truck ran into.

*Chief Arvol Looking Horse*

*Photo: mytwobeadsworth.com*

The two individuals and their dog fled from the truck under heavy RCMP fire. Reports from the site confirm that the RCMP and their military cohorts had been given the "green light" to shoot and kill the "terrorists."

Two days after the shooting, spiritual leader Arvol Looking Horse arrived form South Dakota. The RCMP agreed to let him into the camp if he promised the camp members they would not be hurt; if they would leave the camp of their own volition. At first, the Sundancers were apprehensive: the RCMP had fired on two unarmed people fetching water – what would they do to them if they left the camp? Finally, on September 17, the Gustafsen defenders left the site voluntarily and were taken into police custody.

# ABORIGINAL GANGS IN PRAIRIE PROVINCES IN "CRISIS PROPORTIONS"

**By Lloyd Dolha**                    **Published November, 2003**

Prairie-based aboriginal gangs have reached crisis proportions in major urban centers, supporting larger and more sophisticated gangs – such as the Hells Angels and Asian gangs – and are spreading out into smaller cities and rural areas, moving on and off impoverished reserves recruiting new members.

In the annual report by the Criminal Intelligence Canada (CISC), Aboriginal-Based Organized Crime or ABOC has become one of the national agency's intelligence priorities.

Released on August 22, the report states that aboriginal gangs are present in several urban centers across Canada, particularly in Winnipeg, Regina and Edmonton.

> *"In Alberta, aboriginal gangs that once existed primarily in prisons for protection purposes, have now recognized the financial benefit of trafficking hard drugs, such as cocaine, on the reserves."*
>
> **CISC report.**

# GANG ACTIVITY ON THE RISE

In April, an Edmonton-based task force identified 12 aboriginal gangs operating in the city, with more than 400 members and almost 2,000 known gang associates. The task force warned that gang activity will increase along with the growing aboriginal population if the social and economic problems faced by urban native youth are not addressed.

The local task force identified gangs operating in the city as Redd Alert, Indian Posse, Alberta Warriors, Saskatchewan Warriors, Manitoba Warriors, Native Syndicate, Crypts, West End Boys, Death Do Us Part, Wolf Pack, Mixed Blood and Deuce.

One day before the release of the CISC report on aboriginal gangs, on August 21, the Federation of Saskatchewan Indian Nations (FSIN), released its own report on aboriginal youth gang violence entitled Alter-Natives to Non-Violence Report: Aboriginal Youth Gangs Exploration, the result of a two-year examination of the conditions underlying the growing gang phenomena within Saskatchewan's major urban centers and the communities that are most impacted.

According the FSIN report, aboriginal youth in the prairie provinces join gangs for money, power and excitement. They are characterized by feelings of disenfranchisement from the community and family with no attachment to school.

Youth gangs can be identified by the use of colours, various hand signals, caps/hats worn a certain way, pant-leg rolled up, one glove, an untied shoelace or a bandana worn a certain way.

These gangs are generally involved in street-level trafficking of marihuana, cocaine, crack cocaine and crystal meth.

They are also involved in prostitution, break and enters, robberies, assaults, intimidation, tobacco fraud, home invasions, vehicle thefts, weapons offences illegal gaming and debt collection and enforcement as trench troops for other organized crime groups like the Hells Angels.

Nationally, the primary gangs are the Indian Posse, Redd Alert, Warriors and Native Syndicate, with a number of smaller gangs that frequently form and reform.

The street gang scene in Winnipeg, the birthplace of aboriginal gangs in Canada, is dominated to a large extent by two aboriginal gangs, the Manitoba Warriors and the Indian Posse. A smaller street gang called the Deuce, with connections to the Manitoba Warriors, is a rival gang to the Indian Posse.

"In Alberta, aboriginal gangs that once existed primarily in prisons for protection purposes, have now recognized the financial benefit oftrafficking hard drugs, such as cocaine, on the reserves," states the CISC report.

Many of these gangs have ready access to firearms that has resulted in a number of incidents of violence.

Aboriginal youth are initiated into gangs by the following methods: committing certain crimes at the behest of the leader; "beating in', in some cases an intense beating can last up to three minutes; prostitution; "sexing in" or "banged in', where young females have sex with several members of the gang; a family connection, children who are raised in families in gangs; and, muscling others or intimidation.

## NATIVES PRIME RECRUITS

According to the FSIN report, of the 98,000 youth in Saskatchewan between the ages of 12 to 17 years, approximately 15,000 are aboriginal youth. Based on known risk factors such as poverty, lack of opportunity for employment, institutional racism and discrimination and a sense of hopelessness and despair, many of these 15,000 aboriginal youth are at-risk of being recruited.

The development of gang culture can be understood through the history of aboriginal people in Canada. A widely known aspect of the destruction of aboriginal culture in the residential school system experience and its subsequent intergenerational effects.

As it is widely known, many of the aboriginal children of the 1950s and 1960s suffered extreme physical and sexual abuse. The racism and assimilation efforts of the residential school era has left residual effects on aboriginal youth that provided the underlying social unrest of aboriginal youth leading to gang involvement.

Aboriginal youth gang can be characterized as a "spontaneous youth social movement.'

*Photo: newdirectionsindiscipline.com/gangs.htm*

*B*ased on known risk factors such as poverty, lack of opportunity for employment, institutional racism and discrimination and a sense of hopelessness and despair, many of these 15,000 aboriginal youth are at-risk of being recruited.

"For an undereducated aboriginal youth disenfranchised from society, there are few options for survival. Sheer survival is a strong motivational factor that leads many youth to gangs," states the report.

*According to the FSIN, aboriginal youth comprise at least 75 to 90 per cent of youth in open and closed custody facilities. Of the 3,000 youth that are in the criminal justice system on any given day, about 1,800 are aboriginal.*

## JAIL MORE LIKELY THAN DIPLOMA

In the executive summary, the report notes, "In 1992, the Lynn Report stated that it was said that an aboriginal youth had a better chance of going to jail than graduating from Grade 12. This is still true today."

The report quotes a January 2003 submission to the Commission on First Nations and Métis Peoples Justice Reform that notes Saskatchewan has the highest crime rate in the country. Aboriginal people account for only ten per cent of the population of Regina and Prince Albert combined but accounted for 47 per cent of the victims of crime.

Between 1994 and 2000, aboriginal people accounted for 55 per cent of Saskatchewan's homicide victims as well as 60 per cent of those accused of committing homicides.

Aboriginal youth accounted for about six in ten youth accused ages 12 to 17 years in the three cities of Regina, Saskatoon and Prince Albert in 1997.

According to the FSIN, aboriginal youth comprise at least 75 to 90 per cent of youth in open and closed custody facilities. Of the 3,000 youth that are in the criminal justice system on any given day, about 1,800 are aboriginal.

In one passage, the FSIN report graphically demonstrated the danger of gang affiliation for aboriginal youth from a passage of the Western Reporter magazine.

One of the young people on the corner was a 13-year old Joseph Spence, known to his friends as Beeper. When Johnson asked the group "You IP?" Beeper stepped forward even though he had no gang affiliation.

"Straight up," he bragged. "In full effect!" Johnson jumped up out of his seat and pointed the shotgun at Beeper as a 16 year-old Deuce named Fabian Torres shouted from the back of the van. "Bust a cap in his ass!" As Beeper turned to run, Johnson fired a blast straight into his back. Beeper, who had just completed Grade 7, died in the street where he lay.

The FSIN report hopes to make a compelling case to the federal and provincial government agencies to substantiate the need for enhanced and new resources that can be directed at First Nations to address the gang issue.

## PRISON MENTALITY ON THE REZ

A former resident who did not wish to be identified described the gang phenomena as the result of aboriginal inmates who return from jail and bring a "prison mentality" back onto reserves that makes them "open air prisons.'

To address the exploding gang phenomena, a number of initiatives have been launched.

In November 2001, Corrections Services Canada (CSC), launched an Aboriginal Gang Initiative (AGI), in Winnipeg. The initiative was the result of former AFN national chief Ovide Mercredi, who examined the issue of aboriginal gangs and recommended 23 strategy options to CSC.

The major thrust of the May 2000 Mecredi Report, was the involvement of the aboriginal community, especially elders, to find solutions for the rise of aboriginal gangs.

The AGI team consists of five aboriginal facilitators guided by aboriginal elders. The team works with those involved in or affected by gangs.

"We've come along way in a very short time," said Darrel Phillips, Project Manager for the AGI. "We've established a foundation of trust with gang members themselves and the CSC staff. We've also constructed solid bridges of between CSC and the community and we've mobilized a wide array of resources.

"We realized early in our work that many aboriginal gang members truly want to change, but they don't really have the tools or skills to stabilize themselves," added Phillips. "They're being pulled in so many directions and very often their belief systems are totally at odds with committing to a crime-free lifestyle."

Clayton Sandy, Community Relation Manager of AGI, believes that is where the strength of the elders comes into play.

"Because it's our elders that can help gang members see how their beliefs and values determine the choices they make, which leads them into conflict with law. We help them commit to a spiritual path in life (the 'Red Road'), and support them in their spiritual journey," said Sandy.

As of April 2002, within Manitoba, 163 gang members were either incarcerated at the Stoney Mountain Institution, the Rockwood Institution of on conditional release in the community under the Winnipeg Parole office.

Pat Larocque, a lifer, has a great deal of credibility as a member of the AGI team. Larocque works directly with aboriginal gang members in Stoney Mountain and Rockwood.

"I find it's really making a difference to consistantly interact with the guys inside. Most of them know my experience with the correctional system and this gives them a lot of hope that positive change is possible. We're not only trying to get these guys on a spiritual path, we also need to cooperate with CSC staff to help aboriginal gang members prepare for a job when they get out," said Larocque.

## FEMALE GANGS OF CONCERN

A key area of concern for the future is aboriginal women involved in gangs. The issue will be given greater attention once the AGI is established as an on-going initative.

Recently renamed Bimosewin, Ojibway for "walk your path in life in a good way," the AGI has to date: obtained a written commitment from over 125 gang and ex-gang members to work with Bimosewin; over 12 aboriginal individuals have been "helped out or kept out" of gangs; secured employment for more than 15 aboriginal gang members; a safe house has been supported and is now available to ex-gang members; and, a core group of ex-

*" This is a window of opportunity for us to help them find a new indentity rooted in their own culture. We believe this leads to aboriginal gang members making more positive lifestyle choices. "*
**Darrel Phillips**

gang members is emerging that Bimosewin can mentor and work with.

CSC is currently evaluating the efficacy of Bimosewin and, with the approval of the executive committee, may be extending Bimosewin's mandate to other to other provinces in the Prairies over the next five years.

"Many aboriginal gang members respect their elders and their traditional culture," says Phillips. "This is a window of opportunity for us to help them find a new indentity rooted in their own culture. We believe this leads to aboriginal gang members making more positive lifestyle choices."

## SUPPORT PROGRAMS

In Saskatchewan, Bimosewin has extended an offer to the FSIN to participate in their gang initiative committee. The FSIN has established a Youth Gang Awareness Cultural Camp for aboriginal youth in collaboration with the White Buffalo Youth Centre located in Saskatoon.

The camp provides healthy alternatives for aboriginal youth and opportunities to interact with role models and elders, working towards dispelling the glamourization often associated with gang membership.

*The FSIN is developing a three to five year strategic plan to address the complex issues underlying the development of gang culture...*

The FSIN is developing a three to five year strategic plan to address the complex issues underlying the development of gang culture and a provincial policy that focuses on the root social problems experienced by aboriginal youth who join gangs.

In Edmonton, the Spirit Keeper Youth Society (SKYS), an aboriginal non-profit society was recently formed in June to address the escalation and growth of aboriginal gangs in the city. The board of directors consists of a "hands on daily" group of aboriginal professionals each with their own area of expertise in business, program development and crime prevention.

Spirit Keeper is currently working to establish a crisis line for aboriginal youth and a transition house for 18-25 year olds involved in gangs. Spirit Keeper also wants to establish a Learning Centre for pre- and early teenage aboriginal youth as an intervention and prevention measure against future gang recruitment.

They will also be developing an extensive aftercare and follow-up program of both formal and informal support.

Len Untereiner, president of Spirit Keeper, said the society is currently facing some funding difficulties but is trying to secure a safe house for aboriginal youth seeking to escape the city's gang culture.

"We're dealing with about 60 kids on a regular basis on the street level that want to get out of gangs and we have a deal going to have a safe house in the next few weeks to accommodate some of them."

# NATIVE FILM DIRECTOR SHARES NEW VISION

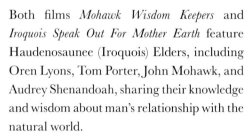

**By Dan Smoke**                    **Published May, 2002**

Two Native American films were shown in Toronto on May 27. Both featured elders sharing their wisdom on respecting and protecting Mother Earth for our future generations. Mohawk director, producer and environmental activist Danny Beaton was present for the screening.

Both films *Mohawk Wisdom Keepers* and *Iroquois Speak Out For Mother Earth* feature Haudenosaunee (Iroquois) Elders, including Oren Lyons, Tom Porter, John Mohawk, and Audrey Shenandoah, sharing their knowledge and wisdom about man's relationship with the natural world.

Welcoming more than two hundred guests to the film screening, Beaton introduced his teacher/advisor, Robertjohn Knapp, Seneca elder and the subject of his next film project, *The Second Thanksgiving*. This film, currently in post-production, was filmed on the Six Nations Reserve.

Both Beaton and Knapp shared their vision of a future world requiring a supreme transformation in our relationship with Mother Earth.

Knapp is a spiritual leader from California, who has been a Sundancer for 30 years.

He brought spiritual teachings into the federal prisons and has been a leader in the struggle for unity amongst all Native Americans. He says, "I believe love is very simple, it's a decision to care or not."

"My effort here is to share with you some things...and bring us together with one mind to create a spiritual force To change the attitudes

so we quit hurting each other... quit hurting the earth," explains Knapp.

He asserts that life is about healing or hurting and our choice between the two:

"Water, air, fire, earth...each has two elements... because they can heal or hurt. We are the water, the air, the fire and the earth. We are made up of those four things. So in that way, we can decide – are we about the healing or the hurting."

*Danny Beaton*
*Photo: Film Assistant*

The sundance taught Knapp how to offer himself in a good way to humanity. "It is his prayer that also has two elements – one to ask and the second to give thanks. So, we are praying all the time whenever we do this ceremony," he says. He learnt from the elders and the ceremonies that "...you only have one decision in life. You have free will, with only one decision to make – stay awake, or go to sleep. If you're awake, then you cannot deny the truth, so there is no decision. But, if you're asleep, anger, jealousy, drugs, alcohol prevail and your decision was to blindfold yourself to deny the truth. So when you see the truth, you can't deny it, it is what it is!"

Beaton has four films that have aired on national television including *Indigenous Restoration* in 1991.

"I've been working with these elders who are in the films for 12 years. The reason for these films is because our elders are speaking out for the sacredness of Mother Earth."

Beaton believes in the way of life of our ancestors and that's why he films Elders. He says the Elders maintain, and are the protectors of, our culture. He has been attending the Youth/Elders Gatherings for the past twelve years and is their official photographer.

This year's ceremonies will take place on Ted Turner's ranch in Montana in August.

"Robertjohn's father is from Six Nations but he was raised in California and has worked with Leon Shenandoah, Thomas Banyaca and works with Corbin Harney, Joe Chasing Horse and others today," said Beaton about why he was working with Knapp.

The working title *The Second Thanksgiving* refers to the spiritual nourishment given by First Nations people to non-Native people "in the same way we provided physical nourishment to the people on the Mayflower and Columbus's voyages."

"We're feeding the non-Native people our spiritual way of life," explained Beaton.

Photo: Danny Beaton

" *Water, air, fire, earth...each has two elements... because they can heal or hurt. We are the water, the air, the fire and the earth. We are made up of those four things. So in that way, we can decide – are we about the healing or the hurting.* "

**Robertjohn Knapp**

# THE WILD HORSES OF THE NEMAIAH VALLEY

**By Lloyd Dolha**                               **Published July, 2000**

Photos courtesy of Friends of the Nemaiah Valley

They are a rare race of wild horses. Descended from the original Colonial Spanish stallions that escaped in Mexico in 1519, they spread through the United States to interior British Columbia's Chilcotin plateau. Once abundant, they are now faced with extinction.

Threatened by a Ministry of Forests (MOF) plan to clearcut 1.3 million hectares of beetle-infested lodgepole pine, the Xeni Gwet'in First Nation Government and the environmentalist group, Friends of the Nemaiah Valley, are launching a campaign to protect the horses. They want to create western Canada's first wild horse sanctuary in the isolated Brittany Triangle – home of the vibrant horse culture of the Xeni Gwet'in people.

On May 16, the Friends of the Nemaiah Valley released a preliminary conservation assessment of the Rainshadow Wild Horse Ecosystem of the Brittany Triangle.

The report's author, wildlife biologist Wayne McCory, provided a preliminary assessment of habitat and conservation values for the grizzly bear, the North American black bear, the wild or feral horse, salmon and other wildlife in the Brittany Triangle.

"The rare horses of the Brittany need full protection if they are to survive," said David Williams of the Friends of the Nemaiah Valley. "This is why we will work with the Xeni Gwet'in First Nation to kick off a campaign to save this area."

*Friends of the Nemaiah Valley… want to create western Canada's first wild horse sanctuary in the isolated Brittany Triangle – home of the vibrant horse culture of the Xeni Gwet'in people.*

The "wild" or feral horse is a herbivore that has returned to ancestral behavioural patterns and now has a survival-oriented life cycle.

The Triangle is formed by the natural boundries of the Chilko and Taseko Rivers, approximately 120 kilometres southwest of Williams Lake. It is approximately 155,000 hectares in size, within a large foothills plateau that is the traditional territory of the Xeni Gwetin. It supports six natural vegetation types that provide varied and abundant plant food sources for the horses. Grizzly and black bears, wolves, mountain lions, Canadian lynx and mule deer also inhabit the area. At higher elevations, California bighorn sheep flourish. The Chilko and Taseko Rivers support·large runs of Sockeye, Coho and Chinook salmon. The average run of Sockeye in the Chiko River is 1.7 million – 27 per cent of the entire Fraser River run. Elkin Creek has an average run of about 600 Chinook. These salmon – and the horses – add to the food supply for carnivores and omnivores, wolves, mountain lions and bears. The Triangle forms a natural corridor, a large intact wilderness with high security for large carnivores.

McCory estimates that 14 bands of wild horses, comprising 140 to 200 animals, inhabit the Triangle. For the past 200 years, the horses have been regarded as a nuisance and shot in government-sanctioned kills. On occasion, they are also shot by local ranchers. Unbelievably, there is no law protecting these rare and magnificent beasts.

The Xeni Gwetin First Nations practice a horse culture and strongly identify themselves with the wild horses. They conduct periodic roundups and train the animals for their own use. The wild horses are both an economic and spiritual resource to the tribe. A main feature of the annual Xeni Gwetin rodeo is a mountain race in which skilled riders race at breakneck

*For the past 200 years, the horses have been regarded as a nuisance and shot in government-sanctioned kills.*

speeds on horses specifically trained for the race. Many band members still use horses to hunt for game, on historic trails.

There is only one road into the Brittany Triangle, built in 1973. The people still speak Chilcotin first and English second.

In 1989, The Xeni Gwet'in First Nation declared their traditional territory protected as the Nemaiah Aboriginal Wilderness Preserve, a declaration ignored by past and present provincial governments. The Nuntsi Provincial Park, established in 1995, comprises 20,898 hectares. The Chilko Lake Provincial Park comprises 247,000 hectares.

The Rainshadow Wild Horse Ecosystem (RWHE) is partially protected by these two parks. Nuntsi is in the southeast section of the RWHE, while a small area of the Chiko Lake park protects the southwest corner. However, there were no provisions made in the 1994 land use plan for a protected corridor between the two isolated parks. In this corridor, extensive logging plans are now in place and large areas of the Aboriginal Preserve, outside the Brittany Triangle, have been logged since the 1989 declaration.

Several forest companies have made applications to build a bridge across the Chilko,

*One of two wild horse herds studied in Nuntsi Provincial Park in 2001.*

*I*n 1989, The Xeni Gwet'in First Nation declared their traditional territory protected as the Nemaiah Aboriginal Wilderness Preserve, a declaration ignored by past and present provincial governments.

upstream from its confluence with the Taseko, to provide logging access to the Brittany Triangle Resource Management Zone. Large areas of clearcutting and road building are planned. If nothing is done to enhance the protection of the wild horses, these protected areas could eventually become "islands of extinction" as clearcut logging and road networks accelerate across the Chilcotin plateau.

The only obstacle facing the clearcut of the Brittany Triangle is a lawsuit scheduled to go before the BC Supreme Court in September of 2002, in which the Xeni Gwetin will argue a claim to aboriginal title as per Delgamuukw.

" To us the Brittany is already a sanctuary for the wild horses, for the people," said Chief Roger William of the Xeni Gwet'in. "It has been the way it is since before European contact and today it's still the same. Our forefathers before us used and trained these wild horses. These wild horses, being a part of us, are something we don't want to lose."

The campaign to create a wild horse preserve in the Brittany Triangle will be launched at a ceremony in the Nemaiah Valley on June 6, 2002.

# THE GANG THAT COULDN'T SHOOT STRAIGHT

## OR,

## WHY THE BC LIBERALS DROPPED THE LEGAL CHALLENGE TO THE NISGA'A TREATY

**By Lloyd Dolha**
**Published September 2001**

It's a good thing for Premier Campbell and his provincial Liberal cronies that they dropped their continuing court challenge to the constitutionality of the self-government provisions of the Nisga'a treaty which came into effect in May 2000.

The court challenge that was launched three years ago bombed big-time in the BC Supreme court on all grounds in *Campbell v. British Columbia (A.G.) 2000*.

In his judgement of July 24, 2000, Justice Paul Williamson affirmed the existence of the aboriginal right to self-government.

*The statue of "Justice" standing outside the Supreme Court of Canada*
*Photo: JD Foy*

Campbell and his cronies Geoff Plant and Mike DeJong, as we all know, ended up in the unusual position of suing themselves after they assumed the mantle of provincial power in the spring election of this year.

But more then that, it was a major legal blunder in terms of political strategy in dealing with BC First Nations.

The Liberals argued that the self-government provisions contained in the treaty were unconstitutional because such powers did not survive the division of powers between the federal and provincial governments in 1867, when the first Constitutional Act was passed.

Not only did the BC Supreme Court reject the argument that the treaty created "a third order of government" which amounted to a "permanent abdication of power by Parliament"; it made a number of rulings on the constitutionality of aboriginal self-government and some general principles for guidance, which we can appropriately call the *Campbell* principles after its progenitor, our premier.

Since the ruling will stand unchallenged, it is now the law of the land in BC.

Let's review the court's findings for our greater edification in our future dealings with the new provincial government.

These are:

- aboriginal rights (including governance powers) formed part of the unwritten principles underlying the constitution "long before" their explicit inclusion in the Constitution Act, 1982;

- the division of powers in the Constitution Act, 1867, only distributed those powers held by the colonies at the time. It was not a comprehensive and exhaustive code of governance powers. Powers outside of these existed and were not touched by the Constitution Act 1867. The court further noted that "the object of the division of powers was not to extinguish diversity (or aboriginal rights), but to ensure that the local and distinct needs of Upper and Lower Canada (Ontario and Québec) and the Maritime provinces were protected in the federal system."

- The division of powers was a division "internal to the Crown" and did not alter the structure of Crown-aboriginal relations.

- an aboriginal right of self-government is "akin to a legislative power to make laws" that survived the division of powers in the Constitution Act, 1867, as an unwritten underlying value of the constitution.

- Traditional aboriginal law, while unwritten and customary, is just as much "law" as is legislation.

*T*he court further noted that since aboriginal title was a community right, it "must of necessity include the right of communal ownership to make decisions about… occupation and use [of the land], in matters commonly described as governmental functions.*"*

*W*hat an interesting and fortuitous turn of events. No wonder Campbell pulled the plug on the court challenge.

The court then turned to the relevant case law and derived the following principles:

- the indigenous nations of North America were recognized as political communities;
- the assertion of sovereignty diminished, but did not extinguish aboriginal powers and rights;
- among the powers retained by aboriginal nations was the authority to make treaties binding on their people;
- any interference with the diminished rights with aboriginal people was to be minimal.

The court further noted that since aboriginal title was a community right, it "must of necessity include the right of communal ownership to make decisions about... occupation and use [of the land], in matters commonly described as governmental functions."

It's an extremely important point.

It reduces the distinction between ownership and jurisdiction which the court found to be overlapping concepts.

What an interesting and fortuitous turn of events. No wonder Campbell pulled the plug on the court challenge.

With principles like that spelled out by the BC Supreme Court, what would the Court of Appeal say or for that matter, the Supreme Court of Canada?

Premier Campbell sure shot himself in the foot with that stupid move just to garner support from the Reformist right. The Nisga'a can now sue the province for court costs.

Even though Campbell has reportedly scaled back his proposed reference to the Supreme Court of Canada on the constitutionality of self-government and will now merely seek the court's opinion on the ambit of aboriginal self-government, the opinion of the Supreme Court will definitely make for some good reading for BC First Nations.

It's one of those great moments in the history of a people when the very foundations of power suddenly shudder.

Not only do BC First Nations have the 1997 Delgamuukw principles, which Attorney-General Geoff Plant conceded "were intended to have the force of law even though they [the courts] did order a new trial," now we have the Campbell, 2000, principles on the constitutionality of aboriginal self-government.

Unwritten aboriginal rights, traditional law as much law as legislation. It means that all the old ways can be recognized as part of Canadian law. The time is now for all BC First Nations to redouble their efforts to meet the test set out in Delagamuukw and set aside our differences – a great undertaking that will require the best in all of us. We have to start documenting these "unwritten aboriginal rights."

*I*t's one of those great moments in the history of a people when the very foundations of power suddenly shudder.

*An audit of the federal justice department recently revealed that there are so few lawyers handling the wave of aboriginal rights cases from BC and the Yukon, that the department is overwhelmed by the workload...*

We can't just sit back while our erstwhile leaders run around from meeting to meeting across the nation with their per diems, travel expenses and excessive consultant-level salaries because there's no way that First Nations will ever get a fair shake at the negotiating table. It's all bullshit.

It will take a definitive statement from the Supreme Court. They waffled on aboriginal title and rights as early as *Calder, 1972*, and as recently as *Delgamuukw, 1997*. But they can't keep avoiding the unscrupulous motives of a right-wing gang like the BC Liberals who have no real interest in social justice for First Nations.

It's all ready happening. An audit of the federal justice department recently revealed that there are so few lawyers handling the wave of aboriginal rights cases from BC and the Yukon, that the department is overwhelmed by the workload and are "seriously" under-prepared for bigger projects.

More lawyers have been hired since the September 2000 report, but some experts are saying that no amount will suffice because there are too many aboriginal rights cases going forward to the courts involving treaty rights, land claims, sex abuse claims, fishing rights and others.

There was a great line in *Halfway River First Nation, 1999*, in which the BC Court of Appeal found the Ministry of Forests had a positive duty to determine the extent of the Halfway Beaver people's right to hunt. We all have a positive duty to assert aboriginal rights on traditional territories.

We all have a positive duty to assert aboriginal rights on the traditional territories. First Nations have to get out there and become a real presence on the land in ways previously unimagined or that need to be relearned from the few elders we have left.

# LEGACY OF A LEGEND: CHIEF JOE MATHIAS

**By Lloyd Dolha**                                        **Published April, 2000**

More than 2,000 people came to mourn the passing of Squamish Chief Joe Mathias on Wednesday, March 15, at the Squamish Recreational Centre in North Vancouver.

The sudden passing of 57-year-old Mathias for undisclosed reasons on March 10 sent shock waves throughout the Canadian aboriginal community.

The First Nations Summit, the group representing the majority of First Nations in the treaty process that Mathias helped to found and lead, immediately cancelled the final day of a critical three-day meeting, which concerned the state of treaty negotiations in the province. A meeting had been scheduled with recently appointed premier Ujjal Dosanjh.

One of Canada's top advocates of aboriginal rights Chief Mathias was a hereditary chief of his people, a natural leader and a powerful, eloquent speaker.

"Joe Mathias was at the pinnacle of his life, happy with loving friends and family surrounding him. We feel anger, shock and confusion that he was taken from us too soon. There will never be another Joe Mathias," eulogized Wendy John, former chief and close personal friend.

**"***Joe Mathias was at the pinnacle of his life, happy with loving friends and family surrounding him. We feel anger, shock and confusion that he was taken from us too soon. There will never be another Joe Mathias.***"**

**Wendy John, former chief and close personal friend**

A tough negotiator, Mathias was a dominant figure on the national political scene, debating the primacy of aboriginal title and rights with premiers, federal ministers and prime ministers from Pierre Trudeau to Jean Chrétien.

Mathias was a member of the AFN's Constitutional Working Group from 1983 to 1987, participating in three First Ministers Conferences following the adoption of the Canadian Constitution in 1982 as well as numerous federal/provincial meetings on aboriginal rights.

From 1985 to 1990 he was BC Regional Vice-Chief of the Assembly of First Nations. Chief Mathias was also involved with the Assembly of First Nations Constitutional Working Group.

Mathias was appointed to the federal task force reviewing Ottawa's Comprehensive Claims policy. Their work resulted in the 1986 report *Living Treaties; Lasting Agreements*, more commonly know as the Coolican Report, which made recommendations to improve the comprehensive claims negotiation process.

In 1990 and 1991 he served as a member of the tripartite BC Claims Task Force. Their work set out 19 recommendations to establish the current treaty negotiations process and the independent BC Treaty Commission to oversee the process.

Mathias served as co-chair of the First Nations Summit from 1991 until his untimely death.

Chief Joe Mathias was buried in a private ceremony at the Capilano Cemetery in North Vancouver. He is survived by his wife of five years Lisa Yoler Ethens, daughter Stefany Mathias, mother Elizabeth Jacobs and 12 brothers and sisters.

# A Nation Mourns the Passing of a National Métis Hero

**By Tina House**　　　　　　　**Published September, 2003**

## A tribute to Fred House 1942 – 2003

The nation mourns the death of the great Métis leader Fred House. His sudden passing on September 29, 2003 marks a monumental chapter in the life of a national Métis hero. Fred was a father, friend, mentor, role model and a well-respected political leader. At the age of 61 he had lived more lifetimes one than most people dream of. He instilled pride and empowered thousands of people to stand up and fight for their inherent Aboriginal rights and recognition. His tenacious and ambitious

spirit combined with the confidence and flair of a wise spoken leader allowed him the opportunity to address Prime Ministers and other leaders on behalf of the Métis people in Canada. Fred believed strongly in self-government for Aboriginal people. He will be forever remembered for his musical talents, easy-going personality, confidence and brilliant mind.

He was a born leader. At the age of twenty-seven he was first elected Provincial

*Fred House and his proud daughter Tina House at the National Aboriginal Achievement Awards in Edmonton, Alberta, March 2001*

*Photo: Tina House*

President of the BC Association of Non-Status Indians and was re-elected consecutively for the next five years. BCANSI was co-founded by his late mother Anne House in 1969 and was the first Métis organization established to represent the non-status Indians and Métis people across BC. During the next decade the organization grew to over 70 chapters across BC and provided many successful programs and services for thousands of people such as social, economic, educational and housing development programs.

In 1978 he became the Founder and President of the Louis Riel Métis Association, a position he held for the next ten years. In 1996 he was elected as vice-president for the Métis Provincial Council of BC.

During his political career Fred was one of the highest profiled Aboriginal leaders in Canadian history. His hard work and determination in lobbying for the rights of the Métis people is evident in many successful organizations and programs that still exist today.

In 2001 Fred received the prestigious *Community Development Award* from the National Aboriginal Achievement Awards, which aired nationally on CBC television.

Fred's daughter Tina is initiating a series of projects in honour of his life and legacy. These include a *Life & Time's Video Biography* and the completion of a book entitled *The History & Legacy of the Métis* that was started by her father. The sales of the video and book will be used towards *The Fred House Trust Fund*. The Trust Fund will invest into the establishment of a *National Aboriginal Leaders Monument* to be placed in Ottawa in honour of her father and other Aboriginal leaders who have fought and died for Aboriginal Rights in this country. The fund will also provide funding for leadership and talent development programs.

For further information, donations or to purchase a copy of the video and/or book:

Contact: Tina House

C/O The Aboriginal Film Industry Development Society

Tel: (604) 736 – 3321

Email: tafids@telus.net

# THROUGH EAGLE EYES

**By Tina House – October 27, 2003**

*Through eagle eyes I see,*
*Flying high in the sky above the trees,*
*I feel the wind brush across my face,*
*Knowing that you are in a heavenly place,*

*I am grateful for the many times we shared,*
*Always with a smile, I know how much you cared,*
*Your magical presence was like a bright starry night,*
*Forever shining like the great northern lights,*

*I was always so proud that you were such a great man,*
*When I watched you on tv and always won every election in which you ran,*
*Your passion for life will always remind me,*
*How much we are to be proud that we are Métis,*

*Now I follow in your path in my own way,*
*Knowing that everything you have taught me will pay off one day,*
*The time has come for me to be strong,*
*I know that you are with me and this is where I belong.*

# MARGARET VICKERS HER STORY OF HEALING

**by Cher Bloom**
**Published July, 2002**

In the contemporary British Columbia Aboriginal Movement, there has hardly been a change implemented in the last thirty years, which has not been touched by the strong, firm, determined but gentle hand of Margaret Vickers. A professional psychotherapist, teacher, healer, singer, designer, artist, athlete, and advocate for the rights of Aboriginal people in many parts of the world, this sensitive woman's clear vision and influence have made her an unsung icon of her generation.

She was born Margaret Ruth Vickers on July 3, 1949, eldest daughter and third born of seven children, into the Eagle tribe of Lach Lan, (the village of Kitkatla) on Dolphin Island. At this time, Natives were considered "non-citizens" of Canada. "At my birth, they used forceps to pull me out. Thus started my struggle with professional medical people for the rest of my life."

*"Margaret means Pearl — it begins with a small agitation and results in a treasure."*

Photo: Cher Bloom

**"*I've always listened to the elders. In my childhood, their words were more important than textbooks.*"**

"I've always listened to the elders. In my childhood, their words were more important than textbooks. At ten, I went to the elders on both my mother's and father's sides. It was the first time I'd met my mother's Vancouver family. I wondered why they were so white, and why they hadn't been part of my childhood. I discovered that neither of my parent's famililies had agreed with the marriage. My mother lost her Canadian citizenship and became a status Indian. Grace was the first white woman to be elected chief counselor of the community."

*Margaret and her brother Matt*

In Edmonton, in 1978, Margaret opened the Eagle Down Gallery, the first Native Indian owned and operated art gallery in Alberta. "Natives use eagle down for ritual cleansing and healing, the same way the Roman Catholics use incense. When eagle down is spread around in ceremony, it means 'Peace be with you.' Participants leave unresolved issues outside the longhouse, they listen and observe. Later, if someone has trouble, they remember the ceremony and know what to do."

Margaret sponsored fifty Canadian Native artists including her eldest brother Roy, who held his first exhibition at her gallery. "Since people weren't used to traditional West Coast art, the gallery became a learning experience for everyone. Many of the gallery's best patrons were Jewish. They contributed hugely to the gallery's success. During that time Margaret created and co-hosted 20-minute educational, promotional television programs featuring the artists, and later co-founded the Edmonton Art Gallery Group for promotion.

"Years ago, Aboriginal artists sculpted stone. The book *Stone Images of B.C.*, by the late Wilson Duff, gave 30,000 years of history to B.C. First Nations. The mask on the cover is from Kitkatla. Wilson Duff had been the Curator of Ethnology at the B.C. Museum. He was the visionary white man who set up the Museum of Anthropology at U.B.C. He requested my help with my people's spiritual history. He later committed suicide. He wished to reincarnate as a First Nations person from Haida Gwai or the Tsimshian Nation."

> **"***Buffy became one of my first teachers in Alberta. That night onstage, she said, 'For all you radicals out there, first get the facts straight before you shoot off your mouth!'***"**

In 1977, Buffy Ste. Marie headlined a huge conference in Edmonton. Margaret attended her concert, and was allowed backstage. "I was dressed in contemporary aboriginal clothing, which I had made. I entered with the authority of my lineage. Buffy was interested in meeting me because of my support of Aboriginal art. She told me to "Help them (the artists),... because artists are like prophets, they tell you what is coming. They tell you what the world is like through their own souls and creativity. They tell the dark as well as the light."

"Buffy became one of my first teachers in Alberta. That night onstage, she said, 'For all you radicals out there, first get the facts straight before you shoot off your mouth!'" It was the best advice she could have given. Research the subject as quickly and efficiently as possible, and then negotiate. It was the desire for reconciliation and restitution that led me into intergovernmental relations."

After selling the gallery a couple of years later, Margaret accepted a contract with the B.C. Museum as an artist and consultant. She developed a kit for blind patrons, using the concept of a bent cedar box containing a mask. "I used different textures for the various colours—gravel in the black, which represented the exterior covering of an animal, a bear, wolf or bird,...(so they could feel the formlines). I used a slippery red paint, which represented the interior, the animal's anatomical structure—the inside formlines. People were able to see with their hands, what the mask looked and felt like, what it represented."

In 1982, Margaret set up a volunteer program at Hospice Victoria, incorporating her own experiences with death and dying. For two years, she and others helped hundreds of

*Margaret and her father*
Photo: Cher Bloom

families go through that turmoil. The approach was spiritual but non-religious. "I am Christian but I integrate traditional ritual, beliefs and customs into my offerrings. I don't call myself a Medicine Woman, — other people do."

In 1989, Margaret became the first and only Aboriginal Woman to be on the Premier's Council for Aboriginal Affairs in B.C., under Bill Van der Zalm. "I had to remind him that he came from a culture who wore wooden shoes and reclaimed land from the sea." She helped the Province of BC come to the treaty negotiating table. Prior to that it had been between the Federal government and Aboriginal people.

Margaret had been on death's door three times. In 1972, she fell into a coma in Kitkatla. Her funeral had already been prepared. In 1975, Margaret again became comatose, this time in Victoria. In this state, she met her dead ancestors. It happened a third time in 1990. "That was a turning point for me. I had come out of a sauna in Skidigate, Haida Gwai, and again fallen into a coma. I met my Mom's mom, who sang to me, and my Dad's dad, who had been killed by a drunk white driver in Prince Rupert. They were both peaceful and happy.

"My life flows like a river. I create time for people of all cultures who desire to direct their behaviours and attitudes into channels of healing."

Margaret Vickers owns a small home in the Tsawout Nation in East Saanich. As a result of the Elder's conference held in Saanichton in July, 2002, she has been invited to facilitate healing seminars, in communities throughout BC.

"Margaret means Pearl — it begins with a small agitation and results in a treasure."

# ONE DEAD INDIAN
## THE IPPERWASH CRISIS AND
## THE ROLE OF PREMIER MIKE HARRIS

**One Dead Indian: The Premier, the Police and the Ipperwash Crisis**
**By Peter Edwards**
**Published by Stoddart Publishing Co. Limited, 2001**

**Reviewed by Len O'Connor**                **Published November, 2000**

*Slippery was now on his back. Someone kicked him in the head. Above him and all around him were forms that didn't look human; they were just dark shapes raining blows down on his body. He had no idea how many there were, just that they were everywhere, swarming him.*

He was beaten and yet soon he could no longer feel any pain. He felt only an odd, dull sensation, before everything went black. He lay face down, his mouth full of sound, and the blows kept coming.

Cecil Bernard "Slippery" George would survive the violent beating he took at the hands of the Ontario Provincial Police (OPP) riot squad Tactical and Rescue Unit (TRU), on September 4, 1995 at Ipperwash. Unfortunately his cousin Dudley wasn't so lucky. He was killed on that fatal night and for six years his family have lobbied for an inquiry into his death and the role played by Premier Mike Harris.

*One Dead Indian*, written by investigative journalist Peter Edwards tells the history of the Dudley George murder, a well-chronicled expose on the unwarranted brutality of the OPP against peaceful protesters.

"The Natives first saw the phalanx of officers when the police rounded a corner just outside the park entrance. It was an eerie sight. Under the three-quarter moon more than 30 officers in dark gray were marching upon them in tight ranks known as 'box formation.'"

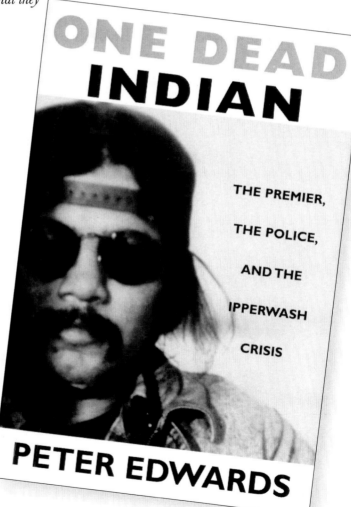

The incident could have been avoided if the OPP had listened to AFN National Chief Ovide Mercredi who requested the police postpone their raid until the next day, which would have given him more time to speak to the protesters. Mercredi was convinced that a confrontation in full daylight had less chance of escalating to violence. The OPP had their own agenda and refused to speak to the AFN chief on the night of September 4, 1995. They had been given orders from the highest office in the province.

Premier Mike Harris denied he was in Toronto on September 4, the first of many lies. He was attending his own benefit party celebrating his election. He also had a meeting that same day with OPP superintendent Ron Fox, a liaison with the Solicitor-General's office and Sergeant Scott Patrick. It was at this meeting that Harris made it clear to the police that the protest at Ipperwash was to be crushed at the cost of whatever action was warranted.

The premier later admitted he was at the meeting but couldn't recall who else attended, and in between memory lapses, he hasn't allowed an inquiry into the incident, which cost the Ontario taxpayers $500,000 in legal fees to keep the case out of court.

The crucial evidence that would either clear Premier Harris or incriminate him was on the files on the meeting of September 4, which should have remained in OPP superintendent Ron Fox's computer, files were requested by the *Globe and Mail,* pursuant to the Freedom of Information Act, by G & M writer Martin Mittelstaedt, who was informed that they had "vanished."

"Efforts by the stall of the Information and Technology division of OPP to retrieve any records which may have been located in the folders were unsuccessful," said deputy Soliciter-General Tim Millard, at the time.

Not only was Millard's department missing files the OPP (claims not to have) had no Polaroid or video record of the arrests that night. There was no audio of Sergeant Ken Deane or any other members of the paramilitary unit responsible for the violence and death at Ipperwash.

This should have been enough to force an inquiry into the shooting death of Dudley George, but the Harris legal team was able to keep Premier Harris a safe distance from the court. Sgt. Ken Deane, the OPP officer in charge on the fatal night went on trial for the murder of Dudley George instead. A veteran police officer, Deane was a senior member of TRU and was highly respected in the OPP force.

---

*T*he OPP… had no Polaroid or video record of the arrests that night. There was no audio of Sergeant Ken Deane or any other members of the paramilitary unit responsible for the violence and death at Ipperwash.

---

> **"** *My brother's life comes too cheap to these people. My brother gets laid in his grave and this guy gets sent home?* **"**
>
> **Dudley's brother Pierre George**

Deane testified that the information police had on the protesters was that they were highly armed and when he saw Dudley George, on the road that night "he thought that Dudley had a rifle.

"He was scanning our position with the rifle. I discharged approximately three rounds at the individual. He faltered, fell to the ground, got up, threw his weapon back to the ditch area," said Deane.

Sgt. Hebblethwaite's testimony not only contradicted Deane's, it left the judge doubting any of Deane's story, Constable Cris Crossitt's testimony was in the judge's words "clearly fabricated and plausible."

Sgt. Deane was found guilty and, for the George family, there was a small sense of retribution which only lasted until the sentencing.

Justice Hugh Fraser handed down a conditional two years less a day, to community service and he could possess a firearm once the sentence is completed.

Sgt. Deane will not even suffer the inconvience of house arrest.

"My brother's life comes too cheap to these people. My brother gets laid in his grave and this guy gets sent home?" said Dudley's brother Pierre.

*A Call For Answers* is one of the chapters in *One Dead Indian* and author Peter Edwards has done an excellent job in showing in great detail both the First Nation and police account of what actually happened.

The fact remains that the OPP did use excessive force that was uncalled for, resulting in Dudley George's death, and that Mike Harris walked away without even an inquiry.

*T he incident could have been avoided if the OPP had listened to AFN National Chief Ovide Mercredi who requested the police postpone their raid until the next day, which would have given him more time to speak to the protesters.*

## ABORIGINAL ACHIEVEMENT AWARD WINNER

# TINA KEEPER

## ARTS AND CULTURE – MANITOBA

**Reprinted with permission from the NAAF**

You can't hear the phrase North of 60 without thinking of Tina Keeper's portrayal of Lynx River's RCMP constable, Michelle Kenidi. Keeper's portrayal of Kenidi on the highly rated CBC series was credited with garnering much of the show's success. "A dream come true television series," is how she describes *North of 60*. Keeper describes Kenidi as "a woman who made a decision to gain control of her life as the result of her pain and struggle. She sought a sense of order, so she became a Mountie – she believes that law and order and a strong sense of community will save Lynx River from itself." Tina was born in Northern Manitoba and moved to Winnipeg with her family when she was four. She completed the acting program at the University of Manitoba while working on a history/theatre double major. In 1982, her sister drafted her into helping with wardrobe for an Aboriginal theatre group. This led to work as a stage manager and later to performing. Keeper supplemented her stage work with mime, improvisation and dance. After only two film parts – one in a NFB short and the other in *Smoked Lizard Lips* – she landed the lead in *North of 60*. The rest is history. She received a Gemini for Best Actress in 1994. She has been a host of the Sharing Circle and Hot Topics and gives much of her time to supporting community-based initiatives and serving as a role model and inspiration to Aboriginal young people.

# INQUIRY INTO THE DEATH OF SASKATOON TEEN

**By Frank Larue**     **Published January, 2004**

The Saskatchewan government says it will hold a public inquiry into the death of Neil Stonechild, a 17-year-old aboriginal teen found frozen to death on the outskirts of Saskatoon more than 12 years ago.

Saskatchewan's newly appointed justice Minister Eric Cline announced the judicial inquiry on February 20, citing unresolved concerns about the way the teen died and the manner in which the Saskatoon city police handled the subsequent investigation.

"I think it necessary because we know that Mr. Stonechild had contact with the police quite close to the time of his passing," said Cline.

"That fact needs to be inquired into so that the public and the family can be assured that all the circumstances surrounding his death are brought to light."

Stonechild's mother, Stella Bignell, has always suspected something terrible happened to her son who was found near the city's prison with only one shoe on, dead from hypothermia.

"I knew he didn't go out there on his own. I knew that something had happened. I just didn't know who or how or why and I still don't know that," said Bignell.

*Left: Neil Stonechild at home.*
*Photo: Noel Martin*

*Below: Neil Stonechild as he was found.*
*Photo: Public*

*Roy said he saw him later that night in a police cruiser, his face bloodied, handcuffed and yelling: "They're going to kill me."*

Bignell said she remembers the night her son disappeared like it was yesterday.

"There was a blizzard that night. I remember telling him to stay inside," she recalled. "I said 'Don't go anywhere, stay put,' but he was going with his friends.

"He said, 'Mom, I'll be fine. You know where I am.' He hugged and kissed me and he left."

## FOUL PLAY SUSPECTED

The teen's family has always maintained that foul play was involved, but Stonechild's death was ruled accidental by the Saskatoon police at the time he was found in November 1990.

One of his friends said he last saw Stonechild in police custody. Jason Roy said the two were partying the night he disappeared, but the two were separated during the night.

Roy said he saw him later that night in a police cruiser, his face bloodied, handcuffed and yelling: "They're going to kill me."

It was the last time anyone admitted to seeing Stonechild alive. His body was found five days later. Roy said he reported the incident twice to the police, but they never followed up on the report.

The death of Neil Stonechild received the renewed attention as part of the largest RCMP task force in the history of Saskatchewan.

The RCMP task force into the conduct of the Saskatoon city police began after an unemployed bricklayer, Darrel Night, walked into police headquarters in February 2000 and filed a complaint.

Night said police picked him up after a drunken brawl. He was handcuffed and driven to a field near a power plant. Dressed in only a jean jacket, Night said the police threw him out of the car and drove off, shouting racist remarks at him.

Night ran to the power plant where he banged on the door until a night watchman let him in to call for a cab. It was -26 Celsius.

The week before, the partially frozen body of 25-year-old Rodney Naistus was found by a member of the provincial legislature out for her daily run in an industrial park in the city's west end. His brother and some friends, that celebrated his release from the Saskatoon Correctional Centre the night before, were the last to see him.

Five days later, the body of Lawrence Wegner, a 30-year-old college student was found near the same power plant that Night had reported being ejected by the police.

After investigating the Darrel Night case, two Saskatoon police officers (Constables Dan Hatchen and Ken Munson) were charged with unlawful confinement and assault by the Saskatchewan Justice Ministry in 2001.

*The week before, the partially frozen body of 25-year-old Rodney Naistus was found by a member of the provincial legislature out for her daily run in an industrial park in the city's west end.*

*F* *ive days later, the body of Lawrence Wegner, a 30-year-old college student was found near the same power plant that Night had reported being ejected by the police.*

No charges were laid in the cases of Naistus and Wegner. Currently, three other deaths under similar circumstances, are under investigation by the RCMP.

## TIMELINES TO BE SET FOR INQUIRY

Justice David Wright of the Queen's Court Bench has been appointed to head the Stonechild inquiry. Justice minister Cline said timelines are to be set once Wright and commission counsel Joel Hesje work out the administrative details.

The Federation of Saskatchewan Indian Nations said they are pleased that another inquest has been called, but are afraid that little will come of it.

"We're pleased ... that they have actually moved on the search for answers, but is this just going to be another process and investigation where we come away with nothing?" asked FSIN Vice-Chief Lawrence Joseph.

Constable Dave Haye, vice-president of the Saskatoon Police Association said that the union also welcomes the inquiry.

"We've been expecting an inquiry on this matter for a while and we're glad it's going to be a public inquiry as opposed to a coroner's inquest," said Haye.

"We want the public to feel confident with us and if this is one of the ways we can accomplish that, then this is what should happen," he said.

## POLICE TRY TO EASE COMMUNITY TENSION

Saskatoon police have tried to ease tensions with the city's aboriginal population in recent years. There is a weekly game of basketball between members of the police union and a local native team, as well as canoe and hiking trips for aboriginal children organized by the force. About one in nine officers on the police force are aboriginal. There is a special liason officer and a First Nations advisory committee.

Nevertheless, the overall statistics are grim. Although aboriginals comprise about 15 percent of the city's 200,000 plus population, they are charged with 50 percent of the crimes and comprise 75 percent of the inmates in the local prison.

Minister Cline cautioned that the purpose of the inquiry "is not to determine civil or criminal responsibility," but he did not rule out the possibility of criminal charges.

*C* *onstable Dave Haye, vice-president of the Saskatoon Police Association said that the union also welcomes the inquiry.*
*"We've been expecting an inquiry on this matter for a while and we're glad it's going to be a public inquiry as opposed to a coroner's inquest."*

> **"** *Through this inquiry, I just hope and pray that it never happens to another parent or any family member. I hope that something will come out of it.* **"**     **Stella Bignell**

"It is always possible that if more facts come to light criminal charges could be laid," said the minister. "If that occurred, then the judicial inquiry would have to be brought to a halt," said Cline.

*Neil Stonechild's body being removed*

Stella Bignell said she is optimistic about the inquiry, but knows it will be difficult to watch.

"I'm glad that it is going where it is going, but I'm also feeling the emotion of losing him again. I can't talk about it without breaking down, especially when I see his picture on TV," said Bignell from her home in Cross Lake, Manitoba.

Bignell said that she will be at the inquiry every day no matter where it is held. The government of Saskatchewan has agreed to pay for her expenses.

"I know there is not going to be closure. You can't find closure when you lose a son or child," she said.

"Through this inquiry, I just hope and pray that it never happens to another parent or any family member. I hope that something will come out of it."

# A MOTHER'S PRAYER FOR SON'S SAFE RETURN

**By George Paul**

**Published April, 2004**

A mother's prayer for her son's or daughter's safe return home echoes throughout the Mi'kmaq Nations of Atlantic Canada and Québec.

The Iraqi War may be far from home, but the harsh reality of war for most Mi'kmaq communities is real and terrifying.

Before there were provinces and borders, the Mi'kmaq people were scattered around what is today eastern Canada. After all the hardships the Mi'kmaq have gone through in the last 400 years, close ties to America still exist.

The 1794 Jay Treaty between George Washington's 13 Colonies and the Mi'kmaq and Maliceet Nations enables Mi'kmaq and Maliceet to freely pass borders. Today First Nations communities across Canada can live freely in America without following immigration laws.

A time-honored tradition of Mi'kmaq men and women enlisting in the American Services (more often the U.S. Marines) represents great honor and prestige within Mi'kmaq communities. Growing up in a Mi'kmaq community young men and women always had the option of enlisting in the United States military.

*Elaine Denny with a picture of her son Charles Francis Jr.*

Photo: George Paul

For one Mi'kmaq family in Eskasoni that option wasn't welcomed but accepted. This is one story of a family coping with a son, a big brother, a role model, in the forefront of the Iraqi War.

Three years ago, at this time, Elaine Denny, a single mother of four, reluctantly said good-bye to his oldest son Charles Francis Jr. Like every mother, Elaine did not want her baby boy to leave home. But Charles, then 20 years old, set his sights on the U.S. Marines and nothing was going to get in his way.

After boot camp Elaine noticed a great change in Charles's attitude. "When he came back, there was a big difference," said Elaine. "He was more sure of himself, confident and he told his brothers to listen to Mom."

Elaine knew Charles had made the right choice in life.

But on September 11 the whole world changed. The war against terrorism eventually led the United States to declare war upon Iraqi President, Saddam Hussein. Then this Christmas Elaine knew something was going on.

Now a Corporal, Charles' Christmas break was abruptly cut when he was told to return to base as soon as possible. Events prior already had Elaine concerned. Charles asked his good friend Nicholas Basque, if he could borrow his late father's U.S. Marine ring. Upon discovering this news, Elaine was in tears, firmly holding Nicholas in her arms saying, "Your father will watch over my son."

Nicholas' father, Will Basque, was a proud Mi'kmaq Sma'knis (soldier) who represented the Mi'kmaq Nation with great honor. Will Basque was a decorated U.S. Marine Veteran of the Vietnam War. He died more than five years ago.

Charles never told his mom that war was about to break out, "He probably didn't want to upset me," said Elaine.

A February 27th letter from Charles confirmed war was soon to begin:

"Well, I'm in Kuwait right now, waiting on our orders to launch the attack on Iraq," wrote Charles. Charles' last letter, dated March 8, said that he was adapting to his environment and missed everyone in Eskasoni.

No word was heard from Charles until Wednesday, April 2nd.

## CHARLES' WHERE-ABOUTS

Elaine knows that Charles is with the Second Battalion 8th Marine along with two other Mi'kmaq Marines, Ronnie Augustine from Indian Brook and Danny Boy Stevens from Millbrook at Nasiriya, Iraq.

Confirmed sources also said the Mi'kmaq men's Battalion also played a major role in the rescue operations of Jessica Lynch, a POW since March 23. The Second Battalion 8th Marine created the diversion for special operations forces of Navy SEALs, Army Rangers and Air Force combat controllers to rescue Lynch at the Nasiriya Hospital.

On CBS This Morning Danny gave a message to his mother saying that the boys are OK.

Elaine was excited to get the message.

# FAMILY SUPPORT

The march to Baghdad is near. The United States is expecting greatest resistance from Iraqi Forces and civilians. Elaine is fearful for his son's safety but gives great credit to the entire community's support and prayers.

"Eskasoni has great people," said Elaine. "People are coming up to me and asking me how I'm doing. And that they are praying for me and Charles. I don't feel alone."

Elaine supports the war and the United States troops. What keeps Elaine strong is what Charles said to her, "I'm in it so you could sleep good, Mom.'

"I believe what my child says," says Elaine

Siblings of Charles are proud of him. Katelyn, 14, looks up to big brother and wants to follow in his footsteps. "He's a role model. I'd like to go into the marines also but Mom won't let me," said Katelyn.

Younger brother Brandon, 21, who is in his third year at UCCB says, "I'm proud of my brother and I hope he comes home safe."

Brandon also emphasized, "But I don't support Bushes actions. It's all just about oil."

Elaine wrapped yellow ribbons, representing hope, around her yard.

She is also waiting for a poster of the Mi'kmaq Flag and the American Flag side by side with the inscription, "God Bless Our Mi'kmaq Troops."

# CANADA'S MILITARY ROLE

In times of war, many Natives have signed up for the Canadian military. At least 4,000 volunteered in the First World War, another 3,000 served in the Second World War and several hundred went to Korea.

In the First World War it is estimated that 93 percent of eligible men from Mi'kmaq communities served for Canada. Many Mi'kmaq men died for Canada.

It is not certain how many Mi'kmaq men and women are currently in the U.S. Military but these are the numbers collected; Eskasoni- 2, Big Cove, NB- 2, Indian Brook, NS- 3, Millbrook, NS- 5, Listuguj, Québec- 2, Burnt Church, NB- 5, and Waycobah- 2; a total of 21 Mi'kmaq men and women. Other reports state there are 29 Mi''kmaq.

To send words of support to Elaine and her family email her at elainedenny@msn.com.

# YUKON MAN CHARGED WITH MURDER

**By Lloyd Dolha**                     **Published February, 2004**

A Yukon man accused of the killing of American Indian Movement activist Anna Mae Pictou Aquash almost 30 years ago is fighting his extradition to the United States.

On March 1, a Canadian judge granted a delay in extradition proceedings against John Boy Graham. The extradition hearing was sheduled to take place, but won't occur until March 29, 2004. U.S. authorities want Graham to be released to face trial in South Dakota.

"The States (are) going to come up with their case and we're going to put up our defense," said Graham. "We're going to fight this to the end. They're not going to pull another Peltier on us."

Graham is to be charged with the murder of the well-known aboriginal activist. The AIM leader was shot in the back of the head in December 1975.

Her decomposed body was found on the Pine Ridge reservation in February 1976. She was among the Indian militants who occupied the village of Wounded Knee for 71 days in 1973.

Graham has consistantly denied his involvement in the murder.

A father of eight, Graham, who has been living in Vancouver for years, was charged on March 30, 2003, along with Arlo Looking Cloud, now a 49-year-old chronic and homeless alcoholic.

A federal jury found Looking Cloud guilty of the murder of Aquash on February 2, 2004. Jurors heard how Looking Cloud and two others took Aquash from Denver, Colorado to South Dakota.

Looking Cloud admitted to being present when Aquash was shot. Witnesses for the prosecution said AIM leaders were responsible for Aquash's death. The jury deliberated for seven hours before reaching their verdict. Looking Cloud will be sentenced April 23rd.

Zand faces a mandatory life prison sentence.

Graham was released on $75,000 bail on January 16, and has been living under house arrest. He was arrested in Vancouver in December of last year.

His lawyer, Terry Laliberte, said he knows the reason why charges have been laid now.

"It's a political situation," said Laliberte. "There's been a change in the leadership, it seems, of the American Indian Movement. People have different vested interests in the United States."

"From what I've seen, from the information that's been provided to me, Mr. Graham is being scapegoated in this," he said outside the court.

Laliberte said there isn't one bit of forensic evidence that links John Graham to Aquash's death.

Graham has attacted an international support group that also proclaims his innocence. He has criticized the conviction of Looking Cloud as a "sham."

# CREE FAMILY ACCUSES JUDGE OF RACISM

**By Lloyd Dolha**

**Published May, 2004**

A Saskatchewan judge drew accusations of racism from the family of a young Cree girl, when he ruled she was a willing participant – or even a sexual aggressor – in sexual activity with a 26-year-old man.

On September 4, Dean Edmondson of Melford, Saskatchewan, received a two-year conditional sentence from Justice Fred Kovatch, for sexually assaulting the (then) 12-year-old girl. He will be confined to his home, rather than face a lengthy jail term.

Judge Kovatch said that he couldn't ignore allegations by the defense that the girl was raised in an abusive home environment. Earlier testimony suggested the girl was frequently abused by her father. During the trial, the girl's underwear was submitted as evidence. Semen belonging to the girl's father was found on it. That evidence, said Kovatch, supported the defense theory that the girl may have been the sexual aggressor.

In September 2001, Edmondson and two friends had been drinking heavily and driving the backwoods country roads near Tisdale; where they came upon the 89-pound girl in front of a local bar. The girl accepted a ride from the three men, all in their twenties, who gave her several beers to drink.

According to testimony, the girl ended up in Edmondson's lap and the two kissed. Shortly thereafter, the truck pulled over and the two attempted to have sex, but Edmondson could not obtain an erection. The other two men also attempted to have sex with the girl but failed as well.

In May, Edmondson was convicted of being party to a sexual assault. His two companions were acquitted in a separate trial. The charge carries a maximum sentence of 14 years in prison.

Kovatch noted that similar sexual assault crimes almost always carry extreme penalties.

"I think it's clear from the authorities that a conditional sentence would be rare indeed," said Kovatch.

The judge then noted earlier testimony that suggested the girl was often abused by her father. He quoted testimony by a pediatrician who said that an abused child may show "unpredictable sexual behaviour."

This suggests the girl may have been a "willing participant" or "the aggressor" in the incident, he said.

"That in no way condones Mr. Edmondson's conduct, [but] in my opinion is a factor in sentencing," said Kovatch.

The judge further noted that the girl got into the men's truck willingly, lied about her age and drank beer.

All of these factors must be taken into

account in sentencing, said Kovatch. It would have been different if the girl had been kidnapped off the street and forced into sexual activity

"No one has any business involving themselves sexually with anyone that age. That being said, there are clearly degrees. There is a difference from a sentencing perspective," said Kovatch. The very unusual facts suggest that a jail term is "not necessarily required."

Defense lawyer Hugh Harradence said the judge made the right decision.

"I think it is justice and it can be defended," he said.

As the judgement was read out, family members and supporters of the now 14-year-old girl stormed out of the courtroom, shouting and accusing the court of racism.

"The young white man was sitting there with the judge protecting him. Who has justice served here? It sure wasn't our aboriginal child," a family spokesperson told reporters outside the courthouse.

One family member, who cannot be named by law, said the sentence reinforces what they already knew.

"This trial has never ever served our aboriginal people. It just goes to show it's a racist system in terms of when it comes to our people. There was a wrong done on our child. The young white man got off scot-free," he said.

Edmondson will have to perform 200 hours of community service, receive alcohol and sexual offender counselling; and pay a $500 fine.

In a brief statement to reporters, Crown prosecutor Gary Parker said he will pass the case file to provincial justice officials in Regina to consider an appeal.

A provincial women's rights organization has also denounced the sentence. The Saskatchewan Action Committee for the Status of Women has been following the case.

"This is a travesty of justice," said Kripa Sekhar, executive director. "This is a verdict against all children in Canada. We should all be very concerned."

Sekhar said her organization will write letters of complaint against the judge and will lobby the provincial Minister of Justice to investigate the manner in which the case was prosecuted.

# OSOYOOS CHIEF CLARENCE LOUIE IS TAKING CARE OF BUSINESS

**By Lloyd Dolha**                    **Published July, 2003**

With nine businesses earning more than $800,000 per year, the Osoyoos Indian Band and its Chief Clarence Louie, are indeed noteworthy in the aboriginal community.

British Columbia entrepreneur Chief Clarence Louis is this year's National Aboriginal Achievement Award winner in the business and commerce category. Chief Louis is among 14 recipients to win the Aboriginal community's highest honour.

"I consider myself a "worker" for OIB. All awards are about the band not about me. I work

*A prime example of the new entrepreneurial class is Chief Clarence Louie of the Osoyoos Indian Band in southern British Columbia.*

*Photo: Richard Lorenzen*

for OIB and OIB has done great things in socio-economic development. But we still have a long ways to go, so the award is great recognition for the band. When I got the news about the award I thought that it is great exposure for OIB and it's businesses," said Chief Louie.

Chief Clarence Louie of the Osoyoos Indian Band has decreased the need for social assistance to almost nil by creating jobs and an economic infrastructure through the establishment of eight businesses that he created and manages. Since the mid-90s the band's welfare branch has been reduced more than half.

These businesses include, a golf course, a construction company, a forestry company, a vineyard, a convenience store, a residential and agriculture leasing company and a winery that recently came out with its first batch of ice-wine. Today, these businesses employ more than 140 people.

The businesses leverage a new stream of revenue to fund costly medications for community members, an adult-in-home care program, a recreational complex, an education fund and a patient travel fund.

Chief Louie was first elected chief of the Osoyoos Indian Band back in 1985. Since becoming chief, Louie has constantly emphasized economic development to improve his people's lot in life. In 1998, he founded the Osoyoos Indian Band Development

*Chief Clarence Louie at the opening of the new Nk'Mip winery*
Photo: Richard Lorenzen

*B esides being a full-time chief, Chief Louie is a member of the federal government's First Nations Forestry Program, the National Child Benefit Committee, and the BC government's Native Economic Development Advisory Board.*

Corporation, serving as its president and CEO. The corporation continues to seek out new economic opportunities for his people.

"When I was a kid the Rez only had one company, Inkameep Vineyards. For most youth, their first job was roughing it in the vineyard, which was a good first tough experience. Work started at 5:00 a.m., so when there were school breaks most youth had to go to work in the vineyard, which made most think school wasn't so bad. Everyone went to work when they were 11 or 12, unlike today because of child labor laws. I think it is a good thing when kids start a job at a very young age, it teaches a work ethic," says Louie.

In 1995 OIB became one of the few bands whereby their self generated revenue surpassed that of federal transfer dollars. In 1995 OIB became financially self sufficient.

The band's lease division ( over 1000 acres leased out) is the "bread and butter" as the money generated from leases provide the funds to subsidize all of the under funded social – cultural programs as well as provide the necessary funds for band business growth (bank loans etc.).

"Today we have nine companies, a pre-school day care, a grade school -modern buildings for both – a new health center building, a new gymnasium and fitness center.

"Our band office has grown to whereby we have made two additions during my time – which

is a reflection of increasing our governance – a measure of our increasing financial strength is that when I first became chief one bookkeeper could handle our transactions. Today we have seven bookkeepers and one full time senior accountant – that's because today we do a lot more business. Today we offer more opportunity for our people and because of our own source revenue we can subsidize under funded social programs. We still have many dysfunctions as a community, but we at least have a fighting chance to improve our peoples' quality of life," says Chief Louie.

Besides being a full-time chief, Chief Louie is a member of the federal government's First Nations Forestry Program, the National Child Benefit Committee and the BC government's Native Economic Development Advisory Board.

Last fall, Chief Louie was appointed vice-chair of the National Aboriginal Economic Development Board. The board consists of some 20 private sector members, the majority of which are of aboriginal heritage. The board works with Industry Canada through Aboriginal Business Canada and various partners to promote aboriginal business development. In addition, the board advises the government of Canada on matters relating to aboriginal economic development.

"It is a very important board made up of some of the most talented people across the

> **❝** *I believe every First Nation comes from a 'working culture.' Our ancestors worked for a living and were self-supporting. That is what all of our people must get back to – getting up early every day and providing for their and their families own needs – a 'working lifestyle is a healthy lifestyle.'* **❞**
> **Clarence Louie**

country – being on the board furthers my message the aboriginal people and organization must focus on economic development and send the message to the federal government that our people need jobs and self-supporting income not more social welfare programs," said Chief Louie on his recent appointment.

Chief Louie's efforts have been widely recognized in the aboriginal community. In 1999, he received the Aboriginal Business Leader Award from the All Nations Trust and Development Company. In 2000, the Council for Advancement of Native Development Officers (CANDO) named Chief Louie the Economic Developer of the Year.

"I believe every First Nation comes from a 'working culture.' Our ancestors worked for a living and were self-supporting. That is what all of our people must get back to – getting up early every day and providing for their and their families own needs – a 'working lifestyle is a healthy lifestyle,'" says Louie.

# CHIPPEWAS OF NAWASH DEFEND LAKE HURON AND GEORGIAN BAY

**By Dr. John Bacher**   Assisted by Danny Beaton, Mohawk Nation   **Published August, 2003**

The majesty of North America's Great Lakes are too often taken for granted, despite their vulnerability from being 99 percent water trapped by the last ice age, with only one per cent of their volume being annually removed.  Even spectacular inland seas such as Central Asia's Aral Sea, can become dried up toxic wastelands, through the blind stupidity of human diversions of their sacred waters. Such an ugly fate for Lake Huron today is being battled by the visionary environmental leadership of the Chippewas of the Nawash.

*The Niagara escarpment at Neyaashiinigmiing.*

The name Nawash is taken from a native Chief who fought beside Tecumseh, to repel the American invasion of Canada in the War of 1812. This community is located on the rugged Niagara Escarpment bluffs of Cape Croker, called by the community Neyaashiinigmiing. They are joined in a struggle to protect their ancestral lands by the neighbouring Chippewas of Saugeen, whose reserve is on the shores of northern Lake Huron.

One of the elders who has guided the Chippewas in their struggle to protect Georgian Bay is the 84 year old former Chief, Wilmer Nadjiwon. He explains that, "From a spiritual point of view, we believe that the Creator has put everything on the earth for our benefit. If humans impose laws over those of the Great Spirit, spirituality is defunct because man is making the laws and not the Great Spirit anymore. For us protecting the environment is automatic."

As part of their spiritual duty to uphold natural law, the Chippewas are in the vanguard of opposition to a network of six water pipelines that would divert Lake Huron water to distant communities. One would pipe water from Georgian Bay along an existing pipeline from Collingwood, to Aliston and to Bond Head (named symbolically to honour the mad Lieutenant Governor of Ontario, who robbed the Chippewas of most of their land in 1836) and then to Bradford. Bradford is a community north of Toronto near the drained Holland Marsh, itself a former wetland doomed by a massive agricultural project which is expected by experts to eventually dry up.

Two pipelines may divert water to Walkerton; one from Southampton on Lake Huron, and another from Wiarton on Georgian Bay. A pipeline is proposed from Kincardine to Tiverton, which would end up at Iverhuron Provincial Park. Several native archaeological sites have been identified along its proposed route. A pipeline is being considered along the southern Bruce Peninsula through the South Bruce Peninsula Water and Sewage Works Study. Another is being considered from Paisely to Chesley. One pipeline alone- a $40 million project from Walkerton to Southampton, could transfer about 12,000 cubic meters of water each day.

The six pipeline diversions are being proposed when Georgian Bay is already experiencing record low water levels, the worst of a situation which has now persisted over four years. Residents are now wondering, "Who pulled the plug?" Many important wetlands are now dry and converting to meadows, destroying important fish spawning habitats, impacting especially the abundance of northern pike and largemouth bass. These fish require wetland conditions for the rearing of juvenile fish.

The drying up of Georgian Bay comes after much of the waters of Lake Huron have been impacted by diversions for the booming, sprawling city of London. This city sucks

---

*T*he six pipeline diversions are being proposed when Georgian Bay is already experiencing record low water levels, the worst of a situation which has now persisted over four years.

---

*T*he Chippewas have encountered great difficulty in their efforts to research the seven water pipeline projects. Municipal officials have disguised key details about the schemes and their status.

water out of Lake Huron, and dumps it into the Thames River, which discharges not back into the Lake Huron, but to Lake St. Clair.

According to the native Delaware of the Thames, banks are caving in from the massive amount of treated water being dumped by two exiting pipelines from Lake Huron to London after use. This erosion is silting fish spawning beds and according the Delaware, devastating pickering populations. Water from a pipeline dumped into the Nottawasaga River, to accommodate a recently constructed Honda plant, is increasing the vulnerability to erosion of the sandy plain that lines its banks.

The Chippewas complain that the proposed diversions have not taken into account their aboriginal and treaty rights to fish. Chief Ralph Akisenzie complains that "It's about time the First Nations point of view is upheld. Any diversion of any water into a pipeline will have an effect on the shore. What good are our boats if there's no water?"

The Chippewas have encountered great difficulty in their efforts to research the seven water pipeline projects. Municipal officials have disguised key details about the schemes and their status.

Many government regulators themselves were unaware of important aspects of the pipeline approval process, since it is being led by the private consulting firm under a Class Environmental Assessment, the Municipal Engineers Association. Experts employed by

the Chippewas have found that, "the general looseness of the process and the lack of scientific scrutiny allows the process and the results to be driven" by these very engineers. In Walkerton, concerned environmentalists have charged complicity between the engineering firm RV Anderson, who work for the Brockton council implicated in the water poisoning, and municipal councilors.

Walkerton environmentalists have joined the Chippewas in their opposition to diversionary pipelines. Rather than pipe water from Lake Huron or Georgian Bay, they have struggled to have the ground water supply for their water cleaned up and protected. One speaker at a public meeting warned, "What if developers around the Great Lakes started building pipelines everywhere?" In a similar fashion 500 residents of Paisely signed a petition against being supplied by a pipeline, arguing for a "made-in-Paisely" solution.

While the recently defeated Assembly of First Nations National Chief, Matthew Coon Come and Québec Cree Grand Chief Ted Moses may have come to accept massive water diversions, approved in their recent deal with the Québec government regarding the diversion

*"The general looseness of the process and the lack of scientific scrutiny allows the process and the results to be driven."*

**Municipal Engineers Association**

of the Rupert River, the Chippewas of Ontario point to the problems of James Bay as reasons to oppose pipelines in their traditional territories. A report prepared by their environmental researcher, David McLaren, sees the destruction of James Bay as a warning for what may happen to Georgian Bay.

Prophetically, McLaren warns that as a result of massive water diversions in James Bay. "At least one sturgeon population has been destroyed. Sea grass beds along the James Bay coast are disappearing...The critical area where salt water meets fresh is a breeding ground for a number of species of animals: now it has been flushed into the Bay. In spite of the treaties and agreements Québec signed with the Cree, very little information on the effects of the diversions is available. What data collection is being done by Hydro Québec, they are not sharing."

The Chippewas warn that, "Sprawl follows the pipeline." Such urban sprawl is fueled by developers. Developers hope to build upon environmentally sensitive groundwater recharge areas. These are needed to provide base flow to feed streams through underground springs in arid summer months. Building over them may cause streams throughout southern Ontario to dry up and die.

The Nawash estimate is based on calculations by the respected American environmental group the Natural Resources Defense Council. They report that after 10 percent of a watershed is paved over fish species, especially trout, begin to decline. Gigantic shopping centers, so characteristic of urban sprawl, are especially deadly to fish. Their massive parking lots make it impossible for large areas of asphalt-covered land to receive water to replenish underground springs. Sprawl has caused runoff pollution and increased erosion and sedimentation from increased periodic flash floods, to become one of the continent's biggest sources of water contamination.

Land developers are already lining up to build subdivisions and golf courses which may be approved after the pipelines are built. One such proposal is a 2,200 residential development being proposed by developer Lou Biffs, near his existing Green Briar retirement community.

The Nawash community is concerned that if the promised source protection legislation the Ontario government has pledged comes about and actually succeeds in prohibiting urban development on environmentally sensitive recharge areas, then it amounts to a deluge in last minute development efforts. They have expressed concern over the apparent "five year window of opportunity for polluters, water takers and intensive farm operators" and warn about the prospect of a "rush of development."

The Chippewas understand how land development in complex ways threatens to destroy habitat for fish, on which they hope to build an economy upon through the principles

---

*T*he Nawash community have expressed concern over the apparent "five year window of opportunity for polluters, water takers and intensive farm operators and warn about the prospect of a "rush of development."*

---

> **"** *Our old ways teach us that the water is the blood of the earth, and the rocks are her bones. Even today, living as we do in the modern world, we find it difficult to separate the land from ourselves. As one elder said when we first began to discuss land claims, it's not what we do with the land that's important, it's the land itself.* **"**   **Chief Akiwenzie**

of ecological sustainability. Much of their breach of trust suit is based on an effort to stop destructive shoreline development that destroys fish habitat. This seeks to recover public lands, which are in road allowances, so that no logging and cottage development can take place on them.

The Nawash land claim seeks to return lake and riverbeds to their control. This would give the nation the opportunity to remove numerous barriers that block fish migration many of which, such as private dams, have been created illegally by landowners. Chief Akiwenzie is concerned that the loss of natural corridors between the Bruce Peninsula and Muskoka "will eventually isolate animal species in this region to the detriment of their genetic diversity and their ability to sustain themselves as wild populations."

Akiweznie explains how a profound connection to the earth has inspired his nation's land claim and conservationist battles. He has recalled how, "Our old ways teach us that the water is the blood of the earth, and the rocks are her bones. Even today, living as we do in the modern world, we find it difficult to separate the land from ourselves. As one elder said when we first began to discuss land claims, it's not what we do with the land that's important, it's the land itself. Our traditional way is to leave nature alone. We took from the earth

what we needed, but otherwise we tried to make our footprints as small as possible. If she were harmed, we knew enough to leave her to heal herself."

Of special concern to the Chippewas are public shoreline allowances. This is a 66-foot strip along the shores of Georgian Bay and Lake Huron. These shoreline allowances, although in formal municipal ownership, are frequently encroached upon by adjoining cottage owners in ecologically destructive ways, notably the construction of break walls that destroy fish habitat.

The Chippewas of Nawash have defeated efforts by the Township of Keppel to give away the ecologically sensitive shoreline allowance, which involve some 55,000 acres of land. Landowners, predominantly those who own expensive homes and cottages near the shore, attempted to wrest quit-claims to the shoreline road allowances from municipalities in response to landowner protests over the Nawash land claim. Keppel Township in November 1992 attempted to order 166 quit claims. This was struck down by the courts twice by the intervention of the Chippewas- once in 1993 and finally on April 24, 1998 by the Ontario Court of Appeal.

A major victory to defend fish habitat was won by the Chippewas of Nawash when they successfully defeated a massive condominium

> **"***We were blamed for not using the land in the good Euro-Christian manner and letting it grow wild...***"**
> **Lenore Keeship-Tobias,**
> **Chair of the Nawash Board of Education**

project that was proposed by a developer with the support of Bruce County and the provincial government on Hay Island. It is just off the southern shore of Cape Croker.

A central marina, 98 condominium units and a garbage dump were all planned for the tiny 100-acre Hay Island. These proposals were the subject of several pre-Ontario Municipal Board (OMB) hearings by the Nawash. The proposal would have severe consequences for fish stocks and habitat between the island and the mainland. Since the developers did not collect any data on natural heritage, the Chippewas argued that it was impossible to judge the impact of the proposal on threatened species such as the eastern massasauga rattlesnake After years of objections by the Nawash the developers gave up before a scheduled March 1998 OMB hearing.

The presence of a sacred burial site was successfully used by the Nawash to defeat a 1,400 acre golf course-condominium development on the shores of Georgian Bay. The development was proposed on the home of Nahneebahweequa. She was an influential 19th

century Nawash political leader who journeyed to Great Britain to meet with Queen Victoria to denounce the injustices of native people not being able to own land outside of reserves.

In an editorial the Owen Sound *Sun Times* lamented in an August 26, 1997 editorial that Natives had "dealt a death blow." to the condo development. In response Lenore Keeship-Tobias, Chair of the Nawash Board of Education replied that in the past "We were blamed for not using the land in the good Euro-Christian manner and letting it grow wild...When is the land not the land? When people believe the land has value only when it is "improved" and are blind to its intrinsic beauty and its innate capacity to replenish the spirit. Even the humble cow pasture has its beauty and power. It's a quiet place where one can steal away for a short while to visit Nahneebahweequa, "The Woman Who Stands Up" for her people, a strong woman whose spirit dwells there still."

The Nawash are struggling to re-naturalize their sacred burial grounds in Owen Sound, which were desecrated by residential development. A burial mound of the community on 6th Avenue in Owen Sound was disturbed in a most sacrilegious way. Graves were looted, artifacts were stolen, including a corpse sent to a museum, and even the soil was taken to make bricks. As a result of Nawash protests, the Department of Indian Affairs did

> **"***... When is the land not the land? When people believe the land has value only when it is "improved" and are blind to its intrinsic beauty and its innate capacity to replenish the spirit. ...where one can steal away for a short time while to visit Nahneebahweequa, ...a strong woman whose spirit dwells there still.***"**
> **Lenore Keeship-Tobias**

undertake to survey the site, confirming that the nation is the legal owner. The Nawash are demanding that the land be restored to its original state including the removal of the illegal houses, but with compensation to the illegal occupants.

One of the most successful struggles of the Nawash has been to improve forestry practices in Bruce County and to buffer the Bruce Peninsula National Park, which protects the wildest lands of the Niagara Escarpment. The nation conducted a long struggle against the clear- cut logging of white cedar forests, much of which took place illegally on lands not owned by the logging corporation, including 100 acres in the national park and municipal road allowances subject to native land claims.  Of particular concern was the operation of the Northern Bruce Timber Company, operated by Chris Rovers in partnership with his father Frank.

Lands logged by the Rovers were piled with slash, sometime over 12 feet deep creating a fire hazard. Large areas where cedars were cut left other trees vulnerable to wind, resulting in a high degree of blow-down, especially for poplars. The combination of slash and wind blown down trees made it impossible for wildlife such as deer and bear to traverse large areas. Critical deer habitat was threatened, including a deer yard located close to reserve land on part of the Rovers' 3,500 acres of land near Bruce National Park. The Rovers cleverly scooped this up shortly before the park authorities had a chance to purchase it and therefore protect it.

Some 1,400 acres of Rovers' corporate tract was purchased by the Nature Conservancy of Canada, after the Nawash defeated efforts by

*"...we believe that the Creator has put everything on the earth for our benefit. If humans impose laws over those of the Great Spirit, spirituality is defunct because man is making the laws and not the Great Spirit anymore."*

**Wilmer Nahjiwon, former Chief**

the Rovers to legalize their logging on public road allowances through complex legal battles involving and environmental assessment. Four hundred acres were incorporated into Bruce National Park, while another 1,000 acres will be held and managed by the Nature Conservancy of Canada. The acquisition protected the Johnson's Harbour Deeryard, the largest deeryard on the upper Bruce Peninsula.

Shortly following the purchase of half of the Rovers' forest tracts, the Nawash led a campaign for a more effective tree by-law for Bruce County. Currently municipal tree regulations offer little protection for the northerly part of the peninsula, safeguarding only sugar maple and white ash. Various draft by-laws issued by the county have improved since 1999 as a result of the continuous lobbying of the Nawash. The current version requires tree-cutters to file a management plan and adhere to a requirement to maintain a minimum amount of forest cover.

The Nawash successfully struggled for over a decade to participate significantly in the Georgian Bay commercial fishery, based on a strategy of a sustainable harvest of native whitefish. This has not been easy. Until their judicial victory in a court case when charges were dismissed against them by Justice David Fairgrieve in April 16, 1993, the native fish harvest on Georgian Bay amounted to only one percent of the entire $1.5 million commercial catch – a tiny $17,000 shared among 12 families. Since this victory the commercial fishery has significantly reduced levels of unemployment.

Despite their court victory, the Nawash faced a difficult struggle to maintain their commercial fishing rights in face of the violent onslaught by supporters of the newly elected Progressive Conservative (PC) government of Mike Harris in the summer of 1995. The foot soldiers of the common sense revolution used the same violent, terroristic tactics against the Nawash, one that Harris' government employed with the help of the Ontario Provincial Police (OPP) against Natives at Ipperwash. On

August 5, 1995 a crowd of 100 anglers from across the Grey-Bruce area, led by one of Harris' minions PC MPP Bill Murdoch, who continues to sit in the provincial legislature, confronted a lone native woman selling fish at the Owen Sound open market. After this protest a violent rampage erupted which involved the destruction of thousands of dollars of nets, damages to equipment and several native boats – one being burned while undergoing repairs at a dock following its sinking.

Less than a month following Murdoch's march, on September 3, 1995 in the early morning hours, four native young men were assaulted by a mob of around 20 non-Natives in Owen Sound. Three were seriously stabbed and one victim, Aron Keeting, had a tooth sliced in half. Each of the Natives had to fight off 4 or 5 attackers. Although one police officer was present he did nothing until police headquarters finally responded after several emergency calls. It took two and a half years before any convictions were obtained against this crime. One of the most serious convictions was that against Aaron Keeting for assaulting Lee Jacobs with a beer bottle.

The violent mob tactics of Harris' common sense revolutionaries were in vain. Seven years after their judicial victory, the Nawash finally were able to get the Ontario government to sign a co-management agreement regarding the Georgian Bay fishery.

*O*n *August 5, 1995 a crowd of 100 anglers from across the Grey-Bruce area, led by one of Harris' minions, PC MPP, Bill Murdoch, who continues to sit in the provincial legislature, confronted a lone native woman selling fish at the Owen Sound open market.*

One of the biggest challenges to the Nawash efforts to earn a modest living from the sustainable harvest of the Georgian Bay fishery based on renewable populations of native fish, is the deliberate stocking of Lake Huron with exotic fish by the provincial government. The Nawash are challenging this stocking with the impressive work of a dedicated group of scientists. They have assembled a formidable team under the dedicated leadership of Dr. Stephen Crawford, a zoologist at the University of Guelph. He originally came in contact with the nation in connection with his work to restore native fish species, while employed at Georgia Bay's Fathom Five National Park. His research concluded that introduced Pacific salmon species pose an ecologically significant threat to non-native Great Lakes fish species.

What scientists are saying regarding the harm caused by exotic species in the Great Lakes is simply confirming the wisdom of native elders. Wilmer Nadjiwon, observes: "You can't put a salmon in a predominately whitefish area. They are predators of the juvenile whitefish." Chief Akiwenzie calls stocking with exotic fish, "playing Russian roulette with the fishery. There are good chances such fish will take diseases into the wild... diseases wild fish have no protections against."

Scientific investigations are being used by the Nawash as evidence for the need to close the Bruce Nuclear Power Plant. They discovered that in the current Environmental Assessment for the Bruce plant, the owners did not count whitefish as a Valued Ecosystem Component. It was also exposed that Ontario Power Generation withheld documentation of large numbers of fish being sucked into the nuclear plant's intake pipes.

> *What scientists are saying regarding the harm caused by exotic species in the Great Lakes is simply confirming the wisdom of native elders.*

Working with the local environmental organization, the Bruce Peninsula Environmental Group, the Chippewas of Nawash organized a day-long educational forum to stimulate more grass roots environmental activism to protect Georgian Bay. At the forum Richard Lindgren, an environmental lawyer with the Canadian Environmental Law Association, explained the tools available to those who care for the earth. Since this forum was held three years ago, the Nawash have provided their members with information updates about new tools, such as the 1-866-663-8477 hot-line established by the Ontario Ministry of Environment to report cases of pollution.

The struggles of the Nawash to defend their land as the basis to provide a sustainable economy for seven generations contrast vividly with the push for "revenue sharing" based on profiting from environmentally destructive resource extraction favoured by the recently rejected National Chief, Matthew Coon Come. Rather than ask for a share in profits from nuclear power plants, for instance, they are exposing the threat this technology poses to their plans for an economy based on a sustainable harvest of native fish. It is to be hoped that this community's heroic nonviolent example of the good mind in defense of the earth, will be imitated and even outdone by nations across Canada.

> *It is to be hoped that this community's heroic nonviolent example of the good mind in defense of the earth, will be imitated and even outdone by nations across Canada.*

## ABORIGINAL ACHIEVEMENT AWARD WINNER

# MARY RICHARD

## COMMUNITY DEVELOPMENT

**Reprinted with permission from the NAAF**

Mary Richard can't even think of slowing down. "I don't have time to retire," this Manitoba Métis, now in her 60s, says cheerfully. And that's a good thing for her province, city and Aboriginal peoples everywhere. To say she has worked tirelessly for Aboriginal people over the years would be understating her accomplishments. The CEO of Circle of Life Thunderbird House in Winnipeg (to name just one of her current activities) Richard's efforts have touched virtually every aspect of Aboriginal life in her province through five decades. She was the Executive Director of the Indian and Métis Friendship Centre of Winnipeg (the first of its kind in Canada). That was just the beginning. Richard, a former President of the Aboriginal Council of Winnipeg -- was instrumental in ensuring the survival of Aboriginal languages in Manitoba. She implemented the Manitoba Language Retention Programs during almost a decade of service as Director of the Manitoba Association for Native Languages. "We were just becoming aware of language loss but had no materials for teaching," she says today of her work during the 1980s. "So, we got Elders together with language speakers and I raised the money to get the books printed." These education kits -- made possible after Richard raised half-a-million-dollars -- are now available in seven Aboriginal languages and sought after by school boards and universities across the country. She's established Native housing, training and cultural projects, built bridges to the private sector and established the plans for an Aboriginal business district in her city. Builder, doer, leader, partner – that's Mary Richard.

# TOOTOO'S TRAIN RIDE TO THE TOP

**By Cam Martin**                    **Published November, 2003**

"Look out for the Tootoo train!" The Nashville crowd cheers ferociously as the attacker with the puck is pummeled by Rankin Inlet's unstoppable hockey hero, the NHL's first and only Inuk player, Jordin Tootoo.

Though smaller than many of the players in the league, Jordin is one of the harder hitters, earning him the name Tootoo Train.

The 5 foot 9-inch, 190-pound, right wing has produced well this season and proved to be a valuable asset to the Nashville Predators. Playing an aggressive style of hockey, Jordin appears fearless on the ice, taking on opponents 30 to 40 pounds heavier than him, and winning.

As you watch Jordin take the ice it may not be easy to see that this huge cultural step is the culmination of a lifetime of achievement. He has worked hard to get to this point, and has maintained his focus throughout. Barney, Jordin's father, recalls how his son's dedication was unwavering while growing up: "Jordin faced every challenge head on, with no fear."

Jordin's life began modestly. He grew up in the small town of Rankin Inlet with his mother and father, his brother Terence, and sister Corinne. Though it is considered the hub of Nunavut, Rankin Inlet is still relatively

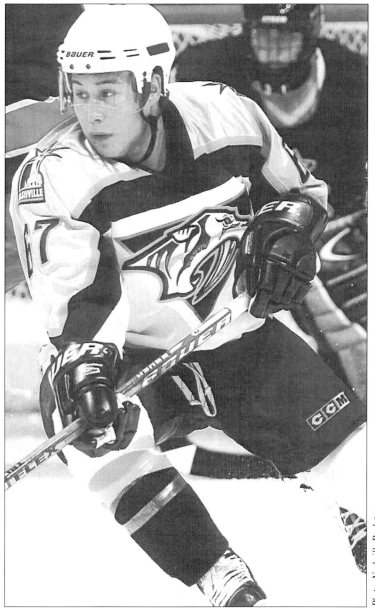

*Photo: Nashville Predators*

*Jordin Tootoo playing for the Nashville Predators*

rural, with a population just over 2000. The climate can be harsh, with some residents living in igloos for part of the year. The climate, however, is ideal for hockey and Jordin and Terence were hooked ever since they were old enough to skate.

Barney recalls how excited the boys would be when he got home from work. "They would nearly knock me over when I got in the door because it would mean that we would get on the Honda [ski-doo] and go to the lake. They loved hockey, all the time."

Both the brothers continued to play hockey, and soon their skills brought them to the Western Hockey League, where they made their mark. Jordin played for the Brandon Wheat Kings and Terence played for the

Roanoke Express. Although both had very successful careers in the juniors, their love for hockey extended past the ice.

In their free time they ran hockey camps together, and visited schools to encourage students to stay on the right path by following what they loved. They also formed a business, Team Tootoo, which continues to sell clothing with the Team Tootoo logo, and unique aboriginal items such as caribou jerky via their web site. Both of the brothers had the idea to use their influence and ingenuity to make a little money, as well as educate others about their culture and their home. In addition, the Team Tootoo web site continues to have regular postings on Jordin's NHL career.

Jordin and Terence's desire to help the youth in the community avoid negative influences was a reaction to the problems they saw in their home town. Because of Rankin Inlet's size, and the lack of resources for the youth, many turn to drugs and crime. There are also continuing problems of racism, which affect many of the Rankin Inlet teens.

*Jordin Tootoo in the Team Canada Jersey*

Photo: Unknown

Barney Tootoo said: "A lot of kids here unfortunately get the short end of the stick. Either by the limitations they set on themselves, or those that others set on them.

*ordin and Terence are symbols, not only to the First Nations community, but to everyone, that if you pursue your dreams with relentless dedication, with the force of a train, then nothing will stop you.*

Terence and Jordin experienced racism, and were exposed to negative influences, but they faced these challenges like any other in their lives, head on and with their characteristic single mindedness."

## A WAY OUT

Jordin and Terence had found a way out of intolerance and limitation; and they wanted to share that dream with their peers. They found it in hockey, their race was not important, and they did not have to pretend to be what they weren't to fit in. No doubt, growing up in such a small town, both of them felt that if would be a great feat to fulfill their dream. The brothers were not wrong, and the message that they spread was that dreams are not out of reach for anyone who has the determination and desire.

Tragically, Jordin's brother Terence took his own life just as they both began to realize their aspirations. In the summer of 2002, Jordin went to summer camp for Team Canada, and Terence had just signed a professional contract with the Roanoke Express. Under a great deal of pressure, they both felt that they were beginning to achieve what they had wanted all their lives.

After an evening of celebration, Terence was charged with driving under the influence. He was understandably upset and though others tried to console him, the rigid standards he had set for himself made him feel like a failure; not only himself, but also all those he had helped. Several days later, his body was found, with a note encouraging his brother to continue, despite what had happened.

The brothers were very close and Jordin was understandably upset but, he persevered in his hockey career, because he knew that Terence would want it that way. The morning of Terence's funeral, Jordin was on the ice, practicing. He faced this challenge like every other in his life, with acceptance and the desire to carry on, despite what he felt.

Jordin and Terence are symbols, not only to the First Nations community, but to everyone, that if you pursue your dreams with relentless dedication, with the force of a train, then nothing will stop you. For more information on Jordin Tootoo, go to www. teamtootoo.com.

# CHEECHOO'S LONG AND SUCCESSFUL JOURNEY

**By Larry Wigge**

*Photos: San Jose Sharks*

Jonathan Cheechoo sat calmly in the San Jose Sharks locker room in St. Louis amidst a group of reporters inquiring about his quantum leap from nine goals as a rookie in the 2002-2003 season to 28 goals this season.

A smile crossed Cheechoo's face.

This 23-year-old right wing smiled because he knew this wasn't the real quantum leap. That came more than a decade ago, when he left his home in Moose Factory, Ontario – an Island community of about 2,000 people about 500 miles north of Toronto – in an attempt to become the first Cree Indian to be drafted and play in the NHL.

Scouts often laugh that the next Bobby Orr or Wayne Gretzky could come from some isolated spot where you need a dogsled to traverse. But finding Cheechoo, the 29th pick in the 1998 Entry Draft, might have been more difficult if his parents hadn't believed in their son's passion to play hockey. They had confidence that by allowing him to leave home with their blessings, one day he could achieve a professional career.

"There are no paved roads in Moose Factory, just some gravel streets," Cheechoo says. "When the Moose River freezes over, a road is constructed across the ice to the mainland town of Moosonee, where the train station is located. In the summer, motorized canoes take residents back and forth. But in the spring and

fall, when the river is thawing, the only travel between the towns is by helicopter."

But it's home to Mervin and Carol Ann Cheechoo and their kids, Jonathan, Kari and Jordan.

"We're a pretty self-sufficient group," Cheechoo explained, with a lot of pride. "We do a lot of hunting: moose, geese, ducks, rabbits and partridge. My dad will probably tell you he has a moose in the freezer right now, in fact."

Now? You will often find the Cheechoos at one of Jonathan's games, whether they have to drive or fly to get there. They are proud of his success and want to share it with him.

"I remember we used to bundle him up and pull him on a sled down the street to his grandfather's house," Mervin told me, while waiting to see his son board the team bus in St. Louis after he helped the Sharks take a 3-1 lead in the first-round series against the Blues.

"His grandfather had the television. There would be 10 or 12 relatives and their friends. They were all into sports, especially hockey. We would put Jonathan in front of the television in a child's chair. We used to joke that that was the only time he was quiet."

# HE SHOOTS, HE SCORES

When Cheechoo was a kid, there was no hockey rink in Moose Factory. So Mervin, a minister at the Cree Gospel Chapel, would wait until it was cold enough every winter, then flood the lot across the street and create a temporary rink.

"It wasn't very big, and sometimes we'd have six or seven guys playing on this little piece of ice, so it could get pretty rough," Jonathan remembered. "Maybe that's where

I got the style that my teammates say is more like football than hockey."

Cheechoo plays with a great deal of grit, though he has the soft hands of a goal scorer.

"He's a gritty goal-scorer," said line mate Mike Ricci. "Yeah that's right — gritty and a goal scorer. He's not the fastest skater in the world, but he finds a way to get to the net — and boy can he shoot."

"I don't think I've ever seen anyone who loves to score goals like Cheech does," said Scott Thornton, Cheechoo's other line mate. "His confidence is contagious – the energy goes right up and down the bench every time he scores."

"I've never seen a player with such character and drive to succeed," said Sharks General Manager Doug Wilson. "He plays with a grit that others can only hope to have. He's almost like a wide receiver who you ask to go across the middle with the possibility he's going to get creamed by a linebacker. With Cheech, you don't have to ask him to do it a second or third time.

"I've had young players come up to me and ask what he has to do to make it in the NHL, I tell him, 'Just watch Jonathan Cheechoo and do what he does.' Cheech is definitely his father's son. He is proud, dedicated to his profession and passionate about how he succeeds in this business. And he never quits on any play."

When I told Cheechoo what Wilson said, he blushed.

"My dad is my hero," he said. "When I look in the mirror, I ask myself what would dad do in this situation and go from there. I owe everything to him. He's the one who told me that I should shoot 500 pucks a day against the plywood wall of the shed.

"I remember being proud of my shot one day when I hit the shed so hard that I broke a hole in the wall. I didn't have the nerve to tell my dad about the hole, but I did anyway — and he just said, 'I guess I'll just have to use stronger wood to rebuild it.'"

## LEAVING HOME IS NEVER EASY

It was Mervin who sat Jonathan down for a talk about moving out of Moose Factory if he was serious about wanting to play hockey.

"He had such passion for the game," Mervin recalled. "I told him there are probably a million kids his age in Canada who have dreamed about playing in the NHL and only a couple of hundred make it. I asked him if he had the dedication to make a go of it."

Cheechoo moved to Timmins, about 190 miles away, and lived with a doctor and his family. He played on a top bantam level team there. Two stops later, he had improved enough to be picked by the Sharks in the second round of the 1998 Entry Draft.

One scout wrote that he skated slower going forward than some prospects skated backward. Cheechoo took that report as a challenge, and so did his town. A collection taken up by the Cree community groups paid his tuition at a skating school to improve his quickness.

Still, skating is more than just learning a few quickness moves.

"To me, his character really came out in the 2001-02 season when he had a concussion that cut his season short," Wilson recalled. "He came to San Jose and worked out with our physical therapist and got stronger and faster.

In fact, he stayed the whole off-season."

"Leg strength, wow!" Cheechoo said. "I never realized how much faster and stronger on my skates I could be. And, in turn, that confidence has helped make me a better player."

A real self-motivated player. And a player who dreamed of playing for the Sharks from the time he was 12. It didn't hurt that one of his uncles gave him a coat with the San Jose logo on it when the Sharks were just coming into the NHL.

"His teacher assigned the class an essay when he was in 7th grade, asking the kids what they would be doing in 2002," Mervin said. "Jonathan wrote that he would be playing for the San Jose Sharks. A couple of years ago, when we were moving, his mom found the essay in a bunch of boxes."

"He also said he would make a million dollars, have a lot of cars and live in a mansion," Carol Ann laughed.

The way Jonathan Cheechoo, who had one goal, two assists and was a plus-3 in five games against St. Louis in the first round of the playoffs, is playing today, the perks he wrote about many years ago will follow very soon.

Not bad for a kid living far away from Toronto, Montreal or San Jose, eh? I asked Jonathan what kind of grade he got on the essay.

"A 'C' I think," Cheechoo said, then he added. "Do you think I could get that changed to an 'A' if I took that back to my teacher today?"

He'd get an 'A' for originality and a real sense of realism from me.

*A real self-motivated player. And a player who dreamed of playing for the Sharks from the time he was 12.*

# Nisga'a Treaty Passes into Canadian History

**By Frank Larue**                    **Published September, 1998**

British Columbia's much anticipated first modern-day treaty came into effect at a signing ceremony in the remote Nass Valley of northern British Columbia on August 4, 1998.

While Nisga'a dancers sang a traditional song of peace, Joe Gosnell, (centre) president of the Nisga'a Tribal Council; Jane Stewart, (left) minister of Indian and Northern Affairs Canada; and BC Premier Glen Clark,(right) held up the treaty document in celebration as more than 2,000 onlookers cheered at the recreation centre in New Aiyansh of the Nass Valley.

*Photo: Nisga'a Tribal Council*

*T*he treaty is expected to be the subject of heated debate in the provincial legislature, the federal House of Commons and the Canadian Senate.

"This ceremony is a triumph for the Nisga'a people, the people of British Columbia and the people of Canada. Today, we make history as we correct the mistakes of the past and send a signal of hope around the world," said Gosnell.

"No longer are we beggars in our own lands, we now go forward with dignity, equipped with the confidence that we can make important contributions – social, political and economic – to Canadian society."

Minister Stewart said the treaty acknowledges a new level of partnership between First Nations and the federal government across the nation. Stewart noted

that much of the multi-million dollar settlement will be used to build important infrastructure such as schools, health care centres and sewage systems.

"It will also be used by the Nisga'a for investment and to create jobs for their people, who will in turn become self-supporting and contribute to the local economy," said the minister.

Premier Glen Clark acknowledged that the treaty still faces a number of hurtles to overcome, but noted that the negotiation process has achieved significant results to bring a sense of closure to the historical injustices of the past.

"We will have to confront the words and deeds of those who would deny our history, those who are blind to the injustice of the past and who reject 30 years of negotiation and compromise," said the premier.

*The original Committee 1913*

The treaty is expected to be the subject of heated debate in the provincial legislature, the federal House of Commons and the Canadian Senate.

The treaty must also be ratified by the Nisga'a people, and the provincial and federal governments before it becomes law. The 5,500 Nisga'a have 90 days in which to ratify the treaty. The ratification vote requires a majority of 50 per cent plus one in order to pass.

The Nisga'a treaty provides for a democratic, accountable government that will include representation for all Nisga'a through a central Nisga'a Lisims government, four village governments, and three urban locals for Nisga'a citizens living outside the Nass Valley. Approximately half of the estimated 5,500 Nisga'a live outside of the Nass Valley.

The Nisga'a Lisims government will have the authority to make laws in several areas such as the administration of government, management of lands and assets, language and culture, and Nisga'a citizenship.

All Nisga'a government laws will operate consistently with federal and provincial laws and the treaty includes rules to address any conflicts that may arise. The Nisga'a government will operate within the Canadian constitution and the Charter of Rights and Freedoms.

Under the terms of the treaty, the Nisga'a will receive:

- $190 million to be paid out over 15 years;
- 2,019 square kilometres of land;
- an average yearly allocation of 44,588 sockeye salmon, 11,797 coho salmon, 6,330 chum salmon, 6,524 chinook salmon, and 4,430 pink salmon, protected by the treaty;

> *The Nisga'a treaty provides for a democratic, accountable government that will include representation for all Nisga'a through a central Nisga'a Lisims government.*

- an annual commercial allocation averaging 28,913 sockeye and 88,526 pink salmon in a separate agreement not covered by the treaty;
- $11.8 million to increase participation in the general commercial fishery;
- $10.3 million in Canada's contribution to the Lisims Fisheries Conservation Trust (to which the Nisga'a contribute $3.1 million);
- limited allocations of moose, grizzly bear and goats, for domestic purposes;
- transition training and one-time funding of $40.6 million;
- funding to help deliver health, education, and social services to their members and other area residents; and
- a water reservation for domestic, agricultural and industrial purposes.

## OPPOSITION SAYS TREATY UNFAIR

The treaty faces a number of opponents who complain that the treaty gives the four Nisga'a clans too much.

Opponents include BC Liberal leader Gordon Campbell, federal Reform M.P. Mike Scott, a grass-roots non-native citizens group, and the neighbouring Gitanyow tribal group.

Campbell said that he has serious concerns about the treaty because the treaty does not treat all British Columbians equally. Non-natives living on Nisga'a lands do not have an equal vote in the election of Nisga'a

**"** *Our detractors do not understand or, practicing a willful ignorance, choose not to understand. Or worse, using a coded language, they are updating a venomous attitude so familiar to First Nations of the world.* **"**                    **Joe Gosnell**

governments. Campbell argues that the treaty allows for some Nisga'a laws to take precedence over federal and provincial laws and enshrines an aboriginal fishery.

Scott said he is planning a campaign to convince the Nisga'a it's a bad deal and said he may use BC's initiative law to force a province-wide referendum.

The Gitanyow argue that 84 per cent of their 65,000 square miles of traditional territory was ceded to the Nisga'a in exclusive negotiations.

The Gitanyow say that the federal and provincial governments violated the BC treaty negotiation process because the Gitanyow were excluded from the Nisga'a treaty negotiations. The Gitanyow claim was set forth before the BC Treaty Commission in 1994 and was accepted by both the federal and provincial governments for negotiation in the BCTC process.

In mid-July, the Gitanyow lost a bid to have the issue of overlapping claims with the Nisga'a settled before the final treaty was signed. They have vowed to carry on their fight in the courts.

The Nisga'a treaty has also been the subject of criticism by other First Nations involved in the BCTC process who reject the notion that the treaty is a template for other treaties under negotiation in the province.

In his address, Gosnell accused critics of perpetrating a "venomous attitude" toward First Nations.

"Our detractors do not understand or, practicing a willful ignorance, choose not to understand. Or worse, using a coded language, they are updating a venomous attitude so familiar to First Nations of the world."

# VIOLA THOMAS: VOICE AND FIGHTER FOR THE DISPOSSESSED

**By Sean Devlin**                    **Published February, 2000**

Viola Thomas is from the Secwepemc Nation and grew up on the Kamloops Reserve. She has dedicated the past 20 years of her life to fighting for social justice for all aboriginal peoples, whether they live on or off reserve.

Her philosophy for life: "If you do not stand for anything, you will fall for everything."

Viola grew up around politics. "My grandfather on my father's side was the last hereditary leader for my Nation, and my grandmother on my mother's side was the first Indian cowboy to win at the Calgary Stampede (in 1923).

"The Late George Manuel was a relative of mine. He was a champion in advocating for the rights and dignities of indigenous peoples internationally. My mother's sister, the late Mildred Gottfriedson, was a founding member of the B.C. Native Women's Society."

Throughout her life, Viola has been influenced by witnessing the advocacy of different people in her family.

"I guess that's what inspired me to get and remain involved in trying to find ways to challenge the stereotypes and myths about our people, systemic racism, and the failure of the Canadian people to live up to their so-called commitment to human rights."

In 1996, she was elected to the presidency of the United Native Nations (UNN), an organization that represents off-reserve Native peoples in British Columbia.

Photo: Sean Devlin

*V*iola grew up around politics. "My grandfather on my father's side was the last hereditary leader for my Nation, and my grandmother on my mother's side was the first Indian cowboy to win at the Calgary Stampede (in 1923)."

Leaving home at 18, Viola went to Prince Albert, Saskatchewan, where she trained with the Department of Indian Affairs to become a Band Development Training Facilitator.

"When my training was finished I came home to B.C. and worked in different parts of the province," she said. "I worked in Canim Lake Reserve, Dog Creek Reserve; I was called out to where ever there were requests from the bands. Quite often I went to the bands that nobody wanted to go to, the isolated ones that nobody else really wanted to take on.

"I took that on as a challenge because it opened up my eyes to the cultural diversity of the Aboriginal peoples of B.C. It also gave me a great sense of humility because of the dire situations that many of the band communities were in at the time. It was a real big eye-opener in many ways. It gave me the privilege to meet different elders from different nations and a lot of Native people from different communities."

Viola then worked for five years as the executive director of the Kermode Friendship Centre in Terrace.

"I do give credit to my past experiences. Without them I could not be in the places that I am now. Meeting the elders I worked with up at Terrace was really amazing to me."

*V*iola has worked as a producer with Aboriginal Artists in Toronto; a para-legal worker with the Aboriginal Justice Centre; an education and cultural programmer at the Carnegie Centre in Vancouver. She was also project coordinator with the Women's Social Policy Review Coalition in Vancouver.

## PETITE, STRONG AND ENERGETIC

Viola Thomas, 42, is petite and strong-willed woman of abundant energy. She is outspoken, opinionated, intent on furthering the social and economic goals of her people.

She speaks, using her hands in emphasis, in a strong-timbered voice that is high-toned yet not strident.

"You see, how I look at my life is that I'm not a specialist of any kind; I'm a generalist. I like to learn many different things and my background has given me that opportunity."

Viola has worked as a producer with Aboriginal Artists in Toronto; a para-legal worker with the Aboriginal Justice Centre; an education and cultural programmer at the Carnegie Centre in Vancouver. She was also project coordinator with the Women's Social Policy Review Coalition in Vancouver.

The woman is passionate about the injustices her people have suffered over the years: "In the treaties we signed, we agreed to live alongside the European peoples, for Aboriginal traditions are based on sharing. We did not agree to give up the right to the lands as our lands meant our very survival. We did not agree to give up the right to speak our language and practice our teachings. We never agreed to sell out or become homogenized by ethnocentric, imperialistic European ideologies."

Her left hand clasps and unclasps in time to her words, beating a fierce rhythm of defiance.

"Where we were once proud and distinctive nations, the Indian Act now defines who we are. There are now 29 definitions of who is Indian! No other group of people is subject to such an Act. Through this legislation our own forms of self-definition and governance and relationship to the land have been eroded. This situation is no better than the former South African apartheid system," she said.

Believing that education is the foundation for informed decision-making, she strives to bring about public awareness and an increased sensitivity to the plight of her people, the First Peoples of this land.

"We need to inform our people so that they are not intimidated by mainstream politics, but at the same time, we also need to democratize mainstream politics to ensure our people's voices are meaningfully respected and reflected in the partisan politics of this country." Viola believes, with vigor, in "people empowerment."

## CULTURAL STRATEGIES NEEDED

"My goodness, if the working poor, regardless of gender or race, ever got involved in the politics of this country we'd have a whole different government. Big time!

"I think that what is really lacking within our community are strategies to address community development that are reflective of our cultural diversity and the historical abuses that our people have been subjected to. We must figure out ways to turn this around. How do we address this issue of poverty?"

But is such a thing possible, asked the skeptical, cynical, world-weary interviewer. The pressures and the propaganda in support of the trans-national corporatist agenda for globalization are enormous.

"I think it is possible," Viola said. "I like to think optimistically all the time. It's easy to think that we're never going to do it. But I like to think "How can we do it?"

As example she mentions the joint initiative of the Indian Homemakers' Association and the University of Victoria to develop a "mother centre" along the lines of the ones in Europe. Such a centre would work with aboriginal single mothers and train them in different capacities to develop a child-minding centre.

The establishment of a glass bead-making factory to supply North American Native beaders is also being explored. At present, all beads used in Amerindian art are from the Czech and Slovak republics.

"So to me, when I look at these kinds of initiatives, driven by single-parent aboriginal mothers, I can see that things are evolving. And I think that these are the kinds of strategies that work best, not a slavish imitation of the mainstream way of doing things, in terms of a colonized fashion," said Viola.

"The challenge is for us to deconstruct that colonization in a contemporary mode and take the values and the dignity that our people have and move them forward into the next century."

*B*elieving that education is the foundation for informed decision-making, she strives to bring about public awareness and an increased sensitivity to the plight of her people, the First Peoples of this land.

## LACK OF POLITICAL MUSCLE

There are 800,000 Native people in Canada; 500,000 of them live off-reserve. Yet, despite their numbers, the political influence they wield is basically nil.

"Even though urban and rural Native people living off-reserve are in the majority, we do not have any political clout. Part of that goes back to the historical lack of capacity-building within our communities – the cynicism and complacency that our people have come to accept, not trusting or believing in a political process that is democratic.

"This is compounded by the challenge for many of our people who really live in poverty to see any connection as to why it is important to get involved, even at a school board level. People who are scratching to put food in their kids' bellies and pay the rent are not at a place to engage in the political process."

Viola Thomas is also highly aware that the disenfranchisement and marginalization forced upon aboriginal people by the white oppressors have been internalized by Native communities.

"How do we interrupt the issues of internalized racism and sexism within our communities?" She asked. "That's another whole challenge. Do you think it's a coincidence that 48 per cent of the 42,000 urban aboriginal people in the Greater Vancouver area are single parent mums?

"You know, there's no doubt in my mind that the idea of sacredness for our children is lost in the context of the aboriginal world view."

She feels that women in Native communities have been disenfranchised by many Native leaders.

"The Assembly of First Nations (AFN) created a Women's Secretariat. But to me that is nothing but window dressing because it is coming from the top down, from Ottawa down. It needs to come from the community up; that's where change happens, with the people within the community."

When the AFN met in Vancouver in 1999, a delegation of urban natives from the city's downtown eastside skid row area asked to meet with the delegates for ten minutes. This was not allowed.

"We had a number of our members, of all ages, and we went and presented tobacco to the AFN elders. We did the protocol thing. When we got there, the AFN called their security guards to the front door and refused to let us into the assembly. We wanted to speak to the chiefs about urban issues, including that of off-reserve voting rights. This is a big concern, in terms of the marginalization of urban aboriginal people," she said.

"This is done by First Nations as well as other levels of government. I don't say that in a mean way. The social reality is that they don't have the capacity to help their people, even if they wanted to."

*❝Even though urban and rural Native people living off-reserve are in the majority, we do not have any political clout. Part of that goes back to the historical lack of capacity-building within our communities❞*

# Robert Davidson's Abstract Edge

**By Shauna Lewis**

Photos by Shauna Lewis

**Published July, 2004**

It was standing room only on the evening of June 22, as more than 400 distinguished guests arrived at the Museum of Anthropology on Musqeam territory at the University of British Columbia. Filling the museum's main gallery, onlookers came from far and wide to share in the opening of premier Haida Gwaii artist Robert Davidson's remarkable exhibit entitled *Abstract Edge*.

Packed into the gallery and overflowing into the museum corridor, the assembly of spectators waited in anticipation for the evening's festivities to commence. With the opening address delivered by museum director Michael Ames, the official welcome and prayer expressed by a Musqueam Elder, and a taste of the night's entertainment provided by Haida Gwaii's Rainbow Creek dancers; the opening ceremony to Davidson's show was a fitting initiation to a night overflowing with cultural veneration and exceptional artistry.

Words of praise and recognition for Davidson's works resonated throughout the opening ceremony as Chief Reynold Russ of Old Masset, Haida Gwaii and the Chief of Skidegate, Clarence Dempsey, conveyed their pride in both Davidson's character and his works.

*Haida salmon dancer*

*Following a beautifully executed prayer song and ornate robe naming ceremony, the evening concluded with a myriad of customary dances and songs*

"He [Davidson] believes in what he does," stated Russ. Davidson's steadfastness and dedication to both his craft and Haida lineage was also illuminated in Chief Russ' address: "Robert you did so much for our Haida people, for showing our culture and artistic work." In finalizing his reverent address to Davidson, Russ concluded on an emotional note: "You are the eagle of the dawn," he said. "We are so proud of you."

Reg Davidson, brother of Davidson, also took to the podium to deliver a short yet poignant speech. Laced with respect for his brother and his works, the younger Davidson touched on elements of the artist's persona, as he relayed personal information to those of us lucky enough to be a part of the culturally lavish affair. Relaying stories of the artist's

youth, Reg's speech touched on how his brother believed it important to balance the symbiotic relationship of civic obligations with his artistry concluding that he passionately made time for both.

Additional comments in the opening address were articulated by a small number of local and national museum delegates. Greg Hill, representative of Ottawa's National Gallery, expressed his pleasure in the exhibit, announcing that Davidson's works will be a part of a nationwide exhibition that will conclude at the National Gallery of Canada in 2007.

Next, Karen Duffec, exhibit curator at the Museum of Anthropology, took to the podium to shed light on the inspiration behind Davidson's innovative exhibit. Addressing the crowd, Duffec began by illuminating the conceptual elements within Davidson's works.

In reference to the *Abstract Edge* exhibit, Duffec acknowledged Davidson's theme as being centered on the space, line, or "edge" between that which is tangible and that which is intangible. Through interpreting the "edge of abstraction" as being the medial space between both the cultural/spiritual and physical/material plain, Duffec referred to Davidson's works as a "meeting at the center" of two distinct realms.

"The duality is always there," said Duffec, in reference to the exhibit. Davidson's art "cannot really be isolated from cultural practices" she said, as his works and their blatant amalgamation of traditional and contemporary elements denote a sort of merger within the edge of physical and cultural space.

## ARTIST TAKES CENTER STAGE

When all of the speeches from family, friends, and museum representatives had concluded, Michael Ames called upon Robert Davidson to take center stage. After initially thanking the Musqueam people for being on their traditional land, Davidson began his address with the formal introduction of his Haida dance group, the Rainbow Creek dancers. Following a beautifully executed prayer song and ornate robe naming ceremony, the evening concluded with a myriad of customary dances and songs that can very well be noted, along with art, as the integral threads of Haida culture.

Before guests were permitted to view the exhibit and sample some of the traditional First Nations foods set up in the outdoor adjacent longhouse, Davidson concluded by delivering expressions of gratitude to those who have walked beside him throughout his artistic journey. Stating that he was "happy to be a part of a team that will make a difference in the world today," Davidson thanked those individuals who have shaped his life personally and publicly.

Conveying that he has been blessed to have such a supportive family, the artist thanked his grandparents, aunts, uncles, brothers, and other extended family members. Calling his family his team, Davidson also expressed his gratitude to his wife Terri-Lynn, his son Ben and daughter Sarah for their undying support.

Last but not least, Davidson thanked the Chiefs and elderly members of his nation, who he said "maintained the thin thread of knowledge...the thin thread of art." In both laying the foundation for First Nations artists and bridging the gap from the past to the present, Davidson also extended special thanks to Robert Davidson Sr, Bill Reid, Victor Adams, Todd Davidson, Pat McQueen, Kim Pearson and others whose guidance and mentorship have been integral in his career.

In reference to our contemporary society, Davidson noted that "we are living in a very blessed time," and he urged us to focus on what we are blessed with rather than what we lack.

"Together collectively we can make a difference individually," he said. Regarding the future, the artist simply stated: "Energy is to rebuild...goal is to rebuild."

*Davidson concluded by delivering expressions of gratitude to those who have walked beside him throughout his artistic journey.*

*While the importance of preserving traditional elements is actively portrayed within his pieces, a contemporary style also emerges; posing the question once again "what is Native art"?*

# PAST AND PRESENT FLOATS THROUGH EXHIBIT

Following the superb opening ceremony, and after partaking of elk, salmon and other savory delights, I made my return to the museum and toward Robert Davidson's *Abstract Edge* exhibit. Unfamiliar with his works, I was excited with what I would soon be viewing. While seasoned within the artistic genre, nothing could have prepared me for the west coast talent that I would soon be appreciating.

A unification of past and present seemed to free float throughout the exhibit, as if there were no old or new styles, but a mixture of both. The duality that Duffec had earlier described was an essential ingredient within every piece, regardless of mediums used.

Although installations of monochromatic aluminum, like that of Davidson's newest work entitled *Meeting at the Center* (2004), were juxtaposed with a low relief red cedar and acrylic piece entitled *Green* (2002); a common theme of mergence, separation and the space in between was visually echoed through each of his works.

While Davidson's active use of negative space, curvilinear contours and rigid lines allude to the traditional attributes of Haida art; the incorporation of postmodern shapes and occasional optical illusions derived from unconventional color hues, enable the marriage of that which is traditional to that which is contemporary.

By creating masterpieces splashed with the rather eccentric hues of avocado green and canary yellow, an avant-garde backdrop floats the execution of traditional shapes in various works. It is within such *duality,* that questions arise in regard to stereotypical First Nations artistry. Is this *true* Native art? And if no, why not? Many individuals all too often idealize Aboriginal art as having a specific style, and in such traditional technique, a way of stereotyping specific methods and approaches is identified.

Davidson, like his mentor Bill Reid, go beyond set ideologies of what is defined traditional art of the northwest coast, and in doing so, an emergence of what is intrinsically Indian is both transformed and catapulted into the 21st century.

Davidson is nothing short of a trailblazer in regard to First Nations artistry, and his works are the very representation of a style in transformation. While the importance of preserving traditional elements is actively portrayed within his pieces, a contemporary style also emerges; posing the question once again "what *is* Native art"? Davidson answers this theoretical question through the implementation of duality in his works.

Native art mustn't solely live within the echelons of historic representation set to adhere to a specific unwavering style; Native art can and does, as seen within Davidson's exhibit, merge fittingly with postmodern style. It is within this fusion of contrasting elements that the increasingly blurred conception of old and new, figurative and conceptual teeters on the Edge of Abstraction.

# INDEX

## A

Akiwenzie, Ralph  211, 215
Alderfer, Eric  12
Alexie, Robert  117
Alford, Richard "Cartoon"  91
Archie, Ernie  162
Arvol Looking Horse  164
Audain, Micheal  126
Augustine, Ronnie  198
Axtl-hix Gibu, Chief  26

## B

Bacher, Dr. John  13, 87, 137, 207
Baker, Simon  23, 24
Banyaca, Thomas  172
Barfett, Raymond  7
Basque, Nicholas  198
Basque, Will  198
Bates, Bernie  118–124
Beach, Adam  *111*, 111–114, *114*
Bear, Jim  46
Beatles  60
Beaton, Danny  87, 129, 141, *171*, 171–172
Benbow, Kia  12
Bennett, Kwan  11, 12
Berg, Allen  79
Berry, Father Thomas  132
Biffs, Lou  210
Bignell, Stella  193, 196
Birkett, Chris  110
Blood Sweat and Tears  59
Bloom, Cher  65, 68, 185, 187
Blunden, Donald  79
Bono  64
Boots, Francis  32, 35, 36, 37
Bourassa, Robert  38, 44, 89, 101, 149
Bradley, Ray  77

Bringhurst, Robert  126
Broeker, Carl  97
Brownbridge, Gar  79, 80
Bush, George  88, 105, 146
Butler, Richard  78

## C

Cage, Nicholas  111, 112
Caille, Andre  139
Campbell, Gordon  177–179, 225–226
Carbonneau, Luc  33, 34
Cardinal, Don  12
Cardinal, Harold  70, 71
Carter, Lauren  53
Cheechoo, Jonathan  *220*, 220–222
Cheechoo, Vern  57
Chrétien, Jean  70, 104, 182
Chrétien, Raymond  146
Ciacca, John  32, 33, 34, 36
Clark, Dr. Bruce  162, 163
Clark, Glen  *223*, 223–224
Cline, Eric  193, 195, 196
Cochrane, Eddy  58
Cohen, Leonard  61
Cole, Brian  99
Cole, Peter  69, 72
Coon Come, Matthew  11, 21, 44, 106, 143, 209, 215
Cory, Reverend  10
Cranmer, Barb  155–159
Crawford, Dr. Stephen  215
Crazy Horse  14, 138, 141
Crossitt, Cris  191
Cuomo, Mario  92
Curtis, Edward  19
Custer, General  16, 138